W9-BSU-161

The Comprehensive Guide To

Largemouth Bass Patterns

The Comprehensive Guide To
Largemouth Bass Patterns
by Babe Winkelman

Published by
Babe Winkelman Productions, Inc.
Brainerd, Minnesota

Book Design	Babe Winkelman
Cover Design	Duane Ryks
Photography	Steve Grooms/Jeff Howard/Mark Strand
Artwork	Duane Ryks/John Norlin
Writing	Babe Winkelman/Steve Grooms
Editing	Steve Grooms/Mark Strand/Duane Ryks
Typesetting	Sentinel Printing
Keyline	Sandra Ryks
Printing	Sentinel Printing

Published by Babe Winkelman Productions
P.O. Box 407, 213 N.W. 4th St., Brainerd, MN 56401

Printed in the United States of America

Reprinted 1988

First edition, 1986
Library of Congress Catalog
Card Number 86-050308

ISBN 0-915405-03-2

Library of Congress Cataloguing in
Publication Data

Winkelman, Babe
The Comprehensive Guide to Bass Patterns

Brainerd, Minnesota: Babe Winkelman Productions
ISBN 0-915405-03-2

It is with love, respect and admiration that I dedicate this book:

to Jake, the largemouth bass who for six years lived in my fish tank and taught me as much as anyone did about the habits and personality of bass;

to Al Amundson, who was with me in the beginning, who shared my earliest bass fishing triumphs and disasters as we stood side-by-side, knee deep in Camp Lake at night, sopping wet but charged with excitement about what we were doing;

to my wife Charlie, who continues to amaze with her abilities and hard work, and my daughters, Tanya, Jennifer, Jasmine and Donielle, who continued to provide the love and understanding that brings our family together;

to the staff of our growing company, whose loyalty and pursuit of quality helps me believe in our dreams;

but mostly to my Creator, for giving me the chance to go fishing.

ACKNOWLEDGEMENTS

When I looked up at the end of this book, I took some time to think about where I am with my life, and where Babe Winkelman Productions is heading. We are growing faster than I ever thought we could, even in optimistic moments. We are busting out of the seams of a building I had thought was too big, and the ideas for new products and new programs makes me wonder whether there's a building anywhere big enough to contain us.

This book holds my best information on how to catch largemouth bass, under every situation we could cover, given the limits of space. It is the combined effort of an awful lot of talented and dedicated people. I especially want to thank Duane Ryks, for his wonderful illustrations that we have all come to expect, and for his steady hand through all the phases of production; and Steve Grooms, for putting down the words to many of my thoughts. Also, a big thanks to John Norlin, a young and skilled illustrator who is on the front end of a long and productive professional career; and to Mark Strand, who provided a steadying influence on the words. Sandy Ryks, whose keylining efforts know no time clock and whose perfectionism shows in every page of everything she does.

There have been so many fishermen who have taught me so much, but I want to mention my brother David, who worked with me in developing many of the patterns you see here, and contributed ideas of his own; and "Big John" Christianson, whose ability to catch largemouths is known far and wide, and who also generously added insight.

I also want to thank the largemouth bass, the beast who inspires so many of us to spend so much time and effort in hot pursuit, and gives all of us such a release from the more mundane things in our lives. I could go on listing all the people who have helped make this book, and all who have shared a day of bass fishing with me, but it would take every page we want to use to talk about bass fishing.

But I want to reserve a special thanks to a group of people who don't get thanked often enough, a group that is the basis for my life's work and accomplishments. You. All of you, who come up to me at sport shows, and in tackle stores, and on boat launches, and who write letters in response to the "Good Fishing" television show. For without your questions, without your shared interest in the sport of fishing, without your sincere desire to become better and more responsible fishermen (and women), it wouldn't matter what this book was about, because nobody would read it.

In the beginning, I had a dream that one day I could build a company whose business it would be to teach people how to fish, and how to love fishing. Through your continued support, it has come true, and continues to come true in bigger and better ways all the time.

TABLE OF CONTENTS

Foreword

Most readers already know that Babe Winkelman is one of America's most skilled multi-species anglers and the host of "Good Fishing," the most popular fishing television series ever to be aired. Those of us who are fortunate enough to know Babe personally will all agree that he has the energy of four or five men. He needs it, to accomplish all the things he does! Years ago, that energy was focussed on the problems of fishing. These days, however, Babe seems less interested in honing his own fishing skills than in teaching others how they can enjoy fishing the way he does.

I met Babe ten years ago, when he submitted a bass fishing article to the magazine I then edited. We made a sort of deal: I'd teach Babe about writing and photography if he'd teach me to catch fish. We both gained from that, but we also learned that I would probably always have more skill with words and Babe would always be better with fish.

So it was natural for us to collaborate on this book. It is *Babe's book*, built on his knowledge of bass and bass fishermen. My job was to set down Babe's ideas in a form that was clear and fun to read, but I've mostly kept out of the way so Babe could talk to the reader in his own voice.

Writing *Bass Patterns* has been a great experience, although one with some frustrations. The limits of space forced us to leave out a wealth of fishing information. We packed as much in as we could, but Babe had so much to say about bass fishing that we could have made another book from the tips that were left over. Perhaps someday we will.

Bass Patterns is a remarkable book. It presents a total system for understanding bass fishing. It is full of detailed information, but that information is presented so that everything works together to show the reader the "big picture."

In a few hours, the sun will be rising on a new day. When it does, I plan to have this foreword in the mail to the printers so I can be on a certain weedy bay of a certain lake, putting some of the lessons of this book into practice. I will have a new sense of purpose and a better strategy than ever before.

Bass, you better watch out!

And Babe, thanks!

Steve Grooms

Chapter 1
The Magic of Bass

A dock on a northwoods lake. A sandy-haired kid with a fly rod is fooling around with the sunfish that live near the end of the dock. Nearby, a dragonfly becomes trapped in the surface film, thrashing its wings furiously. But not for long. A chunky fish explodes through the surface and engulfs the helpless insect in its huge mouth. The kid's eyes almost leave his head, and because of this experience he'll spend countless hours trying to design a lure that beats its wings like a dragonfly. Most models involve a rubber band, wax paper wings and water-soluble tape. None of them work. It won't matter anyway, because what really counts is the raw excitement of that moment, the unforgettable picture of that bass blasting all over the dragonfly, the pure delight in *bass*!

A large Texas reservoir. A gleaming metal-flaked silver bass boat glides into a stumpy cove. A tanned, wiry man in a jump suit darts forward to the troll motor, telling his partner, "One fish, just *one* fish!" The fellow in back nods, knowing one more "weigh fish" will probably put his partner in first place in one of the most important tournaments in the state this year. The troll motor hums, the reel hisses, the chubby crankbait splashes down. As he brings the bait past the shady side of a gnarled stump, the angler lets it pause, then rips it forward. The water boils by the stump, the rod arcs. "There she is!" howls the angler. "*Whooeee*! She might take 'big bass' honors too!" Then the bass shoots through the surface, stands on its tail and rattles a massive set of gills, flinging the crankbait back at the bass boat so fast that both men instinctively duck. *Bass*!

A highland reservoir in Kentucky. Two young men are fishing in a rented boat. Neither is what you'd call a serious fisherman, but this is a pleasant place to drink beer and avoid the weekend Mr. Fixit projects their wives had in mind. Below their boat a monstrous old bass lifts slowly from the blackness of some deep weeds. Seemingly not moving a fin, she glides forward to inspect the plastic worm that is jiggling by. She is awesome. Her eyes are almost as big as quarters and her mouth could accomodate a muskrat. She would make an instant celebrity of anyone lucky enough to land her. Swimming along with the worm, the bass flares her gills to inhale the worm. Blows it out. Sucks it in again. Blows it out. Sucks it in again. Sensing the boat, she spooks, tugging the line slightly as she spits the worm for the last time. Up above, one of the young man frowns thoughtfully and says, "Hey, I just had a little bite." "Naw," says his partner, tipping a beer, "you *always* doin' like that. I'll believe it was a fish when I see it. If then!" Ah, yes, *bass*!

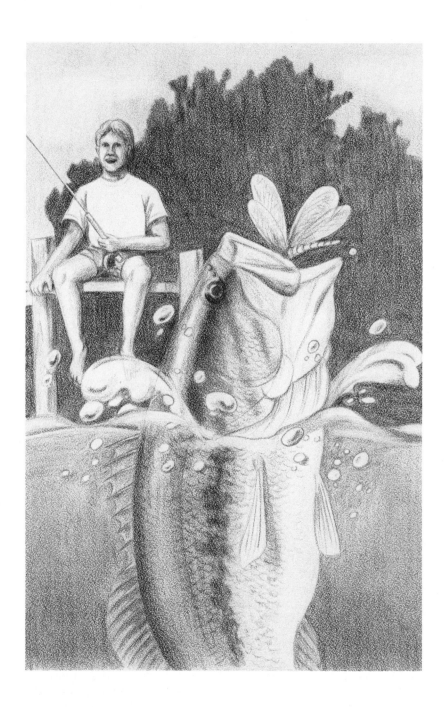

Dark Nights, Big Bass

I don't remember my first bass...that was a *long* time ago, but I sure remember when I really got into bass fishing. My buddy, Al Amundson, and I discovered a little lake not far from our central Minnesota home. This was back in the early 1960s when fishermen were just starting to hear about "structure fishing" and many other new concepts. The lake was a small thing surrounded by hills overgrown with oaks, and we could walk all around it in a night. The southeast shore was a jungle of drowned timber. It held the big bass.

We would wade this little lake on summer evenings when the water was so warm we just wore jeans and sneakers. Our gear was pretty crude, by today's standards, but it did the job. We would throw surface baits like the Jitterbug and the old Heddon Mouse, classic baits that were catching bass before I was alive and they probably always will.

It was exciting fishing if you could forget the mosquitoes. We could hardly see a thing, so everything was done by feel and sound—the click of the bail, the hiss of line going out, the splash of the lure landing and the *bloop-bloop-bloop* of the thing coming back to us. And then the best sound of all, the sharp slash of a bass attacking that lure. Then the fight in the dark!

And, oh boy, were those nice bass! We took stringers that would still make your eyes pop, big fish. I'd caught bass before, but never before had I worked out a particular place and technique—a *pattern*—that produced fast fishing on big fish. I fell in love with bass fishing and I haven't fallen out of love with it since then.

A Love Affair With Bass

From one end of America to the other, it's all the same. People are just wild about bass. You can debate which pro football team is "America's team," but there's no question which is "America's fish." It's the bass, of course.

Bass are popular partly because they're so well distributed geographically. There are at least some bass in every state but Alaska. The Rocky Mountain region is the only area in America where bass don't occur.

You don't have to like the Corps of Engineers or the other dam builders to appreciate the fact they put bass fishing in reach of millions of Americans who just plain didn't have much fishing available to them before the big impoundments were established in the 1950s and 1960s. Apart from the Great Lakes, reservoirs now account for half the standing water in this country. Most of 'em have bass.

People love the way bass fight, too, and no wonder. Bass fight hard. They're like "Rocky"— all heart. They shake their heads, they plunge into cover, they wrap your line around anything handy, they make power runs and they jump. And I'm just like you and every other fisherman: I dearly love to see a big old bass jump, whipping my plug back and forth in a frothy rage. Maybe I'll lose her on that jump, but I love it!

12

The largemouth bass is America's favorite fish. Does anyone have to ask why?

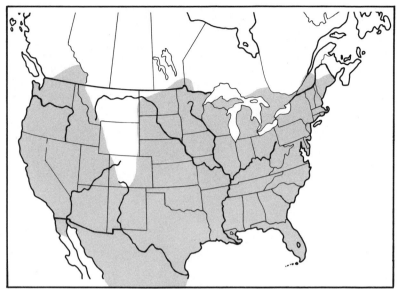

The range of largemouth bass. Eighty percent of the American population lives within ten miles of a body of water with bass in it.

Bass are so *interesting*. They can be real shallow or real deep. They can be shoved way up inside impossible cover or they can be roaming the trackless open water. And they've got moods. Whatever their mood was yesterday, today it's often something else. Last week they wanted a slow bait. This week they want a bait going faster than human hands can move one.

Change is just about the only constant thing about bass fishing. You can hate it if you want to, but that's a little dumb. You might as well learn to like it, because that's bass fishing. If you want everything the same all the time, take up bowling. The pins aren't very moody and you can count on finding them more or less where they were the last time you went bowling. But that's not fishing. It sure isn't bass fishing.

If you aren't a *thinking* bass fisherman, you're almost surely not a very good bass fisherman. One of the reasons there's so much written about bass is that there's a lot to say. This is not a simple fish with set habits. People who go fishing to "relax" and not use their brains are maybe going to find some recreation but they're not likely to find many bass. Not with any consistency.

This is a fish worth spending time studying. I've been fascinated with bass fishing for over 20 years and I'm still learning more about them almost every week. I expect to go on learning more about bass until the day I make my last cast. They're that kind of fish.

Bass have individuality, and that adds to their appeal. Some are loners, while some run in packs. Some spend most of their lives in jungles of vegetation while some haunt more open deep water. Individual bass have different levels of aggression and intelligence. Almost all of them are able to learn from bad experiences with anglers, for bass are smart. Believe it!

14

We anglers also like the fact that bass live in special sorts of places, places that excite an angler's imagination. You'll find bass along logs, back up in abandoned boat houses, in lily pads, etc. Once we've caught a bass from under a dock or by a stump, every dock and stump we see afterwards is more exciting. You look at them and just tell yourself, hey—there *has* to be a big old bass right there!

Those places have been touched by magic, the magic of *bass*!

About This Book

There are bass books and bass books. Why this one? Well, for one thing, I know from all the seminars I give that there are a lot of people who would enjoy bass fishing more if they had the proven, easily-understood system of pattern fishing that I'll be presenting here.

I've spent a lifetime learning about bass fishing. I've fished bass for fun, for food and in tournaments. I've also fished in front of film cameras that are grinding away expensive film while I tried to sweet-talk a bass to audition as a "movie star." (Believe me, trying to catch a good fish when the light is good and the cameras are in place is a special sort of pressure.)

While travelling to fish tournaments or to film my "Good Fishing" television series, I've put hooks into all kinds of water all over this great land. It has been my pleasure to fish with and learn from some of the best bass men in the world. I've even learned from some of the inexperienced fishermen I've guided.

Trying to catch big bass when the camera is running is a special sort of challenge.

I've had a lot of help as I put this book together. On the staff of Babe Winkelman Productions, Inc. there are several top-caliber bass anglers with experience from all over the country. These guys catch a lot of fish and have a lot of fun doing it. They were eager to share the work of putting this book together.

But there's a much more important way in which this book is special: it focuses on *bass patterns*. In this book I want to teach you pattern fishing, the same intelligent approach to fishing used by top bass fishermen everywhere.

Simply stated, a pattern is a combination of *fish location* and *lure presentation* that will catch bass. Pattern fishing is primarily a process of making a good guess about what the best pattern will be and then testing that guess. You move efficiently on the water, constantly refining your notion of what the best pattern might be. As we'll see, the best way to nail down the pattern is to ask the bass. They know!

This book will tell you how to do that. And to help you, we are going to offer a broad assortment of proven patterns that will get you on the winning one sooner. Eventually you'll develop your skills to the point where you'll discover new situations that call for patterns nobody ever developed before. Maybe you'll then be one of the thousands of people who write me to tell me what you've learned. I'll appreciate it.

Learning anything like bass fishing is a combination of fun and work. If you don't work at it by challenging yourself—taking on new waters and new patterns—you just aren't going to grow. If you take the attitude that this is all serious work and you are a failure unless you go out right away and catch a pile of fish...well, you're going to miss the whole point of bass fishing. One of Babe's Rules: if your bass fishing isn't fun, you're doing something wrong. The problem is more likely in your head than in your technique or your equipment.

This is all part of the magic of bass. They are so much fun and yet so much of a challenge. Some days you'll catch them so fast you'll think you're ready to make a living on the professional tournament trail. Then the very next day your fishing will be so tough you'd swear you couldn't get a bass with a stick of dynamite. It's all bass fishing, and it's all fun.

Learning to catch bass like these is a combination of fun and work. You have to work at it...but it's fun!

Chapter 2
Meet the Bass

Let's make the acquaintance of Mr. Bigmouth. Just by looking at him we can learn some important tips about how he operates and how we can catch him.

And this is what we notice:

• For a fish no bigger than he is, a bass has a heckuva big mouth. The size of prey any predator fish can eat is basically determined by what will fit in its mouth (the *height* of the prey, not the length, is what counts). Bass, with their huge mouths, can scarf down a pretty big victim. This is handy, especially when bass dine on their deep-bodied cousins, bluegills and other sunfish. Mind you, bass aren't above knocking off an occasional duck or baby muskrat, either. I've found snakes, blackbirds, salamanders and all sorts of things in bass. A monster bass I recently caught had a bass in its belly that was big enough that a lot of people would have kept *it!* More typical fare includes crayfish, mayfly and other larvae, frogs and—the favorite—minnows.

• Bass are marked and colored in ways that make them hard to see under water. Ask any underwater photographer how hard it is to find a largemouth that stands out from its environment well enough to make a decent picture. The natural camouflage of a bass makes it hard for his enemies to see him. It also makes him almost invisible to the prey he stalks. Bass are green because they have evolved to live in weeds. But they also have a chameleon-like ability to change color and marking so as to better blend in with different surroundings.

• The eyes of bass are located to permit looking upward but not directly downward. Bass are physically adapted to watch for food in the water straight ahead or above them, which is one reason they hit surface lures so readily. Even when you think you are scratching the bottom with a deep lure, like a worm, many bass you catch are picking up that lure as it drops down to them from off a weed or bit of brush. Bass are so agile and aware of what happens above them that they can catch food flying through the air.

You can learn a lot about bass fishing by studying the way a bass is built.

• Bass are squatty and squarish compared to other fish. For their size, bass have a large and not especially streamlined frontal profile. Their tails are not huge, compared to the rest of their bodies. These physical qualities mean bass lack the ability to run down their prey in extended chases the way a salmon can, for example. Bass aren't pokey, mind you. Bass are more like a good football running back than a track star; they have excellent initial acceleration rather than blistering speed over a long course.

Like a running back, a bass excels at quick turns and short bursts of speed.

• Like other members of the sunfish family, bass have a large percentage of fin area for their size. This gives them excellent turning and maneuvering ability, again like a good running back.

It adds up to this. Bass are built to sneak, lie in ambush and chase their prey with short bursts of great speed. They can twist and turn on a dime, darting through a maze of thick cover with the agility of a grouse corkscrewing through the underbrush. Any prey being chased better be awfully quick in the critical first second or two, or it will make a one-way trip down that cavernous mouth!

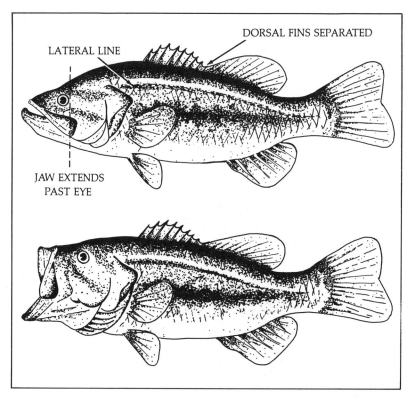

Largemouth bass have large mouths and wide, stocky bodies. They are adapted for feeding in confined cover situations.

Bass Genetics

The largemouth bass (*Micropterus salmoides*) belongs to the overall family of sunfishes. It is not related to sea bass, white bass or striped bass, in spite of similar names. Within the sunfish family is a group called the *black bass*, a group distinguished by their longer (relative to other sunfish) bodies. The other black bass are the smallmouth, spotted (Kentucky), redeye, Suwanee and Guadalupe.

Most anglers know the largemouth bass has a jaw that extends past its eye. That, plus the total separation of the first and second dorsal fins, distinguish the largemouth from the other black basses.

Even when you've identified a fish as being a largemouth there's more to know, for largemouths occur in two "flavors"—the northern subspecies and the Florida subspecies. The main difference is the maximum potential size. Florida bass often get up in the "teens," whereas a northern largemouth that tops six or seven pounds is a mighty big one. These subspecies are similar enough that crosses have naturally occurred in areas where both types inhabit the same waters, and the current world record fish is thought by some authorities to have been such a cross.

That record, unlike so many older angling records, is generally considered authentic. It has also stood for a remarkably long time. As thousands of bass anglers can recite by memory, George Perry caught the 22-pound, 4-ounce fish from Georgia's Montgomery Lake on June 2, 1932. The bait was, by some accounts, an old surface bait called the Creek Chub Fantail. Other accounts have it as a "glass-eyed wooden plug, a Creek Chub Wiggle Fish." Perry caught the fish by casting to a swirl he'd seen near a stump. He used a $1.33 rod-and-reel outfit.

This carved wooden replica of George Perry's world record largemouth is on display at Marv Koep's bait shop in Nisswa, Minnesota. It is held here by James Wentworth.

There is wide speculation that catching the fish to beat that old record might be worth a million dollars to the lucky angler. (Perry won $75 worth of sporting goods.) Matter of fact, there are a few people who have taken up that challenge as their life's work.

When Florida strain bass were planted in San Diego County's deep reservoirs, some awesome bass began to be caught by guys fishing extremely deep waters. The bass world held its breath waiting for Perry's old record to tumble. It almost happened. A 21-pound, 3-ounce bass was taken from Lake Casitas in 1980 by angler Ray Easley. If that fish had been taken in summer or fall instead of right after spawning, it might have topped Perry's fish.

Then there was the monster bass spotted in Lake Miramar by famous underwater photographer Glen Lau. Lau swears that bass would have weighed *28 pounds*—big enough to be a nice musky! That kind of story would be dismissed as "bar talk" if it came from anyone with less experience with big fish. Lau's fish has probably died of old age by now, but we can all hope she had lots of babies before slipping off to her anonymous death.

In an effort to produce larger bass, some state agencies have stocked the Florida strain bass in waters farther north. Those efforts are being criticized by many biologists now. There's evidence that the Florida bass don't do as well in the colder water of the north as the subspecies that has developed there. That's hardly surprising. The northern subspecies has had centuries to get genetically fine-tuned for its environment. When man fools around with Mother Nature, trying to improve on her work, he usually ends up finding out that "Mother knows best!"

Some experienced observers of bass are worried that modern fishing pressure could be modifying the genetics of bass. They argue that intensive pressure on big bass, especially trophy-hunting techniques aimed at catching huge bass when they are shallow to spawn, will eliminate those special fish from the gene pool. The ability to grow to great size is a rare and precious genetic trait. If most of the fish that have that trait are removed, something very special will have gone out of bass fishing.

The Six Senses of Bass

Bass start out with an advantage over you. They have the same five senses you have: smell, taste, touch, hearing and sight. And they have a sixth sense, *lateral line perception*, which allows them to sense the low frequency vibrations put out by predators and prey moving in the water near them.

If you think of these senses in human terms, you'll get it all wrong. Bass live in water, a medium that transmits sound and scent far better than air. The six senses of bass have been specially adapted to the bass's peculiar habitat and survival needs. Let's take a look at the various senses.

Taste.

This sense isn't very important. How do we know? Anatomical studies on bass show there are few taste receptors in the mouth area. Bass don't need a keen sense of taste in order to survive, so they don't have it.

Feel.

The sense of feel is also not highly refined in bass. This sense is most important to you as a bass fisherman by the way it affects how long a bass holds an artificial lure in its mouth. Most of a bass's favorite foods, such as minnows, frogs or salamanders are soft. Crayfish are hard-shelled, so bass must expect them to feel hard in their mouths, but most of their food is soft. Experienced bass anglers agree that bass hang onto natural baits or soft lures longer than they'll hold on to hard artificial lures. So you have more time to set the hook when fishing with live or soft baits.

You can test this. If the bass are in a positive feeding mood, you can really tease 'em with a soft plastic bait. Instead of setting the hook when you sense a pickup, just pull gently. When the bass lets go, wiggle the bait again. You can usually tempt a bass into making many repeat attacks on a soft bait. This does *not* work with crankbaits, spinnerbaits or spoons.

Smell.

Bass do have a keen sense of smell. Most fish do, partly because scent travels extremely well in water. Fish, in tests, have detected the presence of chemicals when they were diluted to the equivalent of one drop of chemical in an Olympic- sized swimming pool.

Yet, compared to such fish as catfish or salmon, bass aren't terribly sensitive sniffers. Given the bass's habitat and feeding habits, the sense of smell is far less important than the sense of sight. That *doesn't* mean you ignore it! Especially if you want to catch big bass.

Big bass have a better sense of smell than small bass. Scientists tell us a fish's sense of smell is related to the number and size of folds in the olfactory organ. Catfish have far more folds than bass, as you'd expect. But would you expect big bass to have a more highly developed smelling system than small bass? They do! Big bass are actually physiologically different, more sensitive to smells.

The sense of smell is tuned in to *danger smells* and *attractive smells*. Here are some smells that turn bass off: 1) predator species smells, 2) the fear scent of other bass, 3) human scent and 4) other foreign odors. Let's look at them.

First, predator smells. If you catch a northern or a musky while bass fishing, don't throw the same bait for bass until you get rid of the predator smell on your lure. Tournament fishermen usually take the time to cut off their lures and retie a fresh lure rather than scaring bass with an offering that stinks like a species that preys on bass. At the very

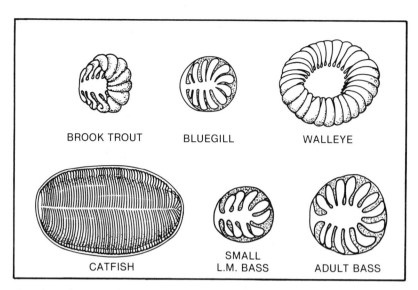

BROOK TROUT   BLUEGILL   WALLEYE

CATFISH   SMALL L.M. BASS   ADULT BASS

Bass have less sensitive scent organs than some fish, but large bass are more aware of scent than small bass.

least, wash the northern slime off the lure and treat it with one of the better commercial fish attracting/masking scents.

The fear scent of injured bass is another turn-off. Scuba diver Bob Underwood did a lot of work on this problem. He found that a bass that was caught and released would attempt to rejoin the school. The school would normally accept the released fish, and often the same lure would even take more bass from that school.

Yet Underwood learned that if a caught bass had been *injured* and attempted to rejoin its school, the school would not tolerate its presence. A bleeding fish caused this sort of response, but so did a fish with a superficial cut in the skin. The injured fish was putting out some kind of scent (known as a pheromone) that frightened other fish. Underwood also rubbed a lure against a shallow cut in a bass's skin. When that lure was put down, all the bass in the area avoided it like it was poison!

Human scent can be a big negative factor. Scientists tell us that all mammalian predators— and that's you and me, as well as bears and seals and others—secrete an amino acid called L-serine through our skin. It repels fish. Some people emit more L-serine than others. Salmon have been shown to be extremely sensitive to this substance, even when it was diluted to a fantastic extent. How much are *bass* bothered by L-serine? Nobody knows for sure. If you want to play things safe and smart, keep your hands clean when fishing (using a soap like Lindy's No-Scent Soap). And use a fish attracting/masking scent.

And bass don't like many foreign odors. In this category we can include suntan lotions, bug dope, motor gas and similar substances that will smell bad to a fish. These scents might not frighten a bass as badly as L-serine because they aren't identified with predators, but common sense tells us they sure can't help your fishing.

Not all smells repel bass. Bass *like* the smell of food and the fear scent of injured prey.

To some extent, bass locate prey by smelling it. This is one reason live bait is sometimes more effective than artificials.

If you break the skin of a minnow, which you do when putting a hook through it, the scent that goes into the water is attractive to bass. In other words, not all pheromones are put-offs. However, the fear scent of forage species is a *turn-on*.

Hearing.

A bass has ears on its head, just like you do, though bass don't have flaps that stick out to show where their ears are. Since bass live in a world that is often dark and hemmed in with dense vegetation, the ability to hear is of life-or-death importance to them.

The bass's ears hear only high frequency sounds—clicks, scrapes, rattles and other similar noises. These are warning sounds, sounds that alert the bass to the presence of nearby danger. These sharp noises are not normal in the bass's environment. Frogs and minnows don't usually click, scrape or rattle. Fishermen and some other predators do occasionally click, scrape and rattle.

There are two lessons here for bass fishermen.

First, be a little cautious about using noisy lures. Some crankbaits have internal rattles to help bass hear them. Fine, but you can get too much of a good thing. Extremely loud rattles are likely to turn off bass in some situations.

What situations? I'd caution you against using extremely noisy lures in very clear or open water, where bass will be used to relying on their sense of sight to locate prey. And any time the bass are spooky or "off" feeling, like after a cold front passes, you aren't helping yourself by using a lure that makes a big racket. On the other hand, noisy lures are often highly attractive to active bass in dingy water or heavy cover.

The second lesson is that we should avoid making sharp noises near bass. That's why carpeted interiors are standard on all bass boats. That's why smart fishermen sometimes put indoor/outdoor carpeting or other soft liners on tackle boxes. That's why you *never* want to make loud sharp noises—like dropping the troll motor roughly into the bracket or kicking over your coffee thermos— when you are near bass.

Ideally, your lure should sound like a minnow or a frog, and your boat should sound like a lily pad.

How about talking in the boat? That's fine, as long as it doesn't interfere with the concentration of your partners. Sounds in the air don't have the impact on bass that sounds in the water do. Sound travels about four times faster in water than in air. Water, in fact, seems to *magnify* sound. Some guys have sound systems in their boats, high fidelity systems with lots of oomph in the speakers. Don't you think the fish hear that music, too?

Lateral line perception.

In a way, this is just an extension of the bass's hearing ability. High pitched, sharp noises are picked up by the bass's ears. Low, soft, pressure-wave noises are picked up by the lateral line. Both perceptions are "hearing" in a sense.

A bass's lateral line is as sensitive as a diseased tooth. If a dying minnow is struggling to maintain equilibrium, a nearby bass feels its erratic throbbing. Or let's say a frog is stroking along in some open water in dense weeds, out of sight of a bass deep in the cover. Nearby bass, by perceiving the special rhythmic pattern of the frog's legs, will know exactly *where* and *what* that frog is. Believe it or not, a pork eel barely crawling along the bottom of a lake sends out waves of pressure that are picked up by nearby bass that cannot see the worm. There's no quieter lure than an eel, yet bass can "hear" it.

This same sense is used by bass to detect danger signals. If you keep stomping on and off the "go" button of your troll motor, nearby bass will be spooked. They'll probably drop into deep water and cease feeding. So does that mean you shouldn't use a troll motor? No way! The energy pulses put out by oars or paddles are far worse than the steadier pulse of a troll motor— they sound exactly like the wave pulses created by panicked fish. But it's better to run the motor in sustained bursts, not a lot of on and off changes. Bass get suspicious about erratic, changing wave patterns. And some troll motors are much better than others, as we'll see later.

You can spook bass by turning the trolling motor on and off too often when close to the fish.

Several underwater observers have witnessed another danger signal picked up by bass through their lateral line. When an angler puts enough effort into a cast to twist the boat, the hull shoots out a pulse of energy that causes all nearby bass to wheel and stare at it with alarm.

How acute is a bass's lateral line perception? A seven-pound bass caught in Florida was found to be totally blind in both eyes, yet the fish was healthy and well-fed. Experiments have been done on bass in tanks in which the fish were blinded. In spite of the loss of vision, these bass were able to locate and capture minnows put in the tank. But notice this. In experiments of this sort where bass taken from extremely dingy water were blindfolded, the bass located and fed on minnows with ease. Bass taken from clear waters (fish that were used to relying on vision for feeding) had trouble feeding without the sense of sight, though they eventually found their prey through lateral line perception.

Bass are adaptable creatures. That's a big part of what makes them bass. They'll use their lateral line sensitivity to locate prey and avoid trouble when they are in places where sight is limited. But where they *can* use their eyes, bass *do* use their eyes.

Vision.

This is a fascinating topic, and we can only hit the high spots here. There are many myths about how bass see. You've probably heard (and believed) several of them.

The underwater world of most bass is murky and dark. Plankton and other suspended particles reflect and filter out sunlight coming into the water. Bass are usually found in dense cover, weeds or timber. No wonder they are basically nearsighted. Bass *can* see about 30 feet through clear water, but most bass are found in places where, because of cover or suspended particles in the water, they can see only 12, eight or five feet away, often even less.

A bass's eyes are normally focussed for short-range vision. With effort, a bass can focus on distant objects, but that is rarely important to them. They care about what is close. Far away stuff can't eat them or feed them. Close stuff is of intense concern to them.

Bass can see objects to the sides, above, in front of, behind and even slightly below them. The only directions they *cannot* see are directly below and directly behind them. Your eyes are located on the front of your face; a bass's eyes are located on the sides of its head. You have a great deal of three dimensional vision (and since you have hands and long arms, that's pretty useful). Bass have three dimensional vision only in a small area right in front of them. All this is part of Mother Nature's plan. Bass can perceive food or danger all around and even behind them. But their *three dimensional vision* is limited to that narrow zone right in front of their noses where they do their feeding.

Bass can see both above and below the surface of the water. Because of the way light rays enter the water, the shallower a bass is, the less it can see above the surface. This is one of several explanations bass view deep water as a haven. Not only are they safe from attacks from the sky, but they can see much more of the above-water world when they

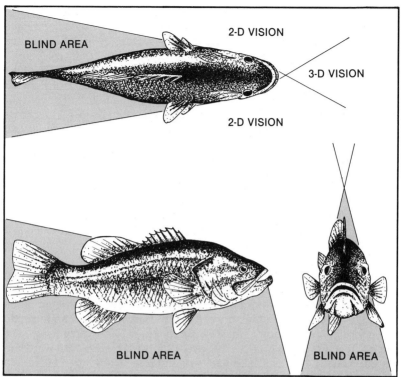

Bass can see most of what is around them, though they have only a small area of three-dimensional vision.

are deep. When a bass spots something suspicious looking above the surface, it naturally drops deeper—both for protection and for a better look.

The higher an object stands above the surface, the easier a bass can see it at any depth. The brighter that object, the more apparent it is to a bass. If you stand up high in the bow of a bass boat wearing a bright yellow hat, you are making yourself visible to all bass in the vicinity. They still might strike...or they might not. If the water is ripply or murky and the cover is heavy, you can stand tall and not worry. But there is logic in wearing dark clothing and keeping your profile low, especially when trophy hunting.

A lot of controversy has centered on the question of whether or not bass can see colors. They can, as we'll discuss in detail a little later. In fact, the bass's eye is pretty much like the human eye—most sensitive to the yellow and red spectrum of the color scale. (This is not universal; walleyes, for example, have eyes that are most sensitive to green and orange.)

The eye of the bass is much better adapted for low light circumstances than the human eye is, although bass don't see as well in darkness as walleyes. For a bass to see an object moving in the water at night, it has to get under that oject to get it highlighted against the sky. Even without a moon, there is always some light coming from the sky.

We should consider another basic fallacy about bass vision, namely that bass can't stand bright light. Have you read that, "Bass don't have eyelids"? In strict anatomical terms, that's true. Nor do bass have contracting irises, as we humans do. All this is true...but misleading.

Bass can tolerate extremely bright surroundings. Though they lack eyelids, bass do have several ways of reducing the impact of light on their eyes. The underwater world is basically dim and full of cover that reduces the impact of bright light. By dropping into deeper water, bass can "turn the lights down." Yet beyond that, bass have the ability to alter the impact of light on their eyes. Bass have rods and cones in their eyes, just as we do. The cones perceive color. The rods perceive objects only in terms of shades of black, white and grey. But they do that very well, being 30 times as sensitive to light as the cones. Bass make different use of rods and cones, depending on how bright the light is.

One of the lessons here is that, while color is important in the daytime, it *isn't* at night. The best night bait color is black...which just means that scientists are confirming what mosquito- bitten night fishermen have known for decades.

Even though bass can stand bright light, it is a fact they often lurk in the shade. Feeding bass, not cruising or dormant fish, usually sit on the shady side of cover. From that position they can see prey swimming in bright areas better than the prey can see the bass waiting in ambush. So even though the fish don't *have* to be in the shade, they often *want* to be there. To you, the fisherman, it's pretty much the same, anyway. You should usually fish *as if* bass hate sun and love shade.

Your hours on the lake will be more productive if you fish quietly and concentrate on shaded areas.

Foxes and Hedgehogs

Biologists classify animals in terms of whether they are a "hedgehog" or a "fox." The hedgehog has just one trick for surviving, but it's a good trick. The fox doesn't have quills to hide behind, but its agile mind is full of different tricks.

Relatively primitive animals of all sorts, including fish, tend to be specialists with one or two ways of making a living and keeping out of trouble. They're hedgehogs. The more recently evolved animals, the foxes, are usually generalists with a big variety of clever strategies in their survival kit. Foxes handle change far better than hedgehogs.

Our friend the bass, of course, is a fox. The bass a highly developed fish and one of the more recent additions to the fish family tree. Bass have many different feeding strategies and feed on a wide variety of prey. Bass make their home in a wide variety of places, and when their environment changes bass usually cope well. They are versatile and flexible.

One reason for this is that bass are smart like a fox. Compared to other fish—trout, for example—bass rate very high in IQ tests. Bass are smart. They learn from experience. Does that mean they learn to avoid anglers and lures? Yes.

The largemouth bass, like a fox, is a smart, flexible, highly-developed predator.

Tracking studies conducted by biologist Mike Lembeck in the San Diego County reservoirs have shown that some bass definitely respond to fishing pressure. Bass that were holding near attractive structure at times when angling was banned would move off that structure shortly after the reservoirs were reopened to angling. Bass also showed that they were aware of boats and anglers. Sometimes a bass would tolerate the presence of a boat until the anglers began to present lures; then the bass would move away. Other bass would drift off toward deep water each time a boat simply came too near them. Bass were highly aware of a refuge area, closed forever to angling, even though it was not marked in any way the fish could detect. Some fish were careful to never leave the refuge area.

Several studies, especially one conducted in a controlled lake in Illinois, have proved another suspicion long held by bass anglers: that bass "get wise" to lures that are used frequently in an area. Baits rarely stay red hot for long when they are used repeatedly on a body of water. Bass become conditioned to them.

Exactly how this happens is not easy to say. Maybe the fish don't actually learn to avoid lures; perhaps those individual bass that are most attracted to popular lures get removed from the population, leaving those whose particular tastes or habitat preferences give them some protection against the lures that worked on their pals. Or maybe fish lose interest in a lure if they see it too often; they might not know it represents danger, yet it might be boring to them. Or maybe fish can communicate distress to each other, through pheromones or their struggles as they are being caught. Bass might possibly learn a certain lure is dangerous by observing other fish being caught on it; don't laugh, some thoughtful underwater observers of bass have come to this conclusion.

I'm convinced that we don't know all there is to know about the ways fish communicate to each other. Let me offer one example. Often, when you first begin fishing an area, the first fish you take will be the biggest fish in that school. But if you move up to a spot, hook that big bass *and lose it*, you might as well leave. In all probability, you aren't going to catch anything there. Somehow, that big fish makes it clear to the other bass in the area that it is time to be cautious. Hooking and losing a small bass won't have the same effect. But if you blow it on the biggest, most dominant fish in the school, unless the fish have a fast and furious "bite" going on, forget *that* spot!

Some lures are easier for bass to become conditioned to than others. The more quiet, soft and natural a lure is, the better it works even after bass have been exposed to it. Noisy, unnatural lures are the fastest to lose effectiveness. If you are the first guy in history to throw a buzz bait in some private pond, plant your feet firmly and hang on to your rod! But if you are going to be fishing a popular lake that gets pounded every day all year, you'd be smart to reach for the soft plastic baits or the jar of pork rind.

A little example of that. A friend keeps about 250 bass in a small pond behind his house. Early in the year, he can catch some of those bass on spinnerbaits, but that stops pretty quickly. Then he catches some on crankbaits for a while, though the bass soon get wise. Plastic worms will tempt them for several weeks, but eventually they lose effectiveness. By the summer's end, even though the fish are often hungry, they can only be taken on live bait...and you better switch live bait at times, or they'll lose interest in those baits. Do bass get conditioned to lures? Well I guess so!

Do Bass Go to School?

You will find frequent references to "schools" of bass. This book will have some, too. What does that mean?

Generally, biologists use the term "school" to refer to a congregation of fish that sticks tightly together and acts in concert. Baitfish school. If they didn't, all the predators would pick them off one by one.

Few fish predator species school, strictly speaking. A typical exception to this rule is the white bass. Packs of white bass running together will herd shad into areas where the bass can really chop them up. But, by and large, predators don't have that degree of social organization and they feed better when they operate individually.

Are bass schooling fish? Yes and no! It's best, most of the time, to assume they are.

Let's make an analogy. In a factory town right after the Friday five o-clock whistle, you'll see a tremendous number of working men gathered in nearby beer joints. Are these "schools" of humans? Or are they aggregations of humans who have come to the same place at the same time because they all want the same thing and it is here?

Bass, especially big bass, don't run in consistent groups like schooling minnows. What they *do* is move about as their needs dictate, making the best use of cover to protect themselves and surprise the forage they are eating.

Sometimes that means a group of bass will spend several days in a certain section of a weedline. Occasionally they'll suddenly "turn on" and feed voraciously. At such times, older structure fishermen used to believe the bass had "made a movement" into the weeds. Yet in many cases they were always there.

You will often find bass, not in schools, but spread out along a shoreline, occupying the best habitat they can find. Under one boat dock there might be one or two. Down the shore, under that big tree that fell into the water, four or five fish might be sitting under the timber. About 30 yards away there is a big stump that holds a single fish. It would be stretching things to call anything here a school, yet this is typical bass behavior.

Nevertheless, bass often act as if they were a schooling fish, so it is both useful and accurate to use the term. Like the factory workers, they often find it advantageous to hang out in the same areas. And the bass will be highly aware of what other nearby bass are doing.

And a key reason they flock up is that food is not distributed evenly throughout the lake. Something will happen—the frogs make a "run" in the fall, a gang of crayfish concentrates in a certain area, a hatch of minnows takes place—that suddenly makes a tremendous amount of food available in a small area. Do the bass know about these things? Is water wet? The school of bass that forms around one of these feeding situations might stay together for hours or days. Usually the school sticks together as long as the food supply holds out.

An exciting example of schooling behavior is found when you see a bass intercepting a lure in the air. Why do bass do such a thing? Well, for one thing, when a bass is feeding actively it can be amazingly aggressive. Just *try* to keep a lure out of its mouth at times like that. You can't! But those bass that snatch lures from the air are mainly trying to get that lure for themselves before other bass around them can get to it.

Worm fishermen see the same thing at times. If a bass picks up a worm with a "ka-thunk" and sits there, other bass might or might not be nearby. When a bass picks up your worm and *runs* with it, chances are that fish is dashing off with a prize it doesn't want to share. That tells you that this area is worth working carefully, and that you should rush hooked fish to the boat rather than letting them run and jump all over the place.

When bass are feeding aggressively they will actually snatch lures from the air.

Bass run in schools at times in southern reservoirs where shad are the predominant forage. This is especially likely to happen in older reservoirs where the original drowned timber has rotted away, leaving vast open spaces. Then "schoolies"—groups of young bass of about two pounds, sometimes larger—will gang up to wreak havoc on schools of shad. The surface will be churning with bass slashing into the helpless shad for a short while, and smart fishermen know they should run quickly to the spot and get a fast- moving lure into it. You can also take bigger bass this way at times. Bass in impoundments in winter often school in deep water, sometimes in awesomely large groups. Those school are created by a special food supply.

So do bass run in schools? Sometimes, but not always. Do they often hang in tight *groups* in the same place, especially to feed, and keep track of each other? Yes. When you catch a bass, should you assume it *is* part of a school and that there are more in the area? Yes again, unless you are dealing with cover that obviously won't hold a group of fish. You'll often catch more fish if you *believe* the bass you catch come from schools and fish accordingly.

It isn't often that you can get into a group of bass that is feeding competitively. When you do, hang on!

Things About Bass

Here are some miscellaneous facts about bass that will help you understand and catch them.

Bass don't like being rocked about. Fisheries crews know they have to take extra measures—giving the bass tranquilizers—before carrying bass around in stocking trucks. For this reason, it isn't usually smart to fish very shallow water when the wind has set the waves crashing into it. Bass often won't stand for being heaved around in water like that. Yet I've known days when I could barely hold my boat on a wild shoreline and still caught bass like crazy!

Bass are very hard to catch in the test nets put out by fisheries crews who sample lakes to assess fish populations. Apparently the bass have such good vision, maneuverability and general awareness of their environment that they avoid nets. This tells you something about bass and the type of environment they call home. It also tells you that it isn't smart to rely on test netting reports to judge the strength of a bass population in a lake. I've frequently caught limits of bass in little lakes that the Minnesota DNR officially lists as having "no largemouth bass present."

Bigger bass are almost always females. Females live quite a bit longer than males. Since fish grow as long as they live, the females naturally attain greater size.

Bass have a complex, modern muscular structure. In animals, including fish, dark muscle is for sustained use and light muscle is for bursts of speed. Pheasants have light muscle in their breasts because this muscle is used for quick bursts of flight. Ducks have dark muscle in their breasts because that muscle has to keep them in the air for long migrations. Bass have *both* muscle types, which reflects their highly-evolved generalist nature.

Bass are capable of extremely fast swimming speeds for short times. Largemouths in warm water can hit speeds of about 12 miles an hour, which is roughly five times as fast as human hands can move a crankbait!

Bass are marked with the classic "countershading" pattern—dark on top, white underneath. People once thought this was like the camouflage painting on fighter planes that were meant to blend with the sky when seen from below and blend with the ground when seen from above. It isn't. Light enters the world of the bass from above. As it comes down, it strikes the upper part of the bass's body. That causes the pigment to darken, but that darkness is overwhelmed by all the light hitting it. The lower part of the body (the white part), which is in shade, naturally looks dark. Thus the bass's dark/light coloring, under the influence of sunlight, blends out to become uniformly hard to see. The green-black sides are marked with a big stripe that can take on the character of spots at times, breaking up the uniformity of color and making it even harder for other fish to see the bass.

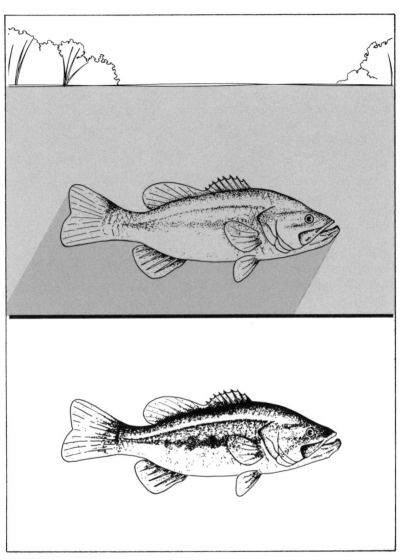

Countershading, in combination with the behavior of light rays, makes a bass blend into the surroundings.

The prettiest bass come from clear or shallow water because they are more brightly colored and distinctly marked. Bass from deep or murky water are usually pale and indistinctly marked.

Chapter 3
A Year In the Life

Early spring. The days are longer than the nights now. The sun has more power, too, so that during the day the fish see the lake's ice as a great gleaming dome of diffused light.

Little of that light makes itself down to where the big female bass lies in her winter hold in 50 feet of water. She is in contact with the bottom, so motionless she appears dead. A northern largemouth weighing just a bit over six pounds, she is 13 years old.

She is the last survivor from the 5,000 eggs her mother laid down over a decade ago. She has defeated astonishing odds to have lived so long. Just being born was a remarkable feat. Most of the eggs deposited by her mother never lived any kind of life except a brief existence as a fertilized egg.

Some survived to become fry, tiny creatures that at least were identifiable as fish. Yet only a small fraction of the fry lived to see their first birthday. A few were caught when quite small by such unlikely predators as insects and crayfish. Some died following an injury. A great many fry were eaten by larger fish, including bass. Some of the fry simply failed at the harsh game of survival. Birds took some.

Indeed, of the whole nest, only six of those 5,000 eggs lived long enough to become bass 12 inches long. Of those six, one suspended too near the surface on a sunny spring day and got nailed by a kingfisher.

Then a new predator became a factor for the remaining five. One fell victim to a gob of worms fished under a dock by a kid who had hoped to catch a sunfish. Another picked up a minnow on a slip sinker rig whose owner intended to catch a walleye. Another of the six grabbed the first spinnerbait she saw. One lived for several years before inhaling a red plastic worm one summer. That fish was released, eventually reaching a weight of three and a half pounds. Worms held a fatal attraction for this fish. He was caught and released again by another worm angler. Finally he hit the worm of an angler who liked to eat bass. Which left only one fish surviving from the original nest.

That lone survivor now rests in deep water where the water is slightly warmer than it is elsewhere in the lake. Her ventral fins are spread out, touching the bottom as if to keep her upright. Her tail fin is collapsed, not perky and spread as you'd expect.

Every once in a while she seems to wake up a little. She stirs, yawns and snaps her jaws vigorously to blow silt and debris free of her gills.

Once an ice fisherman, by accident, gets his minnow right in front of the bass. She ignores it for several minutes. Finally the persistent twitching of the minnow irritates her and she moves away a few feet. The metabolism of the bass in winter is so drastically slowed by cold water that feeding on one small fish will keep her alive for several weeks.

That is about to change. As the sun hits the surface of the ice its heat is concentrated by bits of leaves and bubbles in the ice itself. The ice becomes porous—"rotten"—and weak. Spring breezes cause the ice to flex and buckle, weakening its structure. One day there is more water than ice, and soon all the ice is gone.

The big female does not move, though she senses the pulse of life quickening in the lake. Finally she drifts out of her winter haunt and takes up a position in 25 feet of water on a steep break directly outside a marshy bay.

The water warms by day, cooling down again at night, but warming more than it cools. Spring rains freshen the water and cause the bays to spread their ripe scent outward into the water of the rest of the lake. Windy, sunny weather mixes and spreads the warmth until it is felt more and more by the bass.

She begins to move up into the bay in the late afternoons when the water is warmest, sliding back into 25 feet late in the evenings when the air cools the shallows again. Soon the shallows are warm enough to attract the bass by midday, then by early morning. With more warming, she'll spend all the daylight hours in the shallows, though she'll still seek deeper water at nght.

As water temperatures fluctuate from the low to the high 40s, each day the big female joins a sort of spring picnic, a celebration of rebirth that annually occurs here where the dark, shallow water absorbs the heat of the spring sun, causing the whole area to come to life. Turtles bask on logs. Bugs whirl above the water, crawl through the silt and thrash in the surface film. Frogs emerge from the ooze. Swarms of minnows roam about, along with schools of bluegills and crappies.

And bass. Day by day, the big female and the other bass feed with increasing enthusiasm. This is one time of year when their appetites exceed the ability of the environment to satisfy them. In part, they feed because their increased metabolism demands it. In part, they feed because they are soon to engage in a major activity which will exhaust their strength. This pre-spawn period is a time of vulnerability; bass work hard to fatten up, doing so with a reduced food supply that has not recovered from all of last year's predation.

As water temperatures approach the 60s, the bass increasingly turn their attention to spawning. Though spawning can take place in the same shallow waters that attracted them in the pre-spawning time, there are special requirements for spawning habitat that might draw them to other shallow areas.

Almost a week before the full moon, the big female enters courtship. She seeks out the roots of an underwater stump, banging her distended belly against them. As she does so, a male bass appears and displays interest. Following courtship displays, the two bass cruise the shoreline, seeking a favorable spawning location.

They find an excellent area. It has a firm bottom below the silt, and a fallen tree offers protection from would-be egg robbers. If bluegills can completely surround a nest site, their chances of wiping out the nest are good, no matter how resolutely the male defends the eggs. This site is also protected from any waves that might be generated by winds from most points on the compass. Wave action can cast silt over the nest and destroy it as effectively as hungry sunfish.

With this pair, nest-making is mostly done by the male. He sweeps away debris with vigorous motions of his tail. Eventually, he scours out a depression twice the length of his body. The nest site lies in four feet of water, a bright saucer- shaped area easily seen against the darkness of the surrounding bottom.

This site is near a site she has used before, but not the same. Some bass return exactly to the site or previous spawning efforts. Some spawn nowhere near their former sites. This variability offers some protection against localized disasters that might wipe out a whole year's nesting effort.

Similarly, not all the lake's bass will spawn at the same time as this pair. Some have done so already; others won't spawn for weeks. This, too, is a safeguard. If every bass pair went on the nest at the same time, one bad cold spell could destroy the efforts of *all*.

Like many big females, this one is a persnickety housemaker. The nest prepared for her is not quite good enough. She grooms it again and again after the male has finished. Any little bit of debris seems to annoy her, and she whips the bottom with her tail so vigorously that, weeks later, the lower part of her tail will still be raw, red and partially worn away.

As water temperatures break into the 60s and the full moon arrives, the two bass move over the nest. The male bullies, butts, bites and prods the female, shoving her over the cleared nest and encouraging her to drop the eggs. She finally does, releasing thousands of eggs into the nest as the male wiggles alongside her. He then positions himself over the nest and expels a sticky cloud of sperm.

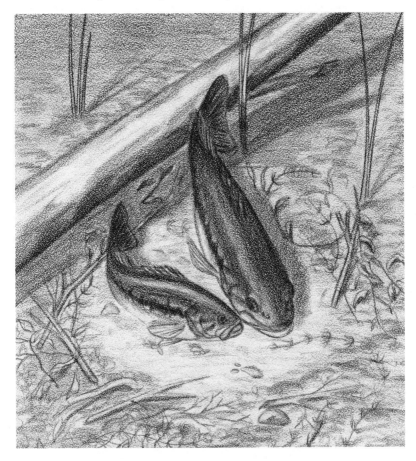

Leaving the male to the difficult task of fanning and protecting the fertilized eggs, the big female drops into deep water. Once again, she sinks to the bottom and appears almost dead. Spawning is extremely difficult on female fish, due to the effort involved, the physical abuse they receive and perhaps even because their bodies must release such a large mass of nutrients. The effort, in fact, is fatal to some females, especially those weakened by age. The big female will feed lightly and sporadically until she has recovered. At night she will make occasional forays into the shallows. During the day she lies mostly in deep water, though occasionally she moves to steep breaks.

It is several weeks before the female re- enters the warm shallows on a more permanent basis. She arrives, in fact, at just about the time the males are finishing their nest-guarding duties.

Not all have hatched. Severe cold snaps can destroy the eggs, as can high winds from a direction that covers the eggs with silt. In many lakes, wolfpacks of stunted bluegills gang up on the male and clean out the nests in spite of his best efforts to drive them away. When fishermen catch males off the nests, even if they release them, usually the nest is lost to sunfish.

The male guards the newly-hatched fry until they reach a certain size...after which he will feed upon them as eagerly as will any other predator.

Back in the shallows, the female finds food and cover for perhaps a week or two. She now feeds along with other bass, including the males who are ravenous after weeks of light feeding while guarding the nests. The deeper weeds have not yet developed, so relatively little is happening in deeper water right after the spawn. For a week or two most of the bass operate around the steeper breaks and little pockets in the thickest of the weeds developing in the shallows.

In time, the weeds develop in deeper water, the water grows warmer and the lake's food supply surges. Food is suddenly abundant and available in much deeper water than before. The big bass drops down into deeper water, where the newly emerging weeds are attracting a wide variety of food. Indeed, for about three weeks, the waters from about six to 14 feet experience an explosion of activity. That's where most of the forage species are congregated. That's where the most intensive mayfly and dragonfly movements occur.

She is eager to feed now, devoting full attention to becoming as strong as possible. For a while, the general lack of young fish encourages her to feed more adventurously than is normal for her.

By some means—acute senses or remembered past experiences—she is at the right place at the right time to take advantage of food abundance. Are baitfish ganging up in the shallows to spawn? The old female will be there to make short, deadly charges that deplete their numbers but improve her vigor. Are the frogs gathering to reproduce? Expect the old female to know it and be at hand. Are perch spawning in the shallows? They'd better be careful, for the old bass will surely be lurking in the shadows nearby.

She roams extensively now, travelling near shore for the most part but occasionally striking out across open water. This northern lake is her home; and she knows its shape, its weeds and its bottom features perfectly well. Her travel routes take her through cover that might hold food, but she also moves from spot to spot in the lake where she has fed successfully in past years.

She remembers, also, places where she has felt threatened before. She avoids those places. Two prominent points used to attract her until she became aware of the fact they attracted anglers, too. She doesn't understand anglers, but has learned to associate the presence of boats with danger. She won't spend time in places where fishing boats are especially common. She avoids some areas because of past close encounters with bigger predator fish.

With the passing weeks, food becomes more abundant, at least for smaller bass. For them, a big difference occurs just before midsummer when the year's whole crop of newly-hatched minnows becomes large enough to be worth pursuing. This has less impact on the big female because she is large enough to take on sizable bluegills, perch, bullheads, young bass and crayfish. While she is now hungrier than at any other time of year, for her body burns up food at a high rate, she has no trouble finding food. She feeds frequently, but each feeding effort is short and productive.

One of the reasons this bass has lived so long is that, for the past four years, she has spent much of her summer way up in a weedy bay. The bay is bigger than many farm ponds, filled with stumps of trees that died when a water level controlling dam was put on the lake in the 1930s. Those stumps make boat access difficult, so that very few anglers have tried to get back into the bay. Those few who have done so failed to notice that way back in, closer to shore than to the main lake, there is a small pocket of deeper water with a stand of rushes in it. The water is kept acceptably cool and oxygenated by the weeds and by an underwater spring that empties into the bay not too far from the rushes. This area is frequently home to the big female throughout the summer.

Her basic needs are well covered by this spot. Because of her great size, she has specialized in eating the mid-sized bluegills that are so common in the lake. With astonishing speed, and at a cost of almost no expended energy, she can strike, snatch and swallow a bluegill from her ambush spot. Sometimes she roams the bay at night, cruising in water scarcely deep enough to cover her back. And many a frog has suddenly felt the water sucked out from under him just before those huge jaws snapped shut and cut off the sight of the starry night sky.

Still, she occasionally leaves the bay, feeding at times around a sunken island that lies well out in front of her bay in deeper water. At other times she strikes out and covers four or five miles a day, moving mostly at night. Three reed banks are favorite hunting grounds. Much of her feeding takes place on a broad weedy flat where coontail mixes with other weed types, an area she knows intimately. She is especially fond of crayfish, and knows several places where they can be captured as they crawl around the tops of the sandgrass or attempt to sneak around in the protection of a rock-rubble pile on the south side.

Her feeding varies. At times she feeds opportunistically, grabbing a perch here and a nymph there. Often enough, though, she finds a chance to mop up on concentrated, vulnerable prey. At times her belly is so full of crayfish, and nothing but crayfish, that she looks the way she did shortly before spawning.

On her travels she sees other bass. At times she feeds along with them when food is concentrated and easily caught. When younger, she ran in schools more than she does now. Her bulk gives her the right to feed first whenever she chooses to, though sometimes caution tells her to let the lesser bass take the risks.

The days grow shorter, the nights longer, and the old bass gradually finds her home in the bay less suitable. The shallow water, which is powerfully influenced by the cold night air, is chilling faster than the deeper water of the main lake. Dying weeds in her favorite shallow bay are a signal that she must shift toward the main lake more permanently.

She still returns periodically to the shallows and those ambush spots she knows so well. When the frogs make their fall "run," swimming to the bottom silt to hide from winter, the old bass is there to meet them. At times she has so many frogs in her belly that it would be physically impossible to force another one in there. Yet she might try, for that is the way of a bass that is feeding voraciously.

Dying weeds deprive the shallow water of oxygen in some areas, so the female hangs around the remaining clumps of green weeds in deeper water. Sometimes she hovers over a deposit of rocks that acts as a solar heat collector on sunny days. Crayfish can still be found there by a fish with enough experience to know where to look.

All over the lake, seasonal changes are altering the makeup of the weeds. Summer's crop of aquatic vegetation is dying and becoming mushy. As the surface water cools, it becomes heavier and begins to sink. Finally the surface water is so cold and dense that it can no longer float on top of the cool, oxygen-poor water below. A total mixing occurs—the "fall turnover."

Like other fish, the big female goes through a period right after turnover when her patterns are unsettled and unpredictable. With water temperatures and oxygen levels constant from top to bottom, suddenly the whole lake is open to her. At times she is in water 60 feet deep. At times she is almost on shore, pouncing on any food she can find there. Her movements now are governed mainly by the need to find warm water and food.

The big bass is now feeding much as she did in the pre-spawn period. She will need food stores to see her through the long winter; if she does not "know" that with her mind, her body knows it in some way. Eggs are beginning to form in her body, too, and they also require nourishment. She eats voraciously now whenever she can, and she is eating larger prey than in spring. Because of the combined effects of natural mortality and the predation of several species of fish, the supply of minnows that was once so bountiful is now depleted. Compared to summer, now her food is much more concentrated in specific spots. The big female, and other bass that know these spots, are still feeding heavily.

She often feeds at the sharp, steeply sloping inside turns in the remaining green weeds of the main lake's weedline. By tucking up in these weeds, she can easily shoot out and grab minnows that expose themselves near the weedline. At other times, on calm and sunny days, she returns to her shallow home bay, and to other shallow spots like it, to dive into the schools of minnows drawn into warm brushy areas.

That's where she is on a sunny October day when a large object passes her, thrashing in distress. Without reflection, the big bass wheels and grabs it. It snaps back at her and begins to pull her toward open water. Her body floods with a sense of panic.

Turning toward deep water, she drives down against heavy resistance, shaking her head and plunging toward the safety of the depths. The resistance does not go away. The big bass makes two more bucking drives that end short of the protection of the weeds, then she slants toward the surface and makes two desperate efforts to shake loose the thing in her jaw.

Finally she is dragged to a boat and, after an effort to run around the troll motor, she is grabbed by the lower jaw and brought into the air. Her body is shocked to find itself deprived of the friendly support of water.

What happens next? Will the old female be dropped in the livewell and eventually take up a position, as a mounted fish, on a den wall? Will she be freed of the hook, held alongside the boat to allow her to recover so she can be released?

Well, I really don't know what happens next. You do. *You're* the successful angler, holding one of nature's rarest creations, a trophy bass. You could tell yourself she is too precious to kill. You could tell yourself a bass so big has very little time left to live anyway. Both positions are true and legitimate. I can't tell you what you are going to do with her.

Until that moment comes—and I hope it does, for that's why I'm taking all this time to write a book—you probably don't know what you would do, either.

Bass In Other Places

It is impossible for one bass in one body of water to be entirely typical of all bass. And that's true of the bass we've been following, too. She was a mighty lucky fish who lived in a healthy, diverse environment in a northern natural lake. That's good for her, and such places do exist.

But don't get the idea *all* bass live this way. Generally speaking, most bass find themselves trying hard to make do with a very imperfect world—the water's too hot much of the summer, larger predator fish hog the best cover, much of the forage is too big or too small, there isn't much cover, the cover and the food aren't in the same places, etc. Be glad you aren't a bass. It isn't an easy life.

If bass environments differ enormously, bass do not. All largemouth bass, no matter what water they live in, have similar priorities. The first priority, *always*, is security. Second is the need to acquire food and to do so in a relatively efficient way. Third, although not as important as the other two, is the desire for "comfort," although that is a human term that isn't altogether accurate when applied to bass. Still, it will do. Finally, at times, the spawning drive absolutely overpowers all other priorities.

As we learn more about bass, we learn that their behavior is more variable than we once thought. For example, spawning behavior is much more individual than was reported earlier. Individual bass have many different patterns of courtship. It is even possible for the female to take the lead in choosing a nest site, for example. As I've pointed out, these variances are a hedge against the disaster that might fall on a population of animals behaving in stereotyped, identical ways.

You can understand and even predict bass. It takes some experience, but it is possible. Every largemouth bass—from Mexico to Canada—has certain basic needs. These basic needs change a little in response to the cycle of the season, but they follow a predictable annual *pattern*, something like the pattern we've just watched in our big female bass.

One thing is true of all bass at all times. You can bet your house *and* your bass boat *and* your retirement fund that they'll be scrapping to make the best of the possibilities their surroundings offer. Oh, they'll surprise you from time to time, but it all makes sense ultimately in terms of their struggle to make the very best deal of what nature offers them.

Chapter 4
Finding Bass

Finding bass is the biggest challenge in catching bass. At any given time, some 70 percent of the water in a lake will be barren of *any* fish. Only a small percentage of the remaining water will hold significant numbers of bass. And the *active* bass might be in a very small percentage of that water.

Don't let that discourage you. It's *good* news that active bass are concentrated. If they weren't, we'd have a heckuva time finding them!

Bass hang out in very specific places *for very specific reasons*. If you understand what is motivating the fish at any given moment, you'll be able to concentrate your search in more productive places.

Don't expect lots of solid rules. For example, bass like water temperatures in the higher 70s, but that's not a rule that will point you inevitably toward where the bass are. Bass have been caught in numbingly cold water by ice fishermen and they've been caught in water in the low 90s in desert reservoirs. *The only rule a bass absolutely obeys is that it will do whatever it must do in order to survive.*

Let's look at some of the important influences on bass location.

Seasonal Movement Cycles

No matter where bass are found, they experience an annual cycle of activity that is much the same. The particular dates are different (for example, bass spawn two or more months earlier in Louisiana than in Wisconsin), yet the cycle is essentially the same.

For bass in Florida or Ohio, winter is a time of inactivity. In water much below 50 degrees, bass do very little feeding. They don't do much else, either—just sit near the bottom in deep water where it's slightly warmer.

Spring warmth triggers a move to the shallows, not to spawn but to feed. Bass stage a pre-spawn pig-out in water from the middle 40s to the high 50s. They are protected by closed seasons in some states, but in most regions this pre-spawn feeding binge offers the best fishing of the year. Daily weather changes have major impact on how active active the bass will be and where they will locate.

Most of the active bass at any given time will be occupying a small percentage of the water.

The fish will be highly concentrated in the areas that warm earliest. Examples: the extreme shallow ends of coves, channels between lakes or bays, little protected bays with dark bottoms and in shallow channels.

Early in the year, bass run up into very shallow water if that is where they can find warmest temperatures.

With warmer water comes the biggest event on the bass's annual calendar—the spawn. Though they are totally concentrating on that act, spawning bass might feed a little. Yet most fish caught during spawning are males that grab lures to move them away from the nest.

The post-spawn period is a time of transition. Some bass will feed in the shallows while others are recuperating from spawning. In the case of natural lakes, weeds are rapidly developing, and bass are quick to stake out feeding stations in these weeds.

This can be a tough time to find bass, and the big ones are especially tightly grouped. But if you can find them, you can have a picnic. Last year, while we were filming a television show, I located a bunch of large bass grouped up like that. I had to find two things together to find bass: bulrushes and clumps of newly forming lily pads. But if I could find those weeds together, I was into some big bass. Oh, it's fun to come across a bunch of nice fish when the camera crew is there to record it!

I was throwing a yellow spinnerbait right into the clumps, and sometimes the bass got it the moment it touched the water. I had one fish that went 6 and-a-half pounds and several others between 5 and 6. My camerman, Larry, got in the water to see if he could get a different kind of shot, with the camera low to the water. Just then I hit a real nice fish while Larry's camera was rolling. The fish swam sideways, right in front of Larry, and came up for a jump next to him, with me in the background. Believe me, fish rarely perform so perfectly for the camera! But on the

56

jump, the bass threw the spinnerbait right at me, hitting me right between the eyes and nearly knocking off both my glasses and my hat! Viewers probably wouldn't want to see television shows full of fish that got away, but this incident was so funny we knew we had to keep it and put it on the air.

In natural lakes, summertime bass will almost always be found in some kind of weeds.

The water warms steadily after the spawn. Often the weather in this transition period is stormy and unstable. It is difficult to find bass in good numbers. When you find them, they might not stay in one spot for long. Gradually, though, they drift toward their summer haunts and begin serious feeding.

Summer bass locate in *the best cover with acceptable water temperatures near food*. Their metabolism keeps increasing with the water temperature, obliging them to feed heavily. Early summer bass wreak havoc on the minnows spawning in the very shallows where the bass just spawned.

In natural lakes, and many rivers, food, shelter and the right temperatures will all be found in the various types of aquatic cover, primarily from the deep weedline to the shoreline. In some cases the thermal layering of water creates a barrier to bass movement. Often enough, though, the too-cold water lies below the level of the cover favored by bass, anyway, so it isn't a major factor.

Bass in reservoirs often use timber and other sorts of cover in moderately deep water. However, there are many weedy plants, such as coontail, in reservoir systems that act as bass magnets just as they do elsewhere. In most lakes and ponds, bass spend the summer months in the best aquatic vegetation they can find. Weeds offer shelter from predators and sunlight, agreeable water temperatures, oxygen and easy feeding opportunities.

Cooling water in the fall brings on more changes. The fall turnover destroys the thermal stratification of the lake, so uniform temperatures top to bottom allow the bass to move up, down or sideways wherever they choose. The fish now stage a feeding spree like the one that preceeded spawning. Food, on the other hand, is not as plentiful. Because the fish can be almost anywhere, finding them isn't easy.

Fall bass are very active, moving from deep water to shallow water to feed. Telemetry studies show them to do more prowling now than at any other time of year. Areas of lakes or reservoirs that are a long distance from deep water will not be good. Even though the fish feed in the shallows, they want deep water nearby. The last surviving green weeds are bass magnets, as are portions of the lake that warm up in response to pleasant fall weather.

Types of Feeding

Bass feed in several distinctively different ways.

Bass *feed to grow* much of the year when water temperatures are favorable. In this type of feeding, they operate very efficiently to capture food large and small. They are looking for advantages that let them take in nutrition without expending much energy.

Fall bass *feed to fatten*. At this time the fish seek out large prey. You might expect them to take smaller food, as the water cool and that would seem to go along with feeding on smaller objects. But they don't.

At other times of the year, as in winter and during the spawn, bass only *feed to sustain life*. These extremely passive bass eat just enough to keep the spark of life glowing.

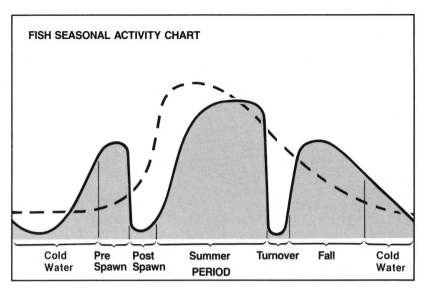

FISH SEASONAL ACTIVITY CHART

| Cold Water | Pre Spawn | Post Spawn | Summer PERIOD | Turnover | Fall | Cold Water |

Throughout the year, bass activity levels rise and fall. Also, food availability rises and falls. The best fishing is usually when bass are active but food is scarce.

Now let's look at a number of influences on bass location that will help you find them.

Water Temperature

Many studies have been done on the preferred temperature of largemouth bass. As I've mentioned, bass can handle a wide range of temperatures. In general, they like the same temperatures that humans like for swimming, maybe slightly higher. Various studies show bass preferring temperatures in the mid-70s to the low 90s.

There's no need to fuss about the exact figure, for it is relative. An Alabama bass will feel at home in warmer temperatures than a New York bass, for this is a fish that accomodates its surroundings. Water at 55 degrees feels a whole lot better to a bass coming out of its winter inactivity than the same water would feel to a September bass that's used to much warmer water. It's a relative thing.

Temperature is relative in another sense. If a bass has been suffering through wintry temperatures in the 40s or low 50s for days or weeks, a shift in water temperature toward 60 degrees will feel great. A shift *downward* to 60 degrees from a warmer temperature in summer, however, would put a chill on bass activity.

You can't find bass by simply locating some theoretical idal temperature.

That *doesn't* mean that temperature makes no difference. In spring, when water temperatures are generally in the 40s or 50s, bass will be trying to get into the warmest water around. A surface temp gauge will then be more important than a sonar unit for locating fish. The same thing happens in fall, when most of the water is too cold for bass. Then more favorable water temperatures in the shallows draw in bass.

When the water is cold, in spring or fall, your surface temperature gauge can help you locate bass.

Things usually get turned around in summer. During this period, water temperatures are often unfavorable to bass in shallow water. The fish are forced down into deeper, cooler water. They may, however, return to the shallows to feed if that's where the best food supply is. In really hot water, they would make such movements into the shallows at night when the shallow water would be as cool as it gets any time of day. Of course, things like light penetration, wind, available cover and the presence of forage species will often mean more to a bass than a "comfortable" temperature.

Many lakes *thermocline*, which means they set up in a three-layered structure. The shallow water will be too warm for bass and the deep water will be too icy cold (and possibly lacking in oxygen). In between is a narrow band of water called the thermocline where water temperatures drop quickly. When and where this three-part structure exists, bass are apt to be in the water *at the thermocline or above.*

Thus, for much of the summer, the bass in shallow, fertile lakes that stratify in this manner may be unable to use deep water. Locating them is made simpler by the fact that they are locked into the water from the thermocline to the surface. They can enter the sterile, chilly water below if they have to, but it's no place for them to spend much time and you can usually ignore it when looking for fish.

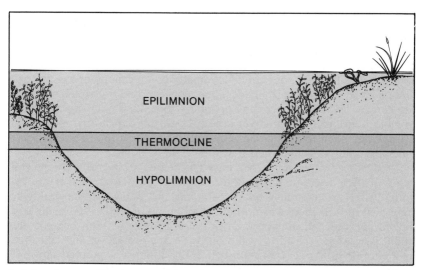

In lakes that stratify, the water lies in layers. At bottom is the cold, oxygen-poor hypolimnion. Above is the warmest water, the epilimnion. The middle layer, or thermocline, lies in between. Summer bass often sit in or just above the thermocline.

When the fall turnover comes, mixing the top and bottom layers, water temperatures and oxygen levels become homogenous throughout the lake. Then bass location is much more complicated. A major barrier to bass movement has been removed, and the fish are exceptionally free to roam. Warming trends will put temperatures higher in the shallows, and the bass often take advantage of those moments to do some feeding close to shore.

Water temperature is more important when it deviates significantly from what is comfortable for bass. In other words, changes of two or three degrees don't mean much to fish except when the water is exceptionally hot or cold. Then, little changes make a big difference.

I remember a tournament I fished down south over ten years ago. It was early January, and it had been cold. Bass pro Roger Moore did very well in that tournament, and he later told me his secret. Roger had flown over the lake *in an airplane* in order to spot areas that might be quick to warm up. He'd spotted a pool of open, shallow water that was isolated from the rest of the lake by a vast field of hydrilla and hyacinths. It took Roger an hour of poling to get his boat into that spot, time lost from fishing, but once he got into that back pocket the water was much warmer and Roger was into a bunch of active bass. Because the main lake's water temperatures were so far from ideal, Roger knew that extreme measures to find warmer water would be repaid.

Similarly, when water temperatures are extreme, especially when they are really cold, it isn't just a matter of how cold things are but *what the trends are.* Spring bass are just as sensitive to trends as to absolute temperatures. The water might be pretty cold, but if it is on a warming trend, the fish can be active. But in chilly water, a downward trend is a big downer for bass.

Cover

Compared to other gamefish, largemouth bass are *obsessed* with the need to get in, under or next to cover. Bass never outgrow the need to find secure cover. The best cover of all is something— a canopy of moss, a tree limb, a dock, a bunch of lily pads, a tangle of exposed tree roots—that the fish can get *under*. If a bass can't get under some kind of cover, it will try to hug up *against* the best cover around. Bass are out of their element in open water, even though some situations cause them to use it. But, give them any kind of shelter, and they'll be right at home.

Take, for example, Jake, the bass I kept in an aquarium for several years. If there was one little log in the aquarium, Jake would try to get under it. If there was one weed in the aquarium, Jake would inevitably be right next to it. If there was nothing at all but bare sand in the tank, Jake looked nervous and unhappy. Once I cleaned out the tank but put one small clamshell on the bottom. It didn't offer any protection, but Jake took up a position right over that clamshell. If I had somehow painted a big "X" in the sand, Jake would have parked right over that "reference point" if he couldn't find anything more significant to relate to.

Jake wanted to be somewhere in particular, not just out in space. He was a bass. Bass like objects. They hate being in the middle of nowhere.

When you assess the cover in the lake, ask *how much* good cover is there? If a lake only has a tiny bit of suitable cover, obviously the fish will be there. If there is a great deal of acceptable cover, as on many lakes I fish, it becomes important to be nitpicky, to look for not just good cover but *the best* cover.

Two things make cover "good" for bass. First is the thickness, the density of the cover. While there are times when bass prefer to move around in open water, they are the rare exceptions that prove the rule: *bass like it thick*, especially in clear water. In an area with pretty good cover, if you see one spot where the cover is exceptionally thick, that's almost surely where the better fish will be. Like a good grouse hunter, an experienced bass angler develops a sharp eye for good cover. With time, you aren't even aware of seeing these spots with your conscious mind. You just *know* where you should put your next cast.

Second, for a bass "good" cover is cover with good access to deep water. Deepness is safety. There are times when bass are in water that barely covers their backs, but big fish don't like spots that are isolated from the depths by a big stretch of shallows. (Although one exception is when fish roam at night.)

Let's talk in more depth about two critical kinds of cover, *drowned brush or timber* and *weeds*.

Timber and Brush

If you could see timber through the eyes of a bass, you'd instantly understand why some trees regularly hold bass and others never do (though they may look identical above water). The same goes for brush.

To our eyes, timber often looks all alike. The bass, however, have strong preferences.

We have to learn to see cover through the eyes of the bass. Where you and I can look out and see hundreds of identical stumps standing in the air, the bass are keyed in on some very different things. Here are some of the key differences between one tree and another, *as seen by bass*:

- In what depth of water is the timber?
- Is it on a flat, on a point, along a creek bed or on a dropoff?
- Are there any holes nearby? Other deep water?
- How bare is the tree—very bare, or does it still have lots of limbs a bass can get under?
- Is there any vegetation nearby? How near? What kind of vegetation?
- Does the tree have roots a bass can get under?
- How many choices of water depths does a particular tree provide? Often bass prefer trees that span a broad range of depths; by relating to a single, comforting object, they can still move up and down at will.

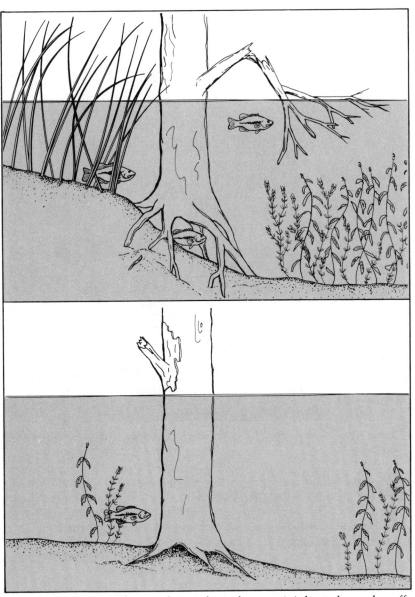

Good and poor trees. The tree above is better because: it is located on a dropoff, has weeds nearby, is more "complex," and has places for bass to get under.

We could go on in quite a bit more detail, but the point should be clear. To nail down bass location, you have to start seeing such things as timber and brush—or docks, or riprap, or beds of wild rice—with the eyes of a bass.

That isn't easy. Start by looking at three things: the *depth* of the cover, the *quality* of the cover (primarily density), and the *location* of the cover with respect to other areas in the lake.

Weeds

In northern natural lakes, it is almost true—almost, not quite—that bass are *always* in the weeds. That doesn't help you very much, though, because there are so many types of weeds that if you search in them randomly, you'll rarely catch a bass. The real question is: *"Which* weeds are they in?"

Again, we've got to see weeds as fish see them. The most important things to learn to recognize are *different species* of weeds and *different holding spots* in the weeds. Incidentally, as more and more of the reservoirs of central and southern America age and lose their original timber, weedy cover there is becoming important to bass and bass fishermen.

You don't have to become a junior scientist to recognize a few common weed species. Each species is different in its appeal to bass. Each species presents different opportunities and challenges to you. Get to know them!

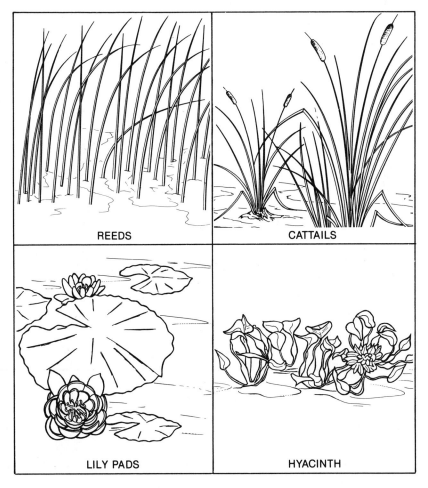

REEDS   CATTAILS

LILY PADS   HYACINTH

Common emergent vegetation.

Don't limit your fishing to emergent weeds, those weeds that stick up above the water. Emergent weeds (like rice, cattails, bulrushes or reeds) can offer great fishing. Some weeds you can see below the surface with the help of polarizing glasses. Others you only see when you bring them up on a lure, or perhaps they register as thin blips on your fishing sonar.

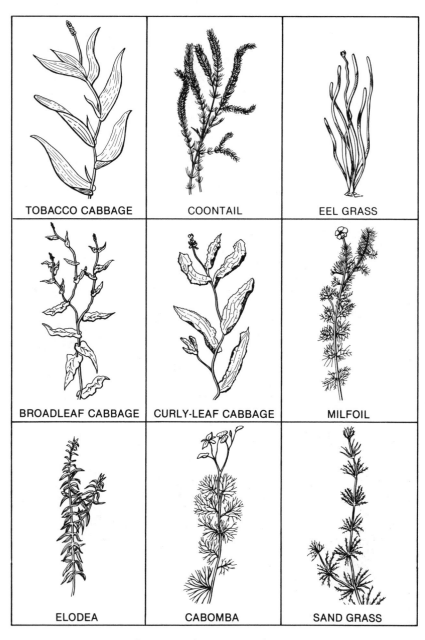

Common submergent vegetation.

Submerged weeds often grow in clumps or beds with many potential sizes and shapes. There are different locations in and along a bed that bass will use. For example, there is a *back edge*, the edge closest to shore. There will be a *front edge*, the edge closest to deep water. The weeds might not grow all the way to the surface, in which case there would be a *top surface* to the bed that you can fish. Bass tend to concentrate along these surfaces—the front edge, the back edge and the top of weeds. While there might be fish deep in the middle of the weeds, they will usually not be the most active fish, so it pays to start your search on the edges, the front, back and top edges of the weeds.

There will be variations in the shape of the weeds, and these can be crucially important. A *point* of weeds sticking out into deep water will often hold bass. An *inside turn* or little concavity in the weedline will often hold bass. Irregularities, either holes or dense clumps within the weedbed, attract bass.

Here's a hint that will save you lots of time when looking for fish. Bass will *either* be on the inside turns or on the points; they won't be holding on both types of cover at the same time. If you hit some fish in an inside turn, start checking out other inside turns. If the fish are on one point in the lake, they'll be on points elsewhere too.

There are also unlimited numbers of ways weedy cover can occur in combination with other elements. Sometimes bass hold in water where two weed species grow together. Sometimes rocks in weeds hold fish. We'll get to more details in the chapter on the specific fishing patterns.

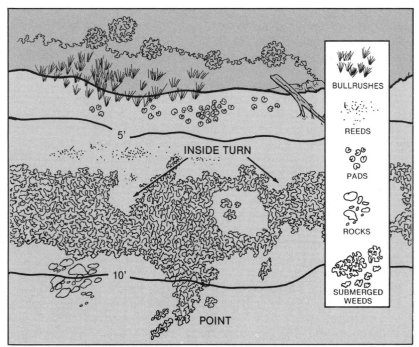

Aerial view of a weedbed. Note that the front and back weedlines are not smooth, but have points and inside turns. These concentrate fish.

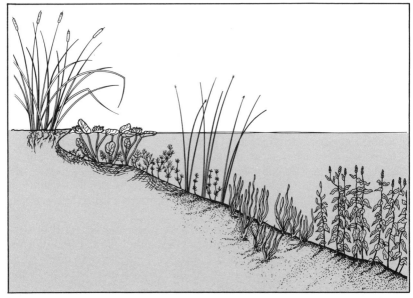

A side view of common weeds. Each weed type tends to grow at certain depths, with cabbage or coontail often being the deepest weed.

Structure

Structure is a term referring to the shape of the bottom of a lake. Points, saddles, holes, islands, reefs, creek beds, flats, dropoffs—all these are structural elements that can attract bass. Most walleye anglers pay close attention to structure, ignoring cover; bass fishermen often pay close attention to cover, ignoring structure.

That can be a mistake, although by concentrating on cover you can find bass much of the time. There will almost always be some bass shallow, and if you peck away at the best shallow cover, you'll catch a few. But largemouth bass, like *all* gamefish, are aware of the bottom contours in their environment. And until you learn to locate and catch bass on structure in deeper water, water where you rely on your sonar instead of your eyes, you're still a beginner.

I just *love* deep water bass fishing! I know that deep fish will often average a better size than they will in the shallows. Bass in deeper water have not seen as many lures (because so few anglers are proficient at deeper presentations). I know, too, that a school of deep bass is more likely to be in the same spot the next time I fish than a school of shallow fish.

The richer a lake is in cover, the less important structure will be. Putting that the other way around, in lakes with poor amounts of cover, structure becomes critically important. A strip pit with poor cover but some interesting points will offer few fish to the fellow who ignores structure. The guy who fishes farm ponds, where structure is often so bland as to be non-existent, better be ready to work his lures in cover.

In natural lakes, any of the classic structural elements can hold bass—*if* food, cover and water temperatures are right, and if the fish have access to deep water. In lakes where bass are the top predator, expect bass to make heavy use of reefs, humps and pronounced points. If muskies, walleyes and northerns are abundant though, bass will be found more often tucked up in the cover of dense weeds along the weedlines or on the flats.

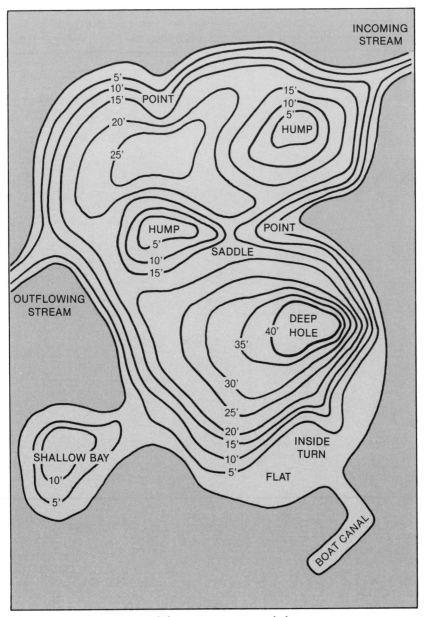

Common fish-attracting structural elements.

On man-made impoundments, structure is often terrifically important to locating bass. In addition to points, dropoffs and other typical structural elements, impoundments have two or three unique and significant types of structure.

Most important is the *main river channel*. Since reservoirs are made by damming rivers, they all have an old river bed running through them. That channel is highly attractive bass at some times of the year. Many of the coves or arms of a reservoir will also have creek channels in them. Those creek or river channels offer the security of depth plus steeper dropoffs than will be found in the surrounding water. Bass sometimes hold in or along the old channels and they often use them as highways for their movements.

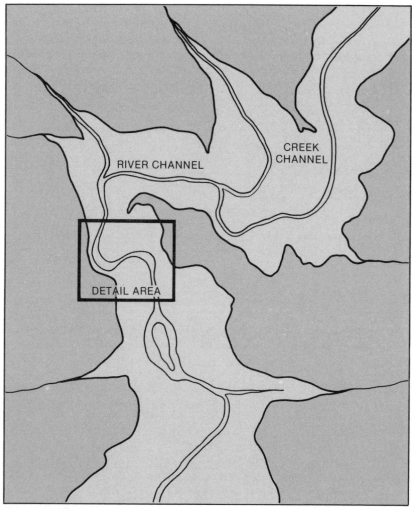

Overview of one arm of a reservoir. Note the main river channel, connected to smaller creek channels.

To find fish along these river or creek channels, you need to understand how a river is shaped. As rivers meander from side to side, one side—the outside of a bend—is deeper than the the inside of the bend. Where a creek turns sharply, the outside of the turn might have been washed out to make an undercut bank. Some of that structure is retained when the gates are closed to flood the impoundment.

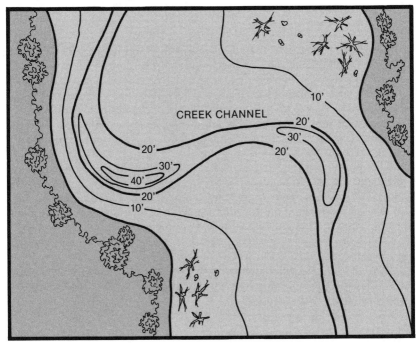

Detail of a creek channel, showing how the meandering of the creek makes steeper breaks on the outside turns.

Reservoirs also have unique structure and cover that is the result of man's activity on the land before it was flooded. Many sorts of flooded objects offer cover and ambush points for bass. Examples include old roads, chicken coops, fence rows and house or barn foundations.

The secret to finding bass on reservoirs is often the ability to visualize what the land looked like before it was flooded. You can then use that picture to help you find bass.

Structure-Cover Combinations

Usually, you find bass by finding that perfect combination of structure *and* cover. Add depth, and you usually will have the whole locational pattern. A locational pattern is a certain kind of *structure* at a certain *depth* with a certain kind of *cover* on it.

So, for example, you might nail the locational pattern down to something like the *tips of points* (structure) in *11 to 13 feet of water* (depth) where there is some *young coontail* (cover) developing.

When bass are really aggressive, you can be loose with your fix on the best structure-cover combinations. Often, though, you have to home in on the best locational pattern with great precision.

Food

Bass have to eat, and they'll go where the food happens to be. That's why bass are taken in the San Diego reservoirs at vast depths where you'd expect lake trout. The prime forage in those reservoirs is stocked rainbow trout; because rainbows live in deep, cold water, that's where the bass go. Don't, however, expect bass to hold in the inky depths of most lakes.

In a great many reservoirs, shad are the most common and preferred forage for bass. The more prevalent shad are, the more bass tend to concentrate on them.

This preference for shad will affect bass location in interesting ways. Shad feed almost exclusively on tiny plankton. Plankton is driven hither and yon by winds. Thus shad—and the bass that chase them—often end up being concentrated on the wind-beaten points and shores of impoundments. These points and shores might or might not have cover on them, but that's often a secondary consideration. Bass go there because the shad are there.

Bass location is governed a great deal by food availability. Unfortunately, it is hard for anglers to know in advance just when and where a food source will suddenly turn on.

Recent Weather

Bass often move in response to weather changes. We'll look at more of these issues in our chapter on weather.

Warm weather can draw bass into the shallows when temperatures have been chilly. The most rapid warming comes when warm air temperatures, sunlight *and* a wind occur together.

Cold fronts, naturally enough, can send shallow bass scooting for the depths if they are in water that was chilly even before the front. This happens most in spring and fall. When the front drives the bass deep, they usually only move to the first significant dropoff.

Wind can create conditions that draw bass in to feed along deeper structure. The pounding of waves stirs up the bottom, reducing water clarity and dislodging food items for minnows. A persistent wind against a point or hump will often trigger bass activity there by setting up currents past those structures.

Conversely, winds and high waves pounding into very shallow water cover will drive bass away. Waves of more than a couple of feet or so are bad news for guys intending to fish shallow water cover.

Wind is lashing waves over a shallow point. Shallow cover is rarely good in wavy weather, especially when the water is cold.

Other Factors

Here, briefly, are several other environmental factors or influences that should be on your mind as you look for fish.

Water Clarity

Water clarity is important to bass location. Dark water reduces light penetration and causes bass to feed in shallow water. Clear water allows light to reach into the depths, so bass will hold deeper.

In part, this is due to the impact of light on weed growth. Submerged weeds grow to whatever depth the light reaches. If sufficient light penetrates to 23 feet, weeds will grow from that depth on inward to the shoreline. If the water is so dark that light penetration is severly limited, the weeds might not be able to take root and grow below six or seven feet.

Bass in clear water will be huddled up tight against cover. They will be influenced by the sun, so that on a bright day they'll be on the shady side of cover, not out truckin' around in open areas. Clear water bass hold in deeper spots than they would if the water did not transmit so much light. In such a clear lake, the bass will move to the shallows to feed when light levels are low.

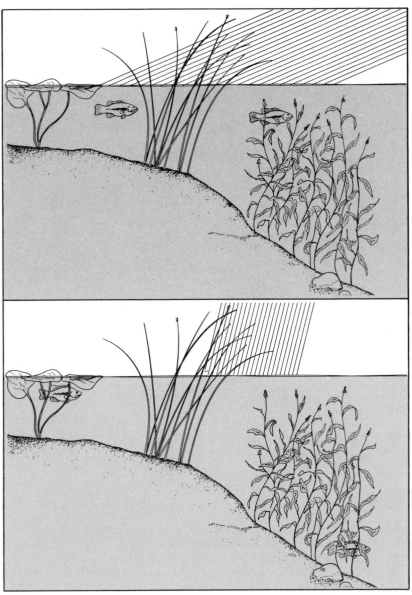

When light levels are low (as at dusk) or when they come in at an oblique angle (as in spring), bass will roam open water and high up over cover. But bright light coming straight into the water forces the fish to seek cover.

Bass in dark, turbid water will be shallow and less tightly tied to cover. Dirty water bass are more confident about roaming around in the shallows. They feel less threatened because the darkness of the water itself offers some protection to them. They will be shallow because there will be no weeds deep and because they cannot see well in deep, dark water. Bass in dark water, obviously enough, are easier to approach.

If you are a beginning bass fisherman, make an effort to avoid super-clear water. Fish the darker water where it is so much easier to get near bass without spooking them.

Sunlight

Sunlight works together with water clarity to influence bass location.

Bass operate more efficiently as predators in areas where the sun does not beat down into the water intensely. They feed most effectively when they can *see* but *not be seen*. This is one reason bass sit under docks, on the shady side of stumps, in weeds and so forth.

Harsh sunlight is rarely a factor early and late in the year. In spring and fall the sun's rays strike earth at a shallower angle than in summer months. Though spring or fall skies might look terribly bright to our eyes, bass will feel freer to use shallow water feeding areas than in summer.

Several factors reduce light penetration. The most obvious is time of day. Yet an overcast or a ruffle on the surface of the water reduce light penetration just as well.

When light levels are reduced in clear lakes, bass will almost always locate shallower than they would under calm conditions that allow the sun to shine right into the water. Similarly, the clearer the water, the more bass will be affected by sunlight levels. In dingy, dark-watered lakes, bass will be shallower and more consistent in their location. In clear water, bass will move around more in response to light as well as being generally deeper.

Oxygen

In fertile lakes, the water below the thermocline is devoid of oxygen because the decomposition of dead plant and animal matter on the bottom consumes oxygen. Thermal stratification seals off the deep water and prevents it from receiving the oxygen introduced into the shallows by wind and the photosynthesis of weeds.

You do not need an oxygen meter to identify these oxygen-poor waters. Expect them in any water that is fertile and rich with algae and plant life. In such lakes, a lack of oxygen in deep water will force all bass into shallow water, especially weedy shallow water.

In lakes where the water is oxygen-poor much of the summer, it can be critical to know where cold, fresh springs or rivers enter the lake.

Other Fish

Where bass are the top predator in a lake, they get first choice of cover. In northern natural lakes, that means they have a free hand to locate anywhere in the weedbeds and on structure in front of the weeds. They might even use open water structure, such as underwater humps, when those are holding food.

But bass are rarely so lucky. Usually they must share habitat with northern pike, muskies or walleyes. And those are fish that aren't fun to share anything with. Where does a 39-pound muskie sleep and eat? *Anywhere it wants to!* Every bass knows that. Depending on the relative strength of the populations, northerns, muskies or walleyes can push the bass around and force them to accept secondary habitat.

Northerns and muskies, of course, will eat any bass they can accommodate in their cavernous mouths. You rarely catch good numbers of bass and pike right together. If the pike are around, the bass will be somewhere else...maybe not far, but somewhere else. It isn't a bad sign to catch an occasional northern when you are bass fishing. After all, they occupy similar habitat, and it is especially common to catch a mixed bag if you work the deepest weedline. But if you get into a whole bunch of northerns, move! You won't catch bass in that spot. Change the kind of cover you're working, especially the depth.

Typically, northerns and muskies dominate the front weedline, forcing the bass into the middle of the weeds or all the way to the back. At times they'll force the bass almost on shore!

Even walleyes can bully bass about. Sometimes walleyes are stocked in big numbers into weedy lakes that lack ordinary walleye habitat. The walleyes go where the food is—the weedline—and they often force the bass to take up shallower positions in the weeds.

Finding panfish tells you something quite different. If you see bluegills or feel them peck- peck-pecking on your worm, bass might be nearby. If you find *scattered* bluegills, there might or might not be bass in the area. If you find a school of bluegills, though, there *will be* bass in the area.

Water Levels

In impoundments and river systems, bass are sensitive to the rising or falling of water levels.

Falling water is a real threat to fish that happen to get caught on large, shallow flats. When the water starts dropping, bass haul out of these broader flats and quickly move to a creek channel, dropoff or some other area where the security of deep water is at hand.

Rising water has the opposite effect. The inundation of areas by high water often makes a great deal of food available *out* of the heavy current areas. Bass move into these food-rich, freshly flooded areas to feed.

Other predators, particularly northerns and muskies, can push bass so shallow they're almost on shore.

Chapter 5
Weather, And What to Do About It

If somehow they passed a law making it illegal for fishermen to grumble about the weather, bass anglers would have very little to say. You'd walk into a tavern after a local tournament and there would be a dozen guys standing around, lips twitching, saying nothing. Well, it isn't going to happen. As long as people have fished for bass, they've griped about the weather.

With reason. If there is a fish that's more sensitive to weather than a big largemouth, I haven't met up with it. And don't want to. On a day-to-day basis, weather is the predominant influence on bass location and feeding attitudes.

The following guidelines will give you a help you find and catch bass, in spite of the weather.

Stability

For the most part, *stable weather is good weather*. Whatever the water conditions are—a certain temperature, certain oxygen level, etc.— bass become acclimated to them. They don't welcome major changes in their environment, the sort of wild changes that are usually caused by sharp changes in weather.

You might expect the bass to simply move when their environment becomes unattractive for some reason. But things aren't so simple for the fish. Because of the limitations of cover or the presence of other predator fish, the bass are often locked in a certain area. They *aren't* simply free to haul fins and change locations whenever they please. When the basic characteristics of the water they are occupying undergoes a change, bass become inactive until their bodies adjust to the new condtions.

Of course, at times bass *are* free to change location. We'll see examples of that in the following discussions.

Low light conditions are often the best times to be on the water. It usually pays to get up early for bass fishing.

Sunlight

Light levels aren't a "weather" condition, strictly speaking. Still, changing light levels, brought about by changing weather, hurt or help your fishing, so I'll mention them here.

As a general rule, bass bite better in low or moderate light conditions. That's when they have a visual advantage over their prey. That means bass see well but perch, shiners, shad and other prey do not. This general rule has to be related to other factors, such as water clarity. If you are fishing extremely turbid water, for example, low light levels are not necessarily good. In gin-clear water, on the other hand, anything that softens the impact of harsh sunlight coming into the water is a positive factor.

An important exception: in spring and fall the water is too cold to encourage feeding during the low-light times, but warmer in mid-afternoon. We've already noted the fact that in spring and fall the sun's rays strike the earth at a less direct angle, so although a day is bright the bass are not being as harshly struck by light as we tend to think they are.

Few anglers realize that different lake bottoms handle light in different ways. Gravel, rock, riprap and similarly broken-up bottoms scatter light rays. Those bottoms can provide good fishing in spite of harsh summer light. Even a clean sand bottom, by reflecting light back, reduces its intensity. On the other hand, strong light coming into a flat, black bottom gets no reduction of impact—which means that light levels get uncomfortable for bass.

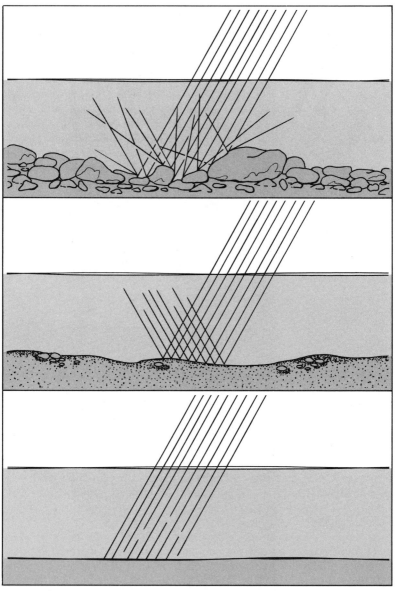

Different lake bottoms handle light in different ways. Bass can be comfortable in bright light if bottom conditions are right.

Algae blooms relate to all this. Say it has been calm and warm for several days. Those conditions favor a big growth of algae. Since it has been calm, that layer of algae will be spread all over. When you get to the lake there's a heavy cloud cover in addition to that layer of algae. Where will the bass be? *Spread out all over the shallows.* Fish fast and keep moving. You can use large baits and faster presentations.

Now you're fishing the same lake under the same circumstances, but there has been a moderate wind from the south. Where are the bass? *Grouped up and active on the north shore.* The algae has been pushed to that shore. Bass will probably be feeding aggressively in the lower light there.

Now you're fishing the same lake right after a storm. There hasn't been much light to encourage algae growth, except that today it is really bright. Where are the bass? *Tight to cover, probably grouped up.* Fish very close to objects today, probing the weeds and skipping casts up under docks. Use small baits and slow retrieves.

There are two obvious strategies for times when water is clear and light levels are high. First, you make an effort to be on the water during the low light hours, at dawn and dusk (or even at night). Second, you concentrate your fishing on shaded areas—the shady side of stumps, very tight to cover, or in deeper weedy cover or, on reservoirs, in deeper timber.

When the water is clear and the light is bright, you should make an effort to be on the water during low-light hours.

Rain

Rain has both primary and secondary impacts on largemouth fishing.

Rain, itself, is usually a plus for anglers. Rain will be accompanied by an overcast sky, plus the raindrops will reduce light penetration. That promotes bass activity and encourages bass to feed steadily throughout the day (rather than concentrating their feeding in the dim light hours of evening and dawn). A warm spring rain in the pre-spawn period is especially good. It warms up the water, reduces light penetration and washes food into the shallows, particularly around any feeder creeks.

A violent rainstorm after a period of calm often hurts fishing. On shallow lakes, a real gullywasher can even cause the lake to turn over, and that always screws up fishing.

Rain also has secondary impacts. Rain washes food into the shallows and causes that water to become silty, especially in reservoirs. The upper ends of coves, clay banks or incoming streams will be the first to become cloudy. Up to a point, this helps you. Bass will move into the silty water, or perhaps along the *mud line* (the edge where clear and roily water meet). Moderately stained water encourages an overall feeding movement; a heavy, distinct stain will encourage feeding right along the mudline. If you are fishing a clear lake or reservoir, a good rain might turn on the bass in the shallows by making the water darker.

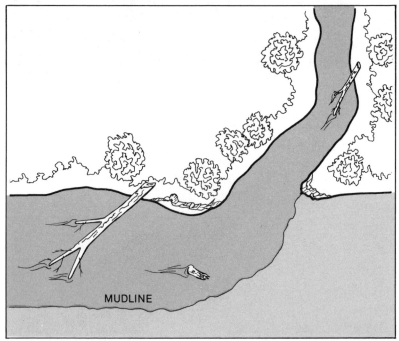

MUDLINE

Muddy rainwater flowing into a reservoir or river will create a mudline. Bass set up feeding stations along this area.

You can get too much of a good thing. Heavy, sustained rains make water so turbid that fishing shuts off until it clears. If you are fishing in water that already looks like heavily creamed coffee, the last thing you need is more rain runoff to come along and murk things up even worse.

As we've noted, rising or falling water levels have a sharp impact on fishing in reservoirs and rivers. When water levels rise, especially in spring, new areas of land are flooded. Bass fishing can be great on areas where, days earlier, butterflies sported on the grass and flowers.

Conversely, at times when rain has been scarce and water levels are falling, shallow water bass in impoundments feel threatened. They act as if they're afraid of being trapped and stranded in a shallow pool away from the reservoir. They usually drop back to the nearest break into deeper water, which will be the nearest creek or river channel.

Bass fishing often turns on early in a rainstorm. But don't risk your life for the chance of catching some fish. Close lightning strikes will put the fish down. And if you don't get off the water promptly, *you* could get put down for good! Graphite rods are excellent conductors of electricity. It is dangerous and *dumb* to fish in an electrical storm.

Newly-flooded areas can provide great bass fishing opportunities.

Wind

Wind, like other weather factors, can be good or bad. And—you guessed it!—a lot depends on whether you get a reasonable amount of wind or too much.

Light or moderate winds can concentrate warm water on the windward shore, which often improves fishing. For example, in early spring you might have a two-day period of calm and warming weather. If a moderate wind follows that, pushing the warmer layer of surface water up against a shore or into a bay, fishing gets hot. Moderate winds also speed the annual spring warm-up process much more than most anglers realize.

After a cold front, the most typical winds are from the west or northwest. Then your fishing, which is always tough after a front, might be better on the south or east sides of the lake because the wind and wave action will kick up material there that diffuses the harsh rays of the post-frontal sun.

Light and moderate winds reduce light penetration by stirring up algae, bottom debris and by ruffling the surface. That encourages bass feeding and spreads activity out over the whole day.

Wind also sets up current effects which concentrate bass. Wind striking a point will cause and eddy behind the point. Baitfish and predators get concentrated there.

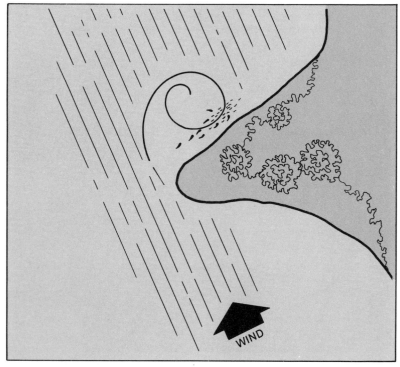

Strong winds striking a point will cause an eddy to form behind the point.

As a general rule, when a light or moderate wind is blowing, *fish the windward shore*. That's where the action is. That's where wave action is exciting the whole food chain. Wind washing over a deeper flat can also be good. Look for flats with one to three feet of water over the tops of the weeds, and fish just above the weeds.

Fierce winds are another matter. They're a pain in the transom, to tell the truth. In higher winds I still like to fish wind-struck shores if I'm working deeper water, if I can hold a boat on structure. I'll often find the fish feeding up high in the weeds then, right below the surface.

Waves washing into shallow cover don't *always* kill the fishing there, but usually that condition will force you to abandon a shallow water pattern that was deadly until the wind came up. For example, if you've been taking bass in a shallow reed bank and a high wind sends waves crashing into the reeds, move out to the best weedbed in deeper water in front of those reeds.

I've also seen the opposite—when wind moved fish from deeper water structure to the shallows. In one case, I'd found a great school of fish feeding on a sharp point in 12 to 20 feet of water, and was leading a tournament. But a hellacious wind came up, sending four-foot rollers smashing on that point, and my bass got pushed off that point all the way up into some shallow weeds about a hundred yards away. That wind probably cost me a state championship.

As a general rule, fish the windy shorelines *in summer but not in spring or fall*. Spring and fall bass have enough to cope with, just moving around and feeding in cold water. They can't blow energy fighting waves. A summer bass, full of energy, doesn't mind tackling turbulent water if that's where the easy food will be.

Generally light or moderate winds will push fish into the windward shore.

I remember old-timers saying "when the wind's from the east, fish bite the least." As a young, hot-shot structure fisherman, I knew better than to believe old wive's tales. After decades of bass fishing in all sorts of weather, I concede that the old-timers were right. I don't understand why, but I accept it: when the wind is directly from the east, fishing for everything but carp is terrible!

However, I like a light *southeast* wind. If a wind stays from the southeast for a day or two, then swings southwest, a front is probably coming...*but you sure want to be on the water until it does!*

Sometimes a wind starts in the southeast and keeps coming out of that compass point for two or three days, with wind velocities building all the time. Fishing will be good for about two days, then it will drop off badly on the third day. Eventually the wind rotates southwest and a front comes. If this pattern occurs, don't expect the good fishing that usually occurs just before the front strikes.

Cold Fronts

As bass anglers already know, cold fronts are our special curse.

Cold fronts are part of a normal weather pattern. About a day or two before a cold front strikes, you will notice mare's tail clouds. That is a tipoff that bass are about to start hitting well. A southeast wind often indicates a change for the worse is coming. The wind keeps rolling clockwise until, after the front, it's from the northwest.

The front itself, often accompanied by wind, arrives with towering thunder clouds. Fishing right before the thunderheads hit will often be terrific. Following the front will be a very high pressure system, together with bluebird skies and mile-high clouds, if there are any clouds at all. Bass fishing is crummy then.

In the typical pattern, fishing gets better a day or two after the front has passed through. It keeps on getting better until the next front comes, which can be almost immediately or not for a long time. Fronts often appear at four or five day intervals. So you see, if you avoid fronts altogether, you're going to be writing off a lot of bass fishing days.

Cold fronts come in all sizes—small, medium and monster. Minor systems don't put bass down as badly as major systems. Monster fronts, with lots of wind and a really high pressure system, will give you trouble for at least two days after passing, maybe three. And if a monster front is followed in a day or two by another front, even a small one, you're on your way to a stretch of lousy fishing.

The pattern of fronts usually causes a year to be good or bad. A bad year of fishing, such as the 1985 season, was bad because fronts came through with great frequency. The fish would be just recovering from one front when the next one would hit, and it went on that way week after week. The absence of fronts can make for great fishing. In 1976, a year of drought where I live, we saw *no cold fronts for several weeks*. The fishing kept building until it was almost unbelievably good.

Fishermen have speculated endlessly about why cold fronts poison bass fishing. Nobody knows for sure, but the bad fishing seems to be related to the harsh, bright light that comes out of the squeaky clean, low humidity post-frontal skies. There's nothing to diffuse the light in the sky. I also believe that fronts cause algae die-offs, so the water loses much of its ability to diffuse the light. One effect of this is that bass move tight to cover, burrowing way up under weed clumps.

After cold fronts, fish tight to cover.

Not all fronts come booming through in the usual way. You might see a lot of spotty little weather systems passing through, with a big front finally coming in behind them. If you have good cloud cover with the earlier systems, fishing will be pretty good until the big front hits.

The worst fronts have a lot of wind in them. The wind itself makes fishing hard (just when you need your sense of feel the most, the boat is tossing around and you have to fish a big weight on your worm to get the bait down). What is even worse is when the winds accompanying a front blow all night long. Those are killer fronts! They really whack the bass fishing. If the wind switches or goes down in the evening, the front won't hurt you much.

I remember one horrible front that came through just before a little club tournament I was going to fish. Nobody could take a fish. The winds were so gusty and the bass were so deep in the weeds that I couldn't feel a fish when I used a worm or a jig. So I put on a little black and white tailspin lure, an Uncle Josh Spinrite. I fished it partly like a worm, partly like a jigging spoon. The bass were in the inside turns, so I tried to get the tailspin to drop right into any tiny crack in the weeds. I'd get hung often, but a snap of the rod would pop the bait free. I only caught three fish, but that was enough for first place. I don't know any other lure that would have worked in that situation, except maybe live bait.

We'll talk about dealing with cold fronts more later on in the book. Meanwhile, here are some basic principles:

- *Slow down your presentation.*
- Fish tight to cover.
- Fish down deep in the cover.
- Use live bait, or life-like artificials (such as plastic worms) with scent.
- Use small lures, light lines and sensitive tackle, except when flipping heavy cover.
- Expect very soft takes and be prepared to set the hook at the slightest touch from a fish.

You can catch fish after a cold front if you slow down your presentations and adjust your tactics.

Chapter 6
Tools of the Trade

Graphs, trolling motors, scent agents, big tackle boxes crammed with thousands of lures, surface temp gauges, bass boats, oxygen meters...and on and on. Today there is a bewildering variety of fishing aids on the market. No wonder one of the questions I hear most often is, "Babe, do I really need all that stuff to catch bass?"

Good question. But I can't answer it for you. In this chapter I'll be talking about a number of fishing aids. Do you *need* them? Well, to tell the truth, that depends entirely on you—how do you fish, how often do you fish, and how good do you want to become at bass fishing?

I'm hardly typical. I've got two boats for bass fishing, each fully rigged with state-of-the-art equipment. I own and sometimes use sophisticated electronic aids. I probably own as many plastic worms, spinnerbaits and crankbaits as many tackle stores, and I couldn't tell you how many rods and reels I have.

But I'm not you. I fish for a living, as well as for fun. I use many fishing aids, not because I "need them" to catch fish, but because I'm fascinated by fish and never feel I can learn enough about them.

How about you? Much depends on how you fish. If you fish bass often in spring and fall, you'll need the surface temp gauge; if you confine your fishing to the warmer months, you can do without on many lakes. And so it goes. Versatile, enthusiastic fishermen will enjoy more fishing aids and accessories than casual anglers who limit themselves to a few situations on a few waters.

You have another basic decision to make. Are you happy with the quality of your fishing? Or are you bothered by the slow days and even more bothered by times when other guys take way more fish than you do? Are you frequently frustrated because you just can't figure out what the fish are up to?

So, again, do you *need* all the modern gear? Again, I can't tell you. You have to tell me! If you are truly enjoying your fishing, you are very fortunate and nobody should tell you you "have" to buy anything. On the other hand, if you have an interest in growing and improving as a bass fisherman, the intelligent use of fishing aids and the best equipment will allow give you more bass fishing pleasure.

You don't have to use a lot of high technology to catch bass, but experimental anglers will enjoy aids that teach them more about the world of the bass.

My Sponsors

Most readers probably know I have sponsors for my television series. I mostly work with their equipment, and that's the equipment mostly mentioned in this book.

That doesn't mean the brand names mentioned here are the "only" equipment you can use. Today there is terrific competition for the angler's dollar, and as a result there is more superb equipment being sold than ever before.

But I'm proud of my association with my sponsors and I'm sure you'd like using their products as much as I have. I've been in this business long enough to be able to pick the firms I work with. I've chosen sponsors whose products I'd want to use and recommend. These products will be mentioned by name at times because I believe in them.

Boats for Bass

There are a whole lot of "bass boats" on the market, plus a bunch of boats with other names that work well for bass fishing. Whatever your bass boat needs might be, somebody makes that boat (if you can only find—and afford—it).

Here are some useful questions to ask yourself before buying a rig:

• Will the boat be used for other types of fishing? Will you ever be backtrolling for walleyes? Any chance you'll want to take the family out for some panfishing every now and then? Waterskiing? If so, you'll have some special requirements for you boat.

• What kind of water will you fish—big wind-blown reservoirs, little stock tanks or stumpy river bottoms? How often will you big stretches of rough water? If you'll mainly fish big waters, you'll surely want the speed and safety of a modern glass bass boat. But if you'll be sneaking around in junk weed bays or shallow drowned timber, a lighter boat that drafts less water will probably suit you better.

• What kinds of launch ramps will you use? In some areas, the difficulties of launching a heavy boat with a V hull will keep you off some of the most interesting, lightly-fished lakes. In other areas the ramps on the best bass waters are so good you could launch the Queen Mary.

• How important is speed? If you fish big impoundments, a slow boat can cut into your fishing time badly. If you will stick to small waters, you hardly need a mile-a-minute rig. I've noticed that few guys feel their boats are too fast.

• Are you interested in fishing tournaments? If so, you're sure going to appreciate the twin livewells and general layout of today's sophisticated bass boats, especially the best glass boats. You'll need a kill switch.

• What kind of vehicle will you use to tow the boat? Some compact cars, especially the front drive models, are limited in terms of what they can pull.

Glass Bass Boats

Today's fiberglass bass boats represent the ultimate in safety, fishing efficiency, comfort and speed. Boy, have I seen a lot of improvement in bass boats in the years I've been fishing! Modern boats have scientifically designed V hulls that offer speed and comfort in rough water that would have been unfishable in the earlier bass boats.

Unfortunately, it's pretty easy for little off-brand makers to put out a glass boat that looks as good as the more expensive boats made by the reputable manufacturers. A good glass boat has a heckuva lot of expensive quality features hidden where you can't see them. After a year or two of fishing, the cheaper boat may have cracked, rotted or broken. Some boats even have hulls that simply aren't safe. Designing a safe hull for high performance use is no simple matter, which is a good reason for sticking to reputable boat makers who have been in the business for a long time. One of Babe's Rules: *an unsafe boat is a bad bargain at any price.*

I'll admit to being almost a fanatic on the importance of flotation. The reason is simple. I wouldn't be alive today if it weren't for the flotation of a boat I once swamped in a chilly Canadian lake. I was taking chances, overloading my boat and not paying enough attention to weather. When a spring storm suddenly blew up, we couldn't get to

The quality of your launch ramps might affect your choice of a bass boat.

shore before swamping. And there I was, in icewater, with hypothermia setting in quickly. It was a very close call, but my buddy and I survived because our boat had upright, level flotation (pretty rare back then). Now I insist on it.

Building a boat with the proper kind of flotation can cost more and result in a slightly heavier (slower) boat. So some guys resist buying the safe boats. What can you say to them? Nobody *expects* to get caught in a life-threatening situation! But it happens. It's happened to me, and to quite a few friends, and they were experienced boaters who didn't expect to be struggling for their lives.

The development of bass boats has paralleled changes in impoundments. Many reservoirs were young in the 1960s. Most young reservoirs are choked with timber and brush. Narrow, short boats are needed to thread through that stuff. As reservoirs have aged, much of that timber has rotted and dropped, allowing waves to build up higher and making it more important to have a seaworthy boat that runs fast from spot to spot.

A "normal" length for a modern glass bass boat is about 17 feet. Boats at that size can comfortably stow all the gear for two hard-fishing anglers and provide an excellent fishing platform. Guys who fish brushy, younger reservoirs often choose 16-footers. Those who frequently work the biggest impoundments are running 18-to 20-foot boats.

I'm currently doing my bass fishing in a Ranger 372V or in my versatile little Ranger 1600 V-II. There are other good glass boats, but nobody has a better reputation for strength, overall quality and refined design. Ranger's Forrest Wood, an old tournament fisherman himself, just won't put his name on a boat that is dangerous, weak or likely to fall apart after it has seen some use.

Modern glass bass boats are unsurpassed for comfort, safety and fishing convenience.

I'm terrifically excited about the boat I'll be using this coming year, a totally new Ranger model I helped design. Ranger will probably call it the 680T Fisherman. It has the versatility of the 1600, but is considerably bigger so it can handle rougher water. A prototype performed so well in heavy seas that the folks at Ranger were amazed. The interior represents my best thoughts on how a fishing boat should be laid out... and I've spent many thousand hours in fishing boats!

The new Ranger 680T Fisherman *was designed to meet the needs of the angler that wants a smaller, lighter boat that can handle rough water.*

I use Mariner motors, and they've delivered dependable perform-ance. The 45-horse on my 1600 is a smooth *four-cylinder* motor. Mariner recently made some changes, listing their four-cylinder motor as a 45-horse. It's the same motor we've known as the Mariner Fifty for years; it's just being rated under a more conservative system. Mariner also now makes a new three-cylinder 50-horse I haven't used yet.

I use stainless steel props and would recommend them to anyone. They cost more initially, but you get back that money in terms of better performance, improved fuel efficiency and ruggedness.

Aluminum bass rigs

For smaller, more protected waters, the modified john boat aluminum bass rigs deserve their popularity. Especially when you buy them pre-rigged, they represent the most bass boat you can get for the dollar. The rigging is all done for you. Of course, sometimes they won't be rigged with just the equipment you'd prefer; that's one of the sacri-fices you make to get that low purchase price.

These boats were originally just john boats dressed up like bass boats. At first, many were unsafe and uncomfortable in waves. Now · the better makers have redesigned the hulls to make them carry weight in the back better and take waves better in front. You can identify these better aluminum boats: they are wider in the stern, have some degree of

V hull effect and have a flared bow to throw water aside. They still run rougher and wetter than a good glass boat, and they lack storage capacity, but not everyone needs to fish from a tournament quality boat.

People mainly buy these boats because they cost less than fiberglass rigs. The trailer-ability and shallow draft of the aluminum bass boats make them a smart choice for many applications if you respect their safety limitations. I wouldn't use one unless I knew—from more than a salesman's promise—that the boat had upright, level flotation.

Go-anywhere Rigs

There's a place in bass fishing for the "go-anywhere" rigs. Some tremendous bass come out of little stock dams, farm ponds and remote lakes with lousy accesses. I know a guy who catches a lot of bass in lakes inside the city limits of Minneapolis where outboards aren't allowed. His canoe carries a portable depth finder and a troll motor; it is a bass boat. The plastic mini pontoons, powered by troll motors, are another "boat" you wouldn't take on wavy waters; but they offer comfort and fishing efficiency for small waters. Regular metal cartoppers or john boats fitted with troll motors and depth finders can be jammed into the water where there isn't any formal launch ramp at all. A lot of guys are starting to realize that belly boats—those inner tube rigs—are real professional gear that let you fish places where nobody else can go.

Little boats like this john boat can give you access to small, lightly-fished waters where bass grow big.

Troll Motors

No matter what kind of boat you've got, it isn't really a bass boat unless it has a good troll motor. Depending on where and how you fish, your troll motor might be the most vital piece of gear you own except your rod and boat, more important even than your sonar in some cases.

Unfortunately, troll motors break down for various reasons, and then the modern bass angler gets an unpleasant reminder of what it was like before we fished with electric power. Which reminds me of a tournament several years ago. I'd found a good school of fish along a bank of heavy weeds. I took enough fish from that school on the first day to be leading. On the second day, however, my troll motor died. Winds came up, the lake began throwing whitecaps at us, and I had one of the most frustrating days of fishing of my life. By slamming my big gas motor in and out of gear I could almost hold position outside the weeds, and every now and then I snaked a bass out of that school. Without a healthy troll motor, it was a lost cause.

A lot of guys buy an electric motor that is underpowered. Modern boats are pretty heavy, and the troll motor that works beautifully in calm weather may be totally inadequate when it is windy. You never hear a bass fisherman complain his troll motor is too powerful.

I prefer a manual front troll motor, and often control it with a foot.

A few years ago, the only way to get enough power was by buying a 24-volt system. But since everything else in your boat is going to be 12 volts, going with 24 volts on your electric motor complicates the electric system. The big breakthrough came when 12-volt motors were geared down and equipped with oversized props. Suddenly, 12-volt motors had the power to jerk around heavy boats.

Scuba observers have watched bass reacting to gas and electric motors. They've noted that troll motors are accepted by bass as long as the motor isn't turned on and off again erratically when it is near the fish. Also, bass are more spooked by small prop motors that run at extremely high rpm's than they are by the newer, slower motors with big props.

On my bass boats I've got Minn Kota 395s—the model that mounts on the bow in a bracket but does not have the remote steering. I've always preferred the simplicity of a troll motor that I steer directly by hand or with my foot as I fish.

I like a stand-up bike seat to help keep my balance. Before I had one, several years ago, I fished a January tournament on Florida's Lake George. This was a big tournment that attracted a lot of big name anglers, and I sure wanted to do my best. My roomate at the resort was David Owens, one of the best guys fishing the tournaments back then. And it was cold, awful cold. It snowed on us one day, so I was fishing in my snowmobile suit. When practice fishing one day I went way back up a boat canal, looking for any little bit of warm water I could find. Back there, I saw a good-looking bush, so I got set to fire a side-armed cast at it. I was standing in the front of the boat, with one foot up on the troll motor to steer it.

As the boat turned, the back end banged up against a dock, causing me to do a neat one-and-a-half gainer into the icy water. When I came up, in shock, I saw the troll motor was still running, pulling the boat steadily away from me. Then I remembered that the rod and reel I just dropped was brand new. I dove, in my snowmobile suit, and began to scramble around for my expensive outfit. Somehow I got my legs tangled in my line. Now my legs couldn't move, so I paddled like mad with my hands and got to the surface. The guy who owned the dock had been lying in a lounge chair up the hill by his cabin, and he began to roar with laughter as he saw me flopping around.

Paddling with my hands, I caught up with the boat and caught hold of the troll motor. I aimed it for the dock I'd hit. Pretty soon I was able to drag myself out of the water, my legs tied together, dragging the rod and reel behind me. That was too much for the cabin owner. He laughed so hard he fell out of his chair and rolled all the way down the hill to the water.

I was as embarrassed as I was cold, which is saying a lot! I got back to the resort as quickly as possible. The wife of the owner promised to wash and dry my clothes without telling anybody that I'd gone in. Fine. I went back out, looking for warm water and bass. When I came back there were wet clothes hanging all over the main area of the lodge. Aaargh! I felt humiliated. I asked the resort owner's wife why she hadn't kept my awful secret. She said, "Those aren't your clothes! They belong to David Owens. He fell in this afternoon!"

Anyway, I appreciate the support of the stand-up bike seats.

Weeds or timber can be a problem. The big plastic weedguards will fill up with weeds until they become more of a nuisance than an aid. Most modern troll motors come with weedless props. These are good. But thick, stringy weeds, can still clog up your prop, so some guys are mounting "Weed Shark" weedcutters on their motors. Because of the power and the weedless props of the Minn Kotas, I've had so little trouble that I haven't bothered to install a Weed Shark.

Be sure you get all the power you paid for. Until very recently, the only good power source for troll motors were the biggest "deep cycle" batteries, the type of battery designed for heavy *extended* use (these same batteries are used in golf carts and for powered wheelchairs). Regular "cranking" batteries, even if labeled "marine" batteries, don't stand up to the abuse of total drawdown and recharging. Deep cycle batteries have extra heavy plates designed for that kind of life.

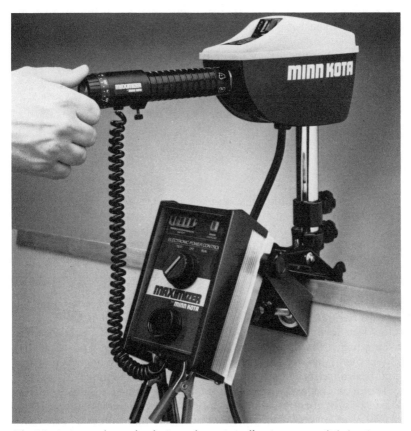

The Maximizer reduces the drain on batteries, allowing you to fish for days in-stead of hours on a charge.

Now there's a new alternative, something called the "dual-purpose" battery. It offers lots of cranking power and yet it withstands the deep cycle punishment of troll motor fishing. These new batteries should make it possible to reduce the number of batteries in your boat.

There is no substitute for big, heavy batteries with lots of lead and acid in them. Some guys are now wiring two deep cycle 6-volt batteries in series to get 12 volts. There's nothing magic about this arrangement, but the two big 6-volt batteries have more guts—more lead and acid— and thus more power than any single 12 volt battery. I've heard of guys fishing this kind of rig for five days consecutively, using the motor *hard*, without recharging.

I've just added a new device to my boats called the Maximizer (from the makers of Minn Kota motors). It does several things, but mainly it reduces draw on the battery to an amazing extent. Conventional troll motor power controls are just rheostats that turn unwanted energy into heat, wasting energy. The Maximizer draws from the battery only as much power as you are actually using. At full power, the Maximizer won't save you anything. But most of us run at reduced power much of the time, and that's where the real energy savings come in. In some tests, batteries lasted two to three times as long when Maximizers were used.

Make sure your wiring does not choke off the flow of power from the battery to the troll motor. If your batteries are in the back of the boat and the troll motor is in front (a common arrangement), the wiring from the battery to the motor *must* be heavy enough so it doesn't impede the flow of energy. Use 4 or 6 gauge wire, and keep it as short as possible.

Sonar

Fishing sonar is a big topic and one that the average angler doesn't understand well. I have put together a course, "The Comprehensive Guide to Fish Locators," that consists of a book and two audio tapes. It goes into details that I won't be able to bring out in this discussion of sonar in bass fishing, so if you're frustrated with your experiences with fishing sonar you might want to order the course (details in back of this book).

No modern bass angler should be without a good sonar unit. At times sonar units let you see bass, but their main value is the way they allow you to *hunt* bass by understanding their world better. Modern fishing began the day anglers began to concentrate less on what they saw above the water and more on what the fish saw below the water. And that happened when sonar was adapted for fishing.

Depth is the key component to location much of the time. We already know location starts by looking for the right combination of *cover, structure and depth*. Unless you're fishing a situation where fish are located near visible objects, your sonar will be useful or even absolutely necessary for determining all three locational keys.

I depended on my front flasher to keep at the right depth to catch big bass on this trip with my friend, Ed Gerchy.

Flasher Units

On the dash of my bigger bass boat I carry an Eagle Silent Sixty flasher. It's handy for checking depths when running at speed. I don't use it for fishing, but it is an important safety feature when running and is good for spotting humps and points that I should stop and fish carefully.

Then, my real bass *fishing* sonar is the Eagle Silent Thirty II flasher bow unit with its transducer attached to my troll motor with a hose clamp. That transducer tells me what is happening *right below me,* and that's critical. If you're running the boat with a front troll motor you don't want to have your depth finder running off a transducer mounted some 16 feet away at the back of the boat. That's not close enough! I use this bow mount flasher for keeping at the right depth for working weedlines, humps or other bass-holding structure.

It is important to choose a sonar with enough power to show weeds. Sonar signals are created when pulses of sound strike objects whose density differs from the density of water. Weeds are almost identically the same density as water, so they are hard to detect. That's where it helps to have more power, which is the same thing as *sensitivity;* a sensitive sonar picks up small differences in density. Fish such as bass return a stronger signal than many weeds, making it possible for an experienced sonar user to spot the fish. But in denser weeds, like coontail, this is really difficult, and not necessary. There are better ways to locate bass...like with a plastic worm!

Graph Recorders

I rely on flasher units for most my bass fishing, but that doesn't mean graphs have no place on a bass boat. The biggest advantage of graphs is that they will print detailed, easily read images of fish. Graphs naturally work better on fish that suspend in deeper, more open water—like crappies, walleyes or salmon. Since bass hold so tight to cover in relatively shallow water much of the time, it is often hard to get a boat and transducer over bass and then it's hard to get the fish to print separately from the cover. This is especially true when you are fishing weeds. You might have a super day of fishing bass in weeds without ever seeing a single fish on your graph.

Graphs shine when bass use deeper, somewhat more open water. Winter bass in impoundments can usually be spotted with graphs. Not surprisingly, guys who fish cold weather bass in the central and southern impoundments often rely on graphs to help them find bass. A graph will show bass holding along deeper structure, such as the edge of a creek bed, and a good graph that prints fine detail will even show bass suspended in timber in deeper water. Graphs also help you locate bass by printing pictures of massed schools of shad or other forage.

Even when bass do use deeper structure, it isn't always easy to see them because they often are tight to cover. If your graph lacks resolution, it won't differentiate between a bass and a nearby tree limb or make three crappies suspended near each other look like one big bass. Bass anglers, even more than other anglers, need superb resolution.

While there's a place for graphs with wide cone angles, bass fishermen need a relatively narrow cone angle. When you are trying to discriminate between fish and cover, the clarity of a more tightly focussed cone angle is desirable. A cone angle of about 22 degrees is about ideal.

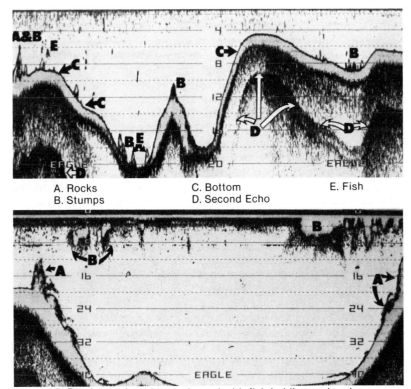

A. Rocks C. Bottom E. Fish
B. Stumps D. Second Echo

A. Brush on edge of river channel with fish holding on brush
B. Bait Fish

There is no match, currently, for the highly detailed displays of the better paper graph recorders.

LCD Units

There's a new type of fishing sonar that is causing a lot of excitement. The LCD (Liquid Crystal Display) units are a sort of hybrid. Like a flasher, they never need paper. Like a graph, they display images of the underwater world that are easier to read than blips of light on a flasher.

They have obvious appeal. Nobody likes the bother and expense of feeding fresh paper into a graph. The most popular LCD units are light and compact, even smaller than a flasher. Because they have no moving parts, they put far less drain on batteries than either paper graphs or flashers. Even some of the cheaper ones let you choose from several depth ranges. Some can be set to automatically change depth settings as the bottom rises and falls. Some have alarms that warn you when you are getting in dangerously shallow water.

All of which sounds great, but can LCDs help you find bass? They all work well enough to basically show you the depth, which is the most important thing. Yet many of the LCD graphs, unfortunately, aren't as useful as an ordinary flasher unit. The problem is the limitations of what some LCD graphs can display. They lack "pixel power."

What's that? Let's say you are organizing the flash card section for a college football game. Your students have cards black on one side, white on the other. Perhaps you want the card section to show a message like "GO VIKINGS!" If you've got 30 or even 130 students in your card section, there's no way on earth you can arrange the cards to spell out that message. Your Gs and Es will look just like your Rs. You lack pixel power. With so few black and white cards, you lack the *detail* needed to shape out those letters. With a couple thousand students you'd probably get your message across, except I sure wouldn't want the job of organizing two thousand college kids.

It's the same with LCD graphs. We're in the infancy of the technology needed to make them as good as they should be. Current efforts to produce a high quality wristwatch television will likely yield the next advances. The best paper graphs have the display equivalent of a *million* pixels per square inch. Some LCD units currently being sold have only *64* pixels per square inch.

With these primitive graphs, a tiny shad will look the same on the display as a 5-pound bass. Weeds will look like trees, and bass holding near bottom will look like square rocks. Who needs that?

We're just seeing the technology that makes purchase of a LCD graph sensible. The Eagle Z-6000 is the first LCD I've seen that I think belongs on a *fishing* boat. It has just less than 2,700 pixels, or 470 pixels per square inch. That's a long way from the million pixels of the best paper graphs, but it clearly takes the Z-6000 way out of the category of a "toy."

That's not the last word. LCD technology is improving so rapidly that units currently on the drawing board will soon offer far more pixels (thus more quality). Some might have the "grayline" feature that makes bottom fish so easy to spot on today's better paper graphs.

I don't expect to quit using paper graphs and flashers for a long time, but I don't doubt that LCD graphs are the fishing sonar of the future, the units likely to supplant flashers and graphs.

With all fishing sonar, the installation *has* to be right, or you won't get acceptable performance. The fishing sonar course mentioned earlier goes into installation in detail. And, of course, there's a fine art to interpreting the signals you get from your sonar, which the course also goes into. I guarantee it—anyone who owns *any* kind of sonar will get more out of that unit if they study this course.

Reels

Reels have become lighter, smoother and more reliable. They have better drags and convenience features that weren't available when I began fishing bass.

Perhaps the most dramatic improvements have come in baitcasting reels, the reels favored by most bass anglers. The bugaboo of baitcasting has always been the backlash. The introduction of reels with magnetic brakes has almost eliminated "professional over-runs." If you haven't tried one yet, you owe it to yourself.

For many types of bass fishing, baitcasting tackle has it all over spinning gear. Baitcasting tackle handles the line sizes most often used by bass fishermen—12 to 25 pounds—better than spinning tackle. Baitcasting also allows more casting accuracy, since you can feather a lure down with your thumb. Most guys who fish baits fast, especially crankbaits, find baitcasting tackle doesn't wreck their muscles the way spinning tackle does.

Manufacturers have worked hard to produce reels specifically for bass anglers. Since bass don't make long runs, compact reels with modest line capacities are best. These light reels balance modern rods. Their small spools are less inclined to backlash than the klutzy spools of older reels. Another improvement appreciated by bass fishermen is the higher (faster) gear ratios that make it easy to really burn a lure through the water.

Modern baitcasting reels are one of the most improved pieces of equipment available to bass anglers.

Manufacturers are also giving today's angler smoother reels built with tighter manufacturing tolerances. To my mind, the Japanese have been in the forefront here, setting a very high standard of quality.

An offshoot of baitcasting is tackle specialized for flipping. Flipping requires a long, stiff rod with specially placed guides. Many "flippers" use regular baitcasting reels, but now several makers have come out with reels designed specifically for flipping. Fish fights with flipping gear are usually settled in the first two or three seconds. Since flipping is usually done in heavy cover, the challenge is to wrestle the bass away from cover before it knows it is hooked. Special flipping reels have a locked drag setting and a slow gear ratio (because slow gearing is more powerful, and flippers need power more than speed).

Spinning tackle has its place in largemouth bass fishing, especially for worming. As one example, if you are casting an unweighted worm up under docks or around shallow cover, a medium weight spinning outfit with eight-pound mono will cast that worm far better than baitcasting tackle could.

Many of the trends noted in baitcasting reels can also be seen in spinning reels. They have become lighter, tougher, smoother and faster. The better ones have graphite bodies, several ball bearings and geartrains that are so smooth and tight that they'll spoil you in a hurry, once you try them. When you crank a modern spinning reel, the only thing you should feel is the lure. I like the reels with triggers that let me open the bail with my right index finger alone (instead of reaching across with my left hand to do the bail). This makes it easy to fire lots of fast, short casts around a stump, for example.

Rods

The best values in rods are the moderately priced graphites from established manufacturers. Boron may have a place in bass fishing, but nobody has proved to me that boron is truly better than the best graphite rods, and boron is more expensive.

While you can buy good quality without buy the most costly, state-of-the-art rods, be careful. Avoid "brand X" boron or graphite rods because there are no accepted standards in the industry. A rod labeled "graphite" or "boron" sometimes has a tiny percentage of those expensive fibers. Stick to the respected brand names in the middle or upper price bracket. You'll get performance and value.

Even if your budget is tight, avoid glass rods. A graphite rod won't make a bad angler into an expert, but most anglers who switch to graphite notice a definite improvement in their ability to cast, feel takes and set hooks.

Like most bass fishermen, I prefer rods with fast actions. *Slow* rods flex more or less uniformly along their length when subjected to a load, such as in casting. A fast rod has a stiffer butt with a more flexible tip; the butt bends less than in a slow rod but the tip bends more. This— in my hands—makes for a rod that is more accurate and easy to handle. I can snap off quick casts with fast rods.

Rod designers have tried for years to make rods more sensitive. Light, single-foot guides helped. Getting rid of ferrules was another advance. Recently, Shimano introduced rods with swelled butts, completely doing away with separate handles. With these rods, your fingers are on the blank itself, for maximum sensitivity. They have been extremely popular.

It takes a stinging blow from a rod to set a hook in a bass's horny mouth tissue. Today's best graphite rods have more power and a much faster tip response than older rods. Modern rods set hooks quicker and with more authority than the best of rods of just a few years ago.

The first graphite rods often sold for over $100. You can still pay that much for some rods, and maybe they're worth it to you, but many rods in the $35 to $70 range are darn nice.

That's good, because a serious bass fisherman needs more than one rod. Using one rod is something like playing a round of golf with a single club. I often fish with three rigs. Maybe I'll have a worm rigged on a spinning rod, a crankbait baitcasting outfit, and a spinnerbait baitcasting outfit. On the water, I can switch outfits and be fishing a different lure without missing a beat.

It isn't just that I don't want to take the time to cut off the old lure and tie on a new one. That's important, especially when I use one lure to locate a fish and then fire a different lure right back to the spot of the swirl. But another reason for working with several outfits is that I can have the right *rod action* and *line* for each lure. Each bass fishing situation has its own special requirements.

If you like to flip, you'll need a rod built just for that. Flipping rods are seven-and-a-half feet long. They have specially placed guides to make it easier to handle the line. The best flipping rods have slow (*not* fast) actions and a stiff tip for setting hooks.

Flipping tackle is excellent for pinpoint fishing to specific targets like dock posts, stumps or weed pockets.

Line

I could enjoy a day of fishing with an antique reel and a sloppy old glass rod, but I wouldn't waste my time fishing with a bad line. Your line is the only link between you and a fish. When that link busts, you lose.

Strength in line is a pretty complicated topic. For one thing, there are several kinds of strength—dry strength, wet strength (always weaker than dry strength), knot strength and abrasion resistance. Abrasion resistance isn't strength, strictly speaking, but it comes to almost the same thing. Bass fishermen are usually throwing lures into rough places—timber, docks, raspy reeds and so forth. One little nick in the skin of monofilament can spell disaster, so bass lines must have tough skins.

People say that bass can't cut mono lines with their teeth. Compared to a northern or musky, a bass has a soft mouth. But check that tissue on a bass's lips. It's pretty gritty. After you've "lipped" a bunch of bass to land them, your thumb will be raw hamburger. The same thing happens to your line, which should tell you something about the need to re-tie lures pretty often. I know. I lost the bass of a lifetime by failing to do this!

Bass anglers need lines with a *balance* of qualities—strength of all sorts, reasonable limpness, low stretch and low memory. Some manufacturers emphasize one quality to the detriment of others, but the bass fisherman wants a line that has total overall fishability.

The worst place, *absolutely*, to economize is on your line. Insist on the very best line for your fishing and keep it fresh. During the day, if your line contacts brush or raspy weeds, keep cutting off and throwing away the last several feet of line. After every six trips, replace the last 50 yards, for that's the line that has experienced the most use. Old line can never be trusted.

More fishermen today understand that there are "premium" and "non-premium" lines. The premium lines are the best lines a manufacturer can produce. They have more expensive chemical makeups and are built with tighter tolerances throughout the manufacturing process.

You can minimize the cost of working with fresh, premium line by buying 1,000 or 3,000 yard spools. The best monos sell for about a penny a yard that way, bringing the cost of a reel refill to half a dollar. You can afford that.

I use several types of Stren, one of America's premium lines. Lately, I've been fishing a lot with Stren's Class line. I appreciate its lack of bulk. In my hands, it feels even better than regular Stren, though it is supposed to be made of the same materials. I also like its fluorescent aqua color.

I've just begun using Prime, DuPont's revolutionary new type of line. It is not a monofilament, but a *cofilament*. That means two line materials are extruded at the same time, one wrapped around the other, to create a line with very distinctive qualities. The sheath, or outer layer, is the same material used to make Stren mono lines. The inner core is polyester, and it gives Prime its remarkable characteristics.

When setting a hook, you want as little stretch in your line as possible.

Prime is in a category all by itself, not just another mono line. What sets it apart is its extremely low stretch in most fishing situations.

Stretch is a critical quality in nylon lines. A line that lacks stretch altogether will be brittle and break suddenly without warning. Line that stretches too much robs you of feel and leads to missed hooksets. With every line *except Prime* you have to compromise, accepting some undesirable stretch to get enough toughness and elasticity.

Thanks to its polyester core, Prime lets you enjoy the best of both worlds. When pulled very hard, it stretches as much as any other premium line, so it's not brittle. But when subjected to low loads, it hardly stretches at all. Those low loads are what count for transmitting the feel of a lure and for setting a hook. In actual tests, Prime set hooks *two or three times faster* than other premium lines.

Line size can make a big difference. When worming or jigging in open water, I'll sometimes drop down to 6-pound test, though I would ordinarily prefer at least 8-pound. For crankbait and spinnerbait fishing, 12-and 14-pound lines are hard to beat. Go down to 10-pound for crankbaiting where cover isn't a problem, and use up to 17-pound whenever you are liable to lose fish or baits to heavy cover. In special situations, like fishing shiners for trophy bass up under floating weed masses, you might need 40-pound line to control the bass.

Heavy lines can cost you in several ways. You lose feel, sometimes the fish are put off by the fat lines, and the stiffness of thick lines can hurt the action of baits. But there's another side to the coin.

A quick story might make the point. A line manufacturer once ran an experiment with about 20 experienced fishermen. The anglers were given identical worming outfits with 8-and 20-pound mono lines and were told to switch outfits every half hour. The experimenters expected the light line would catch more fish because it would present worms more attractively. Just the opposite happened.

In retrospect, the anglers decided they were afraid of hanging up and losing baits when working the lighter line, so with those outfits they nibbled at the edges of cover rather than throwing into the thick stuff...which is where the bass were.

One of Babe's Rules: fish the heaviest line you can, under the circumstances. Another of Babe's Rules: fish the lightest line you can, under the circumstances! In other words, balance *all* the factors when picking a line.

Line color is another matter people ask me about. We can divide monofilaments into the "bright" (fluorescent) and "quiet" (clear or drably colored) lines. I fish bright lines when using a technique that involves watching my line for that tell-tale twitch that signals a take. So I use bright lines for much of my jigging and worm fishing. When throwing crankbaits or spinnerbaits, techniques that depend on feel instead of line-watching, I use quietly colored lines. I also like quiet lines even for worming or jigging when fishing clear water or when bass are negative.

Polarizing Glasses

One of the most useful tools for the bass fisherman is one of the cheapest. We all need *good* sunglasses with polarizing type lenses so we can see down into the water to see fish and cover. At times and places, without a good pair of sunshades you're just about fishing blind.

I often switch lens colors. Grey is best when things are bright. But on overcast days, the amber lenses give objects more contrast. There's a *real* difference. And, yes, you still need good glasses when the light is low because you'll still need to see below the surface. If you watch my television shows you'll see me wearing glasses on dark days. It may look odd, but I'm there to catch fish!

For years, I went through glasses at the rate of about a pair every month. They'd break or get all scratched up. I finally got so frustrated I went directly to a manufacturer to get some made that were *right* for fishing. And I got what I'd been looking for.

These glasses have ground and polished glass lenses that eliminate distortion and almost totally resist scratching. They are very comfortable. They cut out unwanted light and have polarizing panels on the sides that give you good peripheral vision and block out glare coming in from the sides.

I sell these glasses mostly as a service to people who read my books and watch my videos or television series. They aren't a high profit item for me, but I want to be able to get you folks in good glasses. These have my name on them, and that means a lot to me. There are details for ordering them at the back of this book.

Good polarizing glasses are absolutely critical in many shallow water fishing situations.

Color-C-Lector

When I met Dr. Loren Hill to take him fishing last fall, I had to tell him things didn't look promising. We'd had a long run of nasty weather, hardly what we wanted to run a test of his new Color-C-Lector on bass. Here he was, about to go on camera for my "Good Fishing" show in a test of his invention, and I was saying we might not catch a single bass.

"Babe," said Loren patiently, "I've been travelling around the country for months fishing in high pressure tests of the Color-C-Lector. For some reason, I've hardly had decent weather once! Just get me near some bass, and I think we'll show your viewers what this device can do."

We dropped my 1600 in a small lake not far from my office. It's nothing special, just a nice little bass lake that gets a strong algae bloom. I picked it because it was close; a storm was rolling in, and we didn't have much time.

Out on the lake, Loren took a Color-C-Lector reading. "The first thing," he told me, "is to determine how clear this water is. That tells us which scale on the Color-C-Lector to use." Loren determined that this was *stained* water and so we should use the middle scale of the Color-C-Lector.

Since we'd start with spinnerbaits in shallow water, Loren took a reading at three feet. The needle pointed to chartreuse. I thought, "Good! Just what I wanted to use anyway."

Chartreuse turned out to be the color the bass had selected, too. We hadn't fished long when I took a nice fish.

But we soon decided the fish must be deeper, so it was time to switch to crankbaits. Since we'd be fishing a different depth we needed to take another reading. Following the advice of the Color-C-Lector, I put on a red and black Lindy Shadling. It quickly produced two smaller bass and one that went well over five pounds. Hey, this wasn't turning out so bad!

It was Loren who noticed the darkening of the sky as the storm moved toward us. "Babe, I'm taking another reading since the light has gone down," he said. Sure enough, the new recommended color was fluorescent chartreuse. Since I'd just taken three fish on my red and black Shadling, I stuck with it.

Fishing behind me in the back of the boat, Loren caught the next two fish. My hot color had suddenly gone cold. I was still going to hang in there with it when Loren took the third fish in a row, another chunky bass that exceeded five pounds. I wished I hadn't been so stubborn. About the time I broke down and tied on a chartreuse bait, the storm struck and sent us rushing for shelter.

It had been a short trip, but a good one. Especially a good one for the Color-C-Lector. I had to be impressed.

The Color-C-Lector is being called the most exciting innovation in fishing in the past decade or two. Bass fishermen have always recog-

Jerry Hoffnagle takes a Color-C-Lector reading, first noting how clear the water is.

nized that color is a key factor in our fishing. Every now and then we'd see evidence of how touchy bass can be about color.

In a Minnesota tournament, two good fishermen were paired in a boat. One guy caught bass with almost every cast on a chartreuse crankbait. His partner tore apart his tackle box and—what luck!— he found an identical crankbait. But he still couldn't catch squat, no matter how hard he tried. Meanwhile his partner limited out. Finally they compared baits. They were identical, except the deadly lure had a little stripe of orange on its belly that was absent on the worthless lure. With first place safely in hand, the lucky angler let his frustrated partner fish with the orange-bellied crankbait. And he immediately began boating bass. That day, the bass were insisting on that little bit of orange.

Why? Actually, we now have some answers to the mysteries of bass color preference, thanks to Loren Hill's research. Loren probably knows more about the ability of bass to see lures than any other man. Loren is a rare combination of dedicated angler and scientist. He's in the department of zoology at the University of Oklahoma and director of the Bass Research Foundation.

Loren's research turned up some surprising results. Let's say you are about to go fishing early in the morning on a reservoir with stained water. Knowing there are lots of grey minnows here, you decide to throw a little grey crankbait. That seems to make sense, doesn't it?

Not really. According to the research, in stained water under early morning light, grey is the *least* visible of the colors tested. The best colors are orange, yellow, gold or fluorescent orange. In Loren's research, a trained bass, trying as hard as it could, couldn't find a grey panel under those circumstances. If that is true, what are the chances a bass is going to bang your grey crankbait? In that kind of water and light, a grey crankbait is basically "invisible!"

Remember, we're talking about a specific set of conditions—low light, stained water. That doesn't mean you'd never use a grey crankbait on this particular reservoir. In fact, at midday that grey crankbait would be a super choice. The lab research showed that in stained water at midday, grey is extremly visible, second only to green.

Loren found enormous differences in of colors when environmental circumstances were altered. The color that is extremely visible at noon might be almost invisible a few hours later. The color that is most visible in the clear waters of Lake Mary might be impossible for bass to see in the darker waters of Lake Judy, right across the road.

When Loren tested bass to see what colors they *preferred*, the results were fascinating. Bass were presented simultaneously with 11 crayfish painted in 11 colors. Records were made of which colors of crayfish were eaten and which were left alone. The test bass showed strong color preferences, pouncing immediately on some crayfish while totally ignoring others. Moreover, *the colors they preferred were exactly those colors they were best able to see* under those particular environmental conditions.

Let's consider one example. The earlier experiments had shown that three colors are highly visible to bass in muddy water under mid-morning light, namely green, red and gold. When hungry bass were later offered 11 colored crayfish under those circumstances of water and light, they gobbled down the green, red and gold crayfish *and didn't touch any of the other eight colors of crayfish!*

At this point, Loren realized that the right kind of light meter could analyze the environmental variables and tell anglers what color of lure they should use. Thus the Color-C-Lector was invented.

Using the Color-C-Lector is easy. A friend lets his seven year-old daughter take readings for him. However, it is important to take the reading at the right depth because that affects how much light is reaching your lure. As conditions change, you have to take new readings. If you move from the clear main body of a reservoir to a muddy cove, you need a new reading.

Every Color-C-Lector reading gives you a certain "best" color to use. If you don't have a lure with the color indicated, choose a bait with a color nearest the first choice. Or if you don't have an acceptable straight color, use the fluorescent color indicated.

What if you're *surface* fishing? No problem. A reading taken at three feet shows the preferred bait color.

On the Color-C-Lector, you have three scales (for different water clarities), each of which has a fluorescent and a straight band.

Your lure does not have to be *all* the color indicated. If green is the right color, for example, you don't need to fish an all-green crankbait. A bait with the right green mixed in with silver or orange will still produce fish. A green jig with a minnow will do the trick; you don't need to dye the minnow green!

So you don't have to carry lures in all 26 of the colors on the Color-C-Lector. With an assortment of multi-colored patterns, you'll have something good for all occasions. Or use soft-tip markers to doctor lures.

I'm predicting that one major impact of the new interest in color will be to open the minds of bass fishermen about color. How often have you fished with a pink lure? Fluorescent salmon? Powder blue? Olive drab? These colors are on the Color-C-Lector, and they'll start showing up on lures. Do you *know* they aren't good?

For that matter, why are we so stereotyped in our thinking on color? If white spinnerbaits are deadly, why not white worms? Since purple worms work, why not purple spinnerbaits? We're going to discover that our former list of good colors needs a lot of revision.

Meanwhile, I'd advise against fishing a lure that is *all one color* unless you've got the Color-C-Lector to tell you it's the right color. Baits with complex paint schemes have some advantages over baits with unicolor patterns. I believe it is often the contrast of colors that makes a lure visible.

Scent

Bass are famous for their willingness to take artificial baits. This leads anglers to presume bass don't use their sense of smell to any degree, but that's an oversimplification. After all, there are times when live bait will outfish artificials ten-to-one, so bass are certainly capable of using their sense of smell. It is important to them, so it should be important to you.

When do you need to worry about scent in bass fishing? Use scent *any* time it will increase your confidence and concentration, but be sure to use it on *slow presentations*, on *all presentations in very cold water* and *after a cold front*.

In other words, on a hot July day you don't need to put scent on a buzzbait you are racing over the top of the weeds. But take a cold, fall day when you are working a fat crankbait s-l-o-w-l-y over the tops of the dying weeds—*that's* a time scent will give you strikes instead of follows.

I'll give another example. John Christianson, a staffer here at Babe Winkelman Productions, recently won a tournament in which the average guy took a fish or two...but John culled through six limits of bass in one day! John located a rockpile in 22 feet of water where bass occasionally swam by to pick up crayfish. John fished a worm on the bottom, fishing it "dead," with *no action* whatever. He soaked each worm in crayfish scent before putting it down. Every now and then John's line would zip off, and he'd set the hook. In between fish, though, he just sat there fishing that worm as if it were some kind of live bait. Do you think all those bass would have grabbed that motionless worm if it hadn't been putting out a terrific cloud of scent?

There are a whole lot of new scent products on the market, each with its own claims. Nobody, to my knowledge, has really studied the responses of bass to different scents. Fishermen have used anise concoctions for years to mask bad odors, yet no study has proven that anise is more effective than cod liver oil or any other fragrant substance.

There are two trends in scent products that make sense to me. One is the use of natural foods as the odor source. Several new attractants use parts of minnows, nightcrawlers, crayfish or other natural baits as their main scent ingredient.

The other trend is to make the attractant thicker, more viscous, so it sticks to your lure better. The early, oily sprays were frustrating because when your bait hit the water and left that oil slick on the surface, you just knew most of the expensive scent was washing off. One new scent, Chummin' Rub, even sticks to spoons and crankbaits.

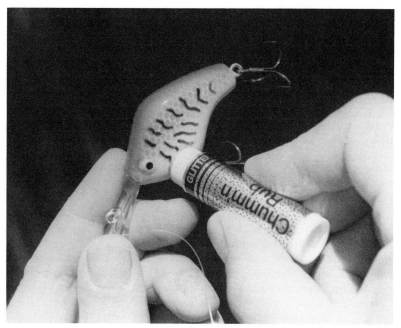

Chummin' Rub can be applied, without waste, to crankbaits or spoons.

Chapter 7
Make 'em An Offer They Can't Refuse

Bass can be awfully touchy about presentation. That's one of the reasons they're so interesting. One of Babe's Rules: no matter how negative the bass are, you can *always* catch a few. If you find the fish and then nail down the presentation perfectly, you can probably catch a bunch!

But not if you "leave your brains on the dock" when you start off. You've got to think. Don't stick with a single presentation or two. It's common to hear another angler say, "I catch two- thirds of my bass on a grape worm." Fine. But watch that guy fish, and you find he hardly uses anything else. He may carry other lures and worms in 14 other colors, but they never get wet unless it is on one of those days when *nothing* is working; then he'll experiment half-heartedly with a bait he has no faith in...before going back to the grape worm.

We all fall into these ruts, me included. The measure of a good bass fisherman is the ability to challenge himself, to grow, to learn new presentations.

Retrieves and Casts

Presentation includes both your choice of a lure and your retrieve. In bass fishing, it often includes the cast, too.

Your *cast* is part of your presentation when you fish shallow water. I've talked about the need for accuracy before. We should also recognize the importance of the way the lure comes to the fish.

Bass in shallow water are naturally spooky. They've left the safety of the depths, and they know it. Perhaps it is instinctual for bass to fear attacks by birds from the sky, but they're aware of danger coming at them from above. Unless they're extremely aggressive, an object flashing over them is frightening. The loud splash of a heavy lure landing nearby is often a turn-off and might be so frightening they scoot for safety.

Whenever you've got bass holding by cover in the shallows, the preferred cast is directly in line with the fish's position but past it. You want to pull the lure past the ambush point, not hit it with the cast.

There are some obvious exceptions. Flipping involves bass in heavy cover where you often can't cast past the fish. Since the best flipping lures (such as a pork frog on a light jig) are soft and not terribly heavy, they enter the water quietly. The flipping cast is inherently gentle, too.

MN 0479

When fishing to objects or visible cover, try to steer your bait left or right with your rod tip to make it go exactly where it should. Or cast, then move the boat with the troll motor so you can steer the bait *under* objects like pontoon boats moored to docks.

When you have to throw a cast into very shallow water, you might need to choose a lure that doesn't land like a load of bricks. A soft plastic bait will plop down like food, not a predator.

In much bass fishing, the first two or three feet of your retrieve will account for 19 bass of 20 you catch. Some people talk about a cast going through a "fish zone" and a "dead zone." The fish zone will be right near cover in many situations. While the odd bass might leave cover to chase a bait and strike it right by the boat, it's often smart to fish that critical first two or three feet as carefully as you can, then *rush* the bait back for another cast.

Few fishermen think about their retrieves as much as they should. Sometimes a little difference in technique works wonders.

A story involving two friends of mine, Randy Amenrud and Gary Roach, might make the point. They were fishing spinnerbaits for bass in a cold rain. Randy didn't have a rainsuit, but Gary did. Gary was comfortable, except Randy was catching all the fish. After Gary studied Randy a while to see what he could be doing differently, he noticed Randy was so cold he was shaking with tremors. On his next cast, Gary shook and shivered...and caught a bass.

Retrieves vary in terms of *speed, action* and *operating depth*. Experiment with all three.

It is less important to play around with retrieves when you are fishing heavy cover. A bass in heavy cover is triggered by *how close* your bait comes. That fish is not accustomed to stalking baits while trying to make up its mind about hitting. He sees it—he grabs it. It's still smart to experiment with retrieve speed, primarily to find one that gets the bait close to the fish.

Bass in more open environments are a very different animal. These are often chasing fish. You'll sometimes see wakes coming from the side after your lure splashes down. When the bass is behind the lure, it moves behind it as it debates striking. Open cover bass definitely challenge you to find just the right retrieve to trigger a strike.

Artificial Lures

There are four major families of bass lures—spinnerbaits, crankbaits, jump baits and live baits. You aren't a *modern* bass fishermen until you have mastered the three families of artificial baits. You aren't a *complete* bass fisherman until you also know how to use live bait.

Of course, you still want to gain proficiency with the lures outside these major groups. The four major families aren't the *whole* answer, but they're sure the place to start. Spinnerbaits, crankbaits, jump baits and live bait will almost always catch fish if you use them properly.

Work on these baits with a variety of retrieves until you have absolute confidence in them. Then make yourself expand and experiment with new presentations. The most consistently successful bass fishermen are the most versatile.

Spinnerbaits

Spinnerbaits do what they do so well that you never want to be without them. What they do is go into the most goshawful jungles of weeds and timber and tell the bass to "come and get it, big boy!" The skirt flutters and pulses; the blade whirls and throbs; the bass strikes!

There's no denying the appeal of spinnerbaits to bass, but their real beauty lies in the way they can be fished in thick cover without hooking anything but fish. Spinnerbaits are one of the best lures for working around timber, docks or weeds. While they can be run deep, they're at their best when fished in water from the surface to about eight feet deep.

I use a single-spin about 90 percent of the time. It's more versatile. Tandem spinnerbaits are better for buzzing just below the surface, but for most other retrieves the single-bladed baits are better.

Reed banks are a classic example of good, weedy cover where spinnerbaits will be effective.

Spinnerbaits will take bass even when you use them without think-ing. Because of that, many guys lapse into "no-brainer" spinnerbaiting. They have no idea how versatile the bait can be. The first step to mastering spinnerbaits is learning different retrieves. Here are several proven ones:

- Fast retrieve, just below the surface. With some spinnerbaits (big blades, tandem spinnerbaits), this retrieve will bulge but not break the surface. For active fish.
- Straight retrieve, average speed. This is unimaginative, but it catches fish.
- Straight retrieve, super slow. This one will often take more fish than a retrieve that flashes by the bass too fast. Slow retrieves are especially important in cold water. In spring, use a light (1/4 ounce) bait; in fall, use a big bait with extra-large blades. With a slow retrieve, The bait runs lower and the fish has a little more time to decide to strike.
- Stop-and-go retrieve. This is a killer when fish are hesitant. A good retrieve for open cover situations.
- Yo-yo retrieve. This is a variant of the stop-and-go, but you let the bait "helicopter" down longer. This will pull bass out of more open situations, such as thinner weeds or timber. Watch for your line to jump, because you'll see strikes before you can feel them. Bass always take the bait while it's dropping. Spin-nerbaits with shorter arms and "rocker arms" with smallish spinners are better for this.
- Drop-in-the pocket retrieve. When working lily pads or big flats with moss or weeds, retrieve the spinnerbait quickly as long as the cover is too thick to fish, then pause to let it drop into any open pockets it comes to. Let it drop a moment or so, watching the line for the twitch of a strike. Then bring it your way again, increasing the speed to aviod snagging when the bait is out of the pocket.
- Jigging retrieve. Work a single spin, maybe with a pork trailer, up and down in deep water, fishing it like a jig.

Modifying Spinnerbaits

There are many ways to modifying spinnerbaits. I like to *modify blades, change skirts* and *add trailers*. It is *not* true that "a spinnerbait is a spinnerbait." You'll be rewarded if you tinker and experiment.

Changing skirts is an easy way to get the colors you want. For a few bucks, you can assemble a big assortment of colored skirts. I like the look of multi-colored skirts, especially blue and chartreuse, green and white or orange and yellow. Avoid plastic skirts in favor of rubber or living rubber skirts, as they have better action. Spinnerbaits with hair or tinsel skirts are usually over-dressed as sold; you can thin or shorten them.

122

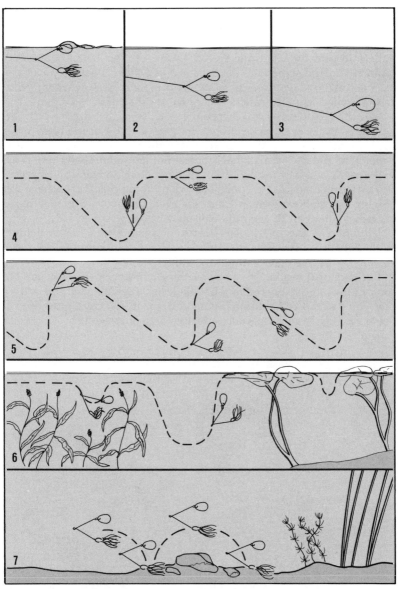

Several spinnerbait retrieves: 1) buzzing the surface, 2) straight retrieve, 3) slow, deep retrieve, 4) stop-and-go retrieve, 5) yo-yo retrieve, 6) drop-in-the pocket retrieve and 7) jigging.

My favorite color for dark water is a chartreuse skirt with a hammered copper blade. Another good one in dark water is a fluorescent orange blade over a black skirt. For clear water on clear days, I like a hammered silver or white blade and a white skirt, maybe white and green. Blue or grape skirts with hammered nickle blades are good in clear water under overcast skies.

Trailers often add to the appeal of spinnerbaits. The best trailer is a piece of pork rind, especially the Uncle Josh Ripple Rind. Pork is so tough it won't scrape off on weeds, timber or brush. However, adding trailers (especially big trailers) can throw off the balance of your spinnerbait. And sometimes it results in a bait that is bigger than a bass in a neutral mood wants. Add a "stinger" or trailer hook when you add a pork trailer, as pork trailers encourage short strikes.

Switching blade sizes has helped me catch some awfully big bass. In fall and at times in summer, I'll put on a #6 or #7 Colorado blade on a single spin. Those big blades put out a thump that brings big bass rushing in. You can't usually reel these modified spinnerbaits very fast, so this retrieve is best for big fish in shallow, colder water. It is smart to add an attracting scent to your bait when doing this. When bass are holding on shallow, weedy flats, I'll even put two #5 blades on a tandem spinnerbait to keep the bait up on slow retrieves.

Vibration is the overlooked factor in spinnerbaits. By switching blade sizes or by switching to a blade with more or less cup to it, you can get the degree of vibration you want.

I've had great results lately by switching to big willow leaf blades on some of my large spinnerbaits. That blade has a special whipping action that you can feel right through your rod (or, if you can't, you need a better rod!). It seems especially effective on aggressive fish.

Two spinnerbaits for big bass. On the left is a lure with an over-sized blade. Next to it a spinnerbait with a huge willow blade.

Spinnerbaits must be in balance. Blade size, head weight, retrieve speed and trailer bulk all have to balance out so the bait runs with the arm directly overhead. Sometimes arms get bent up, down or sideways, and they need to be bent back to the original position.

Every spinnerbait has a certain amount of *lift*—a tendency to ride high in the water when retrieved. Adding trailers or switching to bigger blades will give you more lift. That can be good or bad. A spinnerbait with lots of lift can be worked slower in some spots than one that sinks faster. If you want a spinnerbait that works fast and somewhat deep, keep the blade small and don't add trailers. For really deep work you can wrap lead wire on the arm, but that's rarely the best bait for deep water.

Since I use spinnerbaits in heavy cover, I'm reluctant to add a trailer or stinger hook. They increase your hang-ups. But I'll put up with hang-ups if that's what I have to do to catch bass, and sometimes they're hitting so far back on the skirt that the stinger is necessary. I'll almost always use a stinger hook when I put a pork dressing on a spinnerbait.

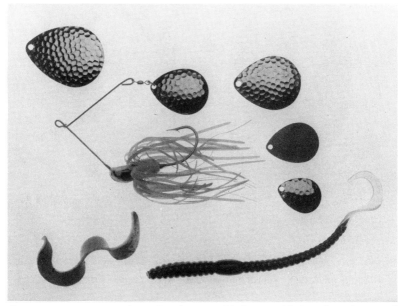

Customize your spinnerbaits by changing blade size, blade color, skirts and trailers.

Crankbaits

Crankbaits, like spinnerbaits, are great for covering a lot of water quickly to find fish. They dive down to work deeper than spinnerbaits. Crankbaits are great for "prospecting" quickly to see if any fish are around. Once you hit a fish it's smart to stop and check the area out more carefully, probably with a worm or other slower bait.

Crankbaits are famous for their ability to catch aggressive, chasing fish. No other bait can put so many fish in the boat in a short time if you locate a school of actively feeding fish.

125

Crankbaits are tops for fast action on aggressive bass, but they can also trigger fish that aren't aggressive.

I also love the way crankbaits trigger violent strikes from neutral to slightly negative fish. Imagine you're half asleeep in your easy chair and your son runs in and throws a football at your stomach. Caught it, didn't you! That's about what happens when a crankbait zips past the nose of a dozing bass. If a bass has more time to mull over the decision to strike, he might let caution rule, but you don't give him that time. Of course, you have to get the bait really close.

Crankbaits dive anywhere from three to 15 feet—even deeper—on a normal retrieve. Fatter crankbaits (like the Bagley B) run shallower than thinner ones (like Lindy's Shadling). Baits with long lips of thin material (like a Hellbender) will run deeper than baits with short lips of thick plastic (like a Rapala).

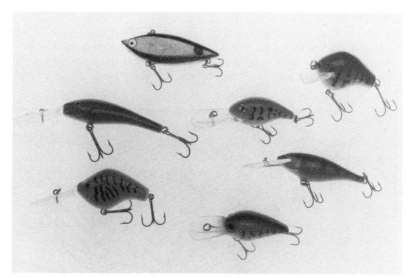

There is no single best crankbait. Each type has a different action and diving depth.

Different situations call for different retrieves. Coontail and ca-bomba are very tough weeds. I like to work baits over and around them, using good polarizing glasses to keep the bait clear of the weed clumps. I'd rather not hang up on these weeds. Cabbage, however, is soft enough you can usually rip the plug free with a sharp snap of the rod tip.

Experiment with speed, too. The straight retrieve used by most anglers most of the time is rarely the most effective. A stop-and-go retrieve is often a killer. Super-fast retrieves trigger reflexive strikes. Remember, you *cannot* reel a crankbait fast enough to keep it away from a bass who wants it.

There are many ways of working these baits. At times you can take a deep-diving crankbait like a Hellbender and just ease it slowly over the tops of weeds; it will have a heavy, slow, wobbling action that can bring bass up. When working a crankbait over brush or weeds you'll sometimes get hung up because the bill of the bait will dig down into the cover. If the bait is buoyant, however, it will naturally float free if you give it some slack.

I often begin a retrieve with an explosive snap that rushes the bait down to its working depth. Then I work it slower. At the end of the retrieve, when the bait is changing angles to come to my rod tip, I'll often speed things up to make the bait appear to be escaping. This little trick has turned lots of "followers" into "strikers" for me over the years.

The biggest mistake beginners make is trying to keep their crankbaits free of weeds. A good crankbait can come through quite a few weeds or even timber without fouling up too often. If you aren't contacting cover with your bait, you usually aren't fishing close enough to the fish. If keeping your bait-tangle free is your biggest objective, fish in your

127

bathtub! No guts, no glory. If catching bass is important to you, *go for it!* Throw that bait in places that scare you. Let it bang into timber. Often, in dark water, bass won't locate a crankbait well enough to hit it unless it is noisily slamming into cover. When you weed up, rip the bait free; you'll catch a lot of fish that hit the bait reflexively just as it comes free.

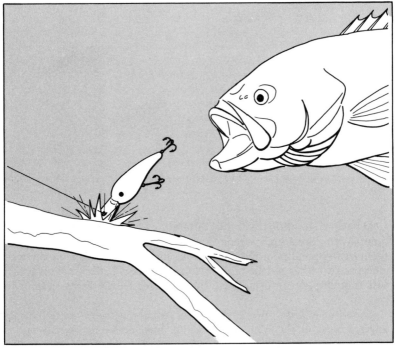

Instead of avoiding cover with your bait, make a special point of banging the bait into cover. You'll trigger strikes.

Sometimes it pays to get your bait down that extra foot or two. The kneel-and-reel technique receiving publicity now has actually been around for a long time. Even without kneeling, you can get your bait down deeper by holding the rod tip low as you retrieve. You can also get deeper by adding a little lead to the line, either right against the knot or clamped to the line a few inches up. Experiment.

Some guys think the faster they reel, the deeper the bait goes. Not so. In fact, it's almost the other way around. Once a deep diver gets to its running depth it will run deeper at slower retrieve speeds than at high speeds.

Line size affects running depth. Use the *lightest line possible*, if getting deep is important (8-pound if you can get away with it, 10-or 12-pound if the cover is heavy). Thick lines fight to keep a crankbait running shallow. Thick lines also bog down lure action and reduce your sense of feel. Prime is a super crankbait line because it transmits such a definite sense of what is happening to the bait.

Fat lines resist the efforts of the crankbait to dive deep. You'll be fishing shallow, and with a big bow in your line.

Feel is *way* more important in crankbaiting than most fishermen seem to know. We get *far* more strikes than we'd ever guess; we just don't feel them. Unless you sense that little "something different" about the way your lure is working, you'll miss fish you could have caught. Good tackle helps, although concentration is more important.

Crankbaits should be tied directly to the line whenever possible. If you want to use a snap, make it a *small* Crosslock or Coastlock snap, *with* a symmetrically bent loop and *without* a swivel. I like crankbaits that come fitted with split rings, for you can tie to the ring and get good action. If your crankbait doesn't have a split ring, consider a loop knot like the King Sling or Duncan Loop.

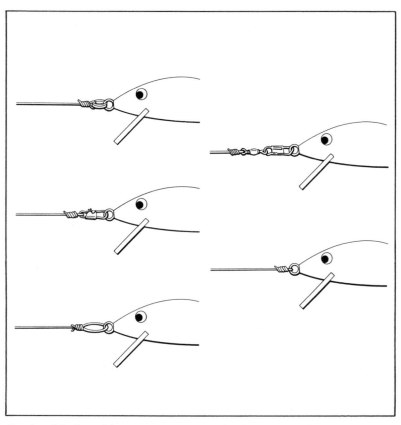

Good and bad crankbait connections. Good: split ring, small snap, loop knot.
Bad: clumsy snap swivel, direct to eye.

Unfortunately, many crankbaits don't run true (they pull left or right) until they've been tuned. The faster you work the bait, the more troublesome this is. The solution is to *bend* and/or *twist* the screw eye. If the lure runs right, bend and/or twist the eye *slightly* to the right, using a needle-nose pliers. Which should you do—bending or twisting? Sight down the bill to see how the screw eye looks in relation to the rest of the bait. The front edge of the screw eye has to be perfectly dead center. If the eye was drilled in at an angle, bend it back to the true position. If it was drilled in straight but off-center, twist the eye.

Don't waste precious fishing time tuning baits. Tune your baits in the off-season, working on a swimming pool with some friends, until you have a whole box of baits you *know* run true. That also gives you the chance to see how deep your baits run with different retrieves. Some individual crankbaits just refuse to be tuned, even if you have an exorcist work on 'em. Bury them where nobody will ever find them again.

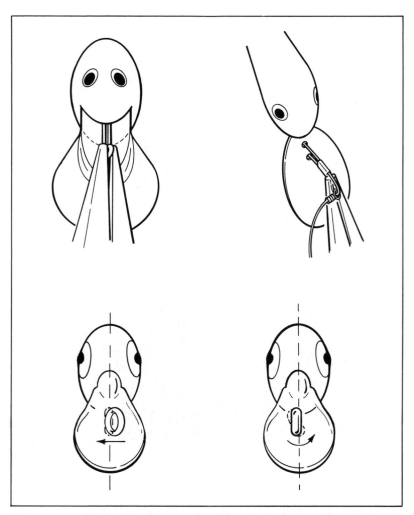

To tune a crankbait, twist the eye or bend the wire in the same direction it runs to. If the eye has been drilled in off-center, bend it.

There is some mysterious quality—a certain vibration pattern—that sometimes occurs in individual crankbaits. A dozen crankbaits might be identical in every respect, yet one of them will be unbelievably deadly. Maybe some day the manufacturers will understand this quality and build it into all baits. Until then, if you find one of those "magic" crankbaits, treasure it and use it carefully!

Color is almost as important in crankbaits as it is in worms—maybe slightly less so because bass don't get as good a look at the bait. Generally, in clear water I like quieter colors with less pronounced pattern. In dark water I go to brighter, harsher colors and finishes. I usually like a certain amount of contrast in my finishes at all times.

Some crankbaits have a special vibration that makes them more effective than apparently identical baits.

I'm not a fan of the photo finish "natural" finishes. Of them, my favorite is the Lindy's baby bass finish, and with it I scrape the lower part of the finish to give me a dark green lure with a contrasting white belly. Remember, the true natural patterns on baitfish are nature's way of protecting those fish from predators. Why fish with a lure designed to be hard to see?

I like contrasty patterns when bass are aggressive, but sometimes use more muted, mellow patterns when bass are negative. I can't prove this makes sense, but it seems to work for me. In general, when water is clear and bass are shy, I think you should avoid lures that are "too much"—too visible, too big, too wiggly or too loud. When the water is dark and the bass are snapping, give them lots of bright color, contrast, noise, speed and heavy action.

Jump Baits

Jump baits are a group of baits that are fished much the same way. The group includes plastic worms, jigs with soft plastics, and jigs with pork. This family has in common the fact that the lures have little action of their own. You put the action on them. Compared to other baits, they're generally fished slower and require more skill to use effectively. It is skill that pays off *big*.

Worms

If you limited me to one family of artificial baits for fishing bass, this would be it. Worms can go anywhere bass go. You can fish a worm at the surface, at 50 feet, or anywhere in between. Worms can be rigged to be as weedless as a bait can be.

No getting around it—effective use of worms takes some learning. You've got to work with them enough to develop technique and confidence. And you need reasonably stout tackle to get the hook buried in a bass's jaw. Unfortunately, the most publicized rig—the slip-sinker Texas rig—is the most troublesome of all worm rigs to use well. No wonder many people have tried worms and given them up as too hard to use. They aren't. Try learning worm fishing with an exposed hook rig. You'll be amazed!

It used to be difficult to buy a worm with the right softness because so many were too hard, but most of today's worms are flexibile and lively. The only place for a hard worm is in reeds, which are very raspy, or some kinds of timber or brush. I'd rather fish soft, wiggly worms and replace them more often than to fish with a thing that acts like a stick. Worms are cheap. My fishing time is not.

Worms come with *straight* or *action* tails of different lengths. I mostly prefer action tails, but straight worms are good in the thickest cover where action tails might wrap themselves on the cover. Straight worms drop a little faster than worms with action tails.

Color is super critical in worms because the bass have so much time to inspect the worm. I normally start with a solid color, but carry an arsenal of straight and mixed colors and let the bass decide what I should use on a given day. Bass may not know much, but they sure know what color of worm I should use. I'm all in favor of listening to them on that topic!

Water clarity should guide your choice of color. In super-clear water, I've done best with ice blue, purple, kelly green and strawberry. In moderately clear water—which is a lot of the water I fish—I like grape and purple. In dirty, muddy water, I turn to black or brown, usually with an orange firetail.

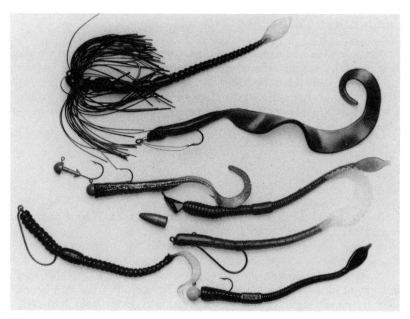

Plastic worms are tremendously versatile. This photo shows just some of the various ways they can be rigged.

Lately, I've been doctoring up my worms with scent. Scent is almost always a positive factor when fishing jump baits. The slower you fish a worm, the more important scent becomes.

Next to color, the most important quality of worms is their drop speed. The size and type of worm affect that. A big action tail, twin tails or legs on your worm will all cause it to drop slower. But the main factor is the amount of weight you use.

Bass usually hit a worm as it falls. If your drop speed is too quick, the worm will plummet past the fish so fast they may not give it a second look. But if you fish a weight that's too light, you can have three problems. Your worm might be too light for efficient casting. Your worm might be too light to give you that sense of what your worm is doing. And sometimes a light worm hangs up high in the cover, never dropping to where the bass are.

I remember a tournament on a central Minnesota lake a few years back. I'd found bass huddled near the base of big clumps of coontail, a very thick weed that grows in huge bunches that look like shrubs. To get a worm down to those bass, I needed a sinker weighing 3/16-ounce. With that much weight I could throw right in the middle of these clumps and then jiggle it until the worm would finally get down to the fish, dropping slowly enough to draw strikes. A sinker of 3/8-ounces dropped so fast the bass ignored the worm. A 1/8-ounce sinker was so light the worm wouldn't get down. My partner didn't ask me what

Charlie Winkelman with a worm-caught Florida bass.

sinker I was using (I would have told him, if he'd asked!) and he was quietly going nuts while I caught fish. How important can sinker weight be? I placed first and set a tournament weight record that day; my partner, fishing the same water with the same worms, boated one bass.

Sometimes the best weight is no weight at all. When prospecting around docks, weedy pockets or brush, it's hard to beat an unweighted worm that you skitter and snake along the surface, letting it drop at key spots where bass might be. You can fish this kind of rig very quickly, though worming is usually a slow form of fishing. For this kind of fishing I like a short, moderately stiff graphite spinning rod with flex in the tip.

You can rig worms many ways. Rig with an exposed hook point unless the cover is so snaggy that you lose too many rigs. Then, and only then, consider a snagless rig.

The classic snagless rig is the Texas rig. It is best for working around stiff brush, timber and certain types of weeds. Some of what you gain in snagless qualities you lose in the difficulty of setting a hook. To get a hook planted, you need to slam it through the width of the worm (perhaps more than once, if the worm is balled up in the bass's mouth) and *then* through the bass's bony mouth tissue.

Accompanying sketches show how to be sure your worm will lie straight on the hook. When placing the hook in the worm, push the point all the way through, then back it up until it lies just under the skin of the worm.

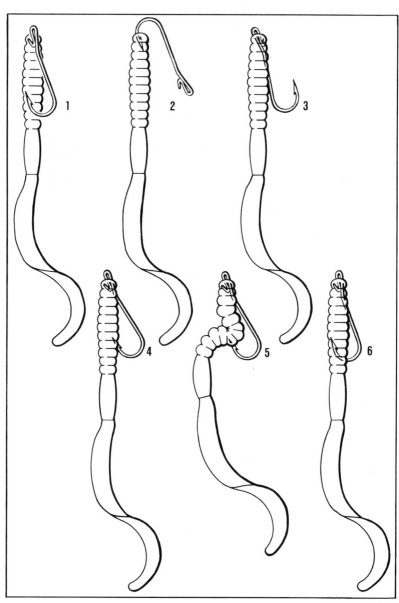

Worms must be rigged to hang straight. If you lay the hook along the worm, you'll see exactly where the point has to go in and come out. In light cover, have the point end near the skin. In heavy cover, keep the point centered in the worm.

With a Texas-rigged worm, use the heaviest rod that will still throw that worm. When you feel a take, carefully lower the rod tip to the water, then whip it up *hard*. Set with an explosive snap of the rod; then set again. Good worm fishermen often peg their sinkers in place by inserting a toothpick in the line hole and bending it off. That reduces tangles resulting from the sinker and the worm coming down on different sides of an obstruction.

Weedless hooks deserve more use than they get. Eagle Claw makes them weighted (249WWR) and unweighted (449WR). These wire weedguards are probably easier to set a hook with than Texas rigs, especially if you play with the wire guards until they are just barely snagless. They aren't quite as weedless as the Texas rig.

Whenever possible, I'll fish a worm on a jighead with an exposed hook. The jig should have a "keeper barb" (a prong that holds the worm in place) and a good hook. The new "mushroom jighead" is the best I've used. These little heads snug up tight against the worm (I usually bite off a tiny bit of worm head to make the fit better) so they are as snagless as possible while having the exposed hook for easier setting. A light mushroom jighead with a six-inch worm on light line is a *super* bass taker on weedline bass. Some good ones are made by the Gopher Tackle Company of Cuyuna, Minnesota.

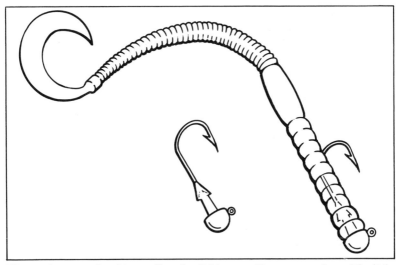

The mushroom jighead is excellent for fishing weedline summer bass. The light hooks set easily, but can be bent.

Worm size isn't usually a big problem. The six-inch worm will take small bass *and* big bass in most situations. It's best choice most of the time, and when the fish are really negative I might nip off part of the worm to make it shorter. In the fall when the bass go on a binge to fatten for the winter, bigger baits definitely draw bigger fish. Then a nine-inch worm isn't large.

Fishing a tournament on Santee Cooper about ten years ago, I found some bass that would work around a flat early in the morning, then drop down to rest in deep water (about 28 feet) when the light came up. When they were up, I caught them with my usual six-inch worms. But though I knew where they were later in the day, I couldn't get them to hit. I kept making my worm smaller, which is a smart thing to try when fish seem negative. Finally I got desperate enough to try something flaky—a fat, nine-inch worm. And, boy, did that get 'em! I've occasionally triggered sulky fish with huge worms on natural lakes and elsewhere since then.

Uncle Josh has a new line of pork worms that is an important addition to the worm field. Pork worms are indestructable, hold scent better than plastic and are flexible even in cold water. The new worm has a special weedless hook system designed by respected pro fishermen, Bobby and Billy Murray. The worm itself has a thick, fleshy body and a special curly tail that wriggles when the worm is moved. The worms come in six colors. To my eye, no plastic bait has ever had quite the action of pork rind.

Soft Plastic Lures

There are several soft plastic lures that are worth fishing.

Plastic "lizards" or salamanders deserve special mention. Most of the time, worms will catch as many bass as the other soft plastics, but around the spawn you can often do more business with a lizard. It just looks like something coming in to eat eggs, and bass will be quicker to grab a plastic lizard than another jump bait.

The whole group of soft plastic baits is good. The only one I don't like is a soft plastic frog, which imitates a superior bait, the pork frog.

Jig-and-Eel

Another deadly pork jump bait is the famous jig and eel. This can be fished in the same water you'd use a worm, but is often used in deeper and more open water. Jig and eel rigs get a lot of use right along the edge of cover (like a weedline or timber line) or on deeper structure.

Grub Jigs

Grub jigs are small and quiet in action. The common twister tails are one example, and another one I've used a lot is the Tom Mann Sting Ray grub. I'll use these little jigs sometimes after a front has shut bass feeding down. In quieter colors, like root beer or smoke, you can turn some big fish on with these tiny morsels.

Jig-and-pigs are known, with reason, as big fish catchers. Since the jigs used usually have a weedguard, the jig and pig combination can be fished almost anywhere. A common setup is a 3/8-ounce black jig with a living rubber skirt and a brown #11 Uncle Josh pork frog. By whittling the frog with a knife you can modify the action. Jig and-pigs are deadly when fished on deeper structure or when worked in weeds, timber or other places.

In fact, I'm fishing these baits in more and more kinds of cover. The more I use this bait, the more I like it. It is a big fish bait that doesn't necessarily cut down on the number of bass you'll take. I believe some bass take a jig-and-pig to be a crayfish. The rig is just dynamite when you find a school of bass that is beating up on crayfish. You'll know this is happening when your livewell gets filled up with crayfish parts or you see bass regurgitate crayfish as they fight.

The more I fish jig-and-pig baits, the more I like them. This is a versatile, big bass bait.

Reaper Worms

Reaper worms are so deadly they have become something of a "cult" bait. These eel-shaped plastic baits are usually fished on a stand-up jig with a triangular head that slips between weeds or cuts free of those it snags on. Reapers are especially effective when fished as a drop bait along the edge of cover. More than any other jump bait, Reapers work when fished with a violent hopping movement called "ripping." But you can take fish by crawling a Reaper slowly on the bottom, too. A five-inch Reaper on a 3/8-ounce jighead is an excellent bait for working deep water *quickly* when searching for fish.

Other Important Artificial Baits

These baits are important to own and use, though they account for fewer fish, probably, than the major groups of lures mentioned above.

Spoons

Most of my spoon fishing is for shallow bass, although on reservoirs at times I'll work deep water with a jigging spoon. Two spoons work especially well in shallow weeds, the Johnson Silver Minnow and the light, plastic Heddon Moss Boss.

The Moss Boss is best at fishing over moss and sloppy weeds. It's light enough to stay on the surface even with extremely slow retrieves. You can throw a Moss Boss into the very worst stuff and skid it from open spot to open spot, jiggling it in place when it comes to one of the rare openings where a bass could grab it. This is one of the best lily pad lures.

The Silver Minnow is more versatile. It is a faster, deeper running spoon. It works in the same kind of water that spinnerbaits do well in— thick weeds or brushy cover in about two to eight feet of water. Silver Minnows are also "at home" in the thickest cover.

I add a trailer to my Silver Minnows almost all the time. Sometimes I use a spinnerbait skirt or plastic worm, but more often I like pork— especially the Uncle Josh Ripple Rind. The Silver Minnow casts like a bullet and is capable of punching down through surface weeds to get where the bass lie beneath. I always carry an assortment of Silver Minnows and trailers when bass fishing. I sometimes feel the need for a different look, so I'll color these spoons with felt tip markers or tape.

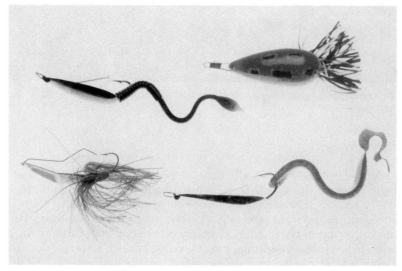

Some shallow water spoons with different sorts of trailers. Often, the best trailer is Ripple Rind.

You'll hook more bass on a spoon if you delay the set just slightly. Above all, sharpen the hook!

Striking bass sometimes miss a spoon, so keep a second outfit ready with a lightly weighted plastic worm. When a bass misses your spoon, immediately throw the worm right on the bass's nose. Seconds count, so be quick! Dance the worm around without pulling it toward you, and you'll almost always get a follow-up strike.

Some people have trouble hooking bass on spoons, but it isn't so hard. Just delay the set for a moment until the bass has turned its head. This same hookset procedure is necessary when fishing topwater baits.

I sharpen the hooks of most baits before I use them, as most hooks are dull when they are brand new. But I make a special point of sharpening the hook on the Silver Minnows. The heavy plating process that gives the spoon its good looks makes for a dull hook until you bear down on it with a file for a while.

Buzz Baits

Buzzers are a variant of spinnerbaits. The big delta blades have much more lift than ordinary blades, so the bait runs at the surface, sounding like a runaway egg beater. There probably isn't a better bait when bass are shallow and aggressive. Buzzbaits are a good choice in warm water and when bass are aggressive. Don't try them in cold water or after a front. Buzzers work best when bass are shallow, yet they can pull fish up from 15 feet down.

Experiment with speed. The original buzzer, the Harkins Lunker Lure, is still a good one, but you have to fish it fast to keep it up. Many buzzbait fans like baits with triple blades (like Norman's Triple Wing) because they can be worked really slow without sinking.

Buzzbaits are great for fishing hot, muggy midsummer nights. Use a black-skirted buzzer with two blades or a triple-wing blade, and keep retrieves slow and steady.

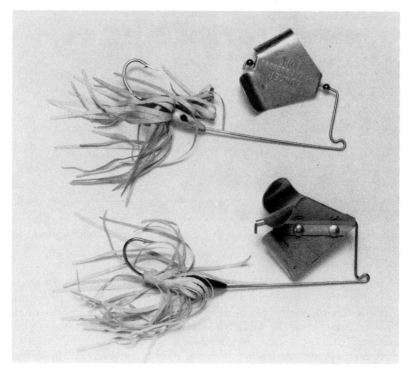

The buzzbait at top has a twin blade, good for fast work. The treble-bladed buzzer below is better when the fish want a slow buzzer.

Bass frequently hit short on buzzers, so a trailer hook is needed more often than not. These stinger hooks don't often get you fouled up since the bait runs mostly up above snags. Don't encourage short-striking by adding trailers.

Sometimes, when fish are aggressive, I tune my buzzbait (by bending the wire) so the blade strikes the body, making more noise. Speed, noise and color are the three elements of buzzers to experiment with.

Buzz baits are often most effective when they strike some object, like a dock post or the exposed part of a stump. As you reel them in, steer the buzzer around with your rod tip to put it in contact with cover whenever possible.

Surface Baits

Surface baits are fun to use. At the right time and place, they're very effective. In the weeks immediately before spawning or after the bass come out of their post-spawn recuperation, they patrol the shallows for food. Or sometimes in the low light of evening or morning in the dead heat of summer, surface baits dragged over the tops of timber, brush or emerging weeds will really pull bass up.

The Zara Spook takes some learning, but it is worth the effort. The walk-the-dog retrieve is especially deadly.

I primarily use four surface baits.

The Smithwick Devil's Horse (or Heddon's Tiny Torpedo) has spinners in front and behind its body. You can fish these *prop baits* with slow twitches and long pauses, or you can make a moderate racket with the spinners.

The old Heddon Zara Spook is designed for the "walking the dog" retrieve. It can be a killer, and I won a tournament walking a Zara. You have to learn the rhythmn to get the bait kicking from side to side. The line must go slack in between twitches. Most guys like to hold the rod tip low, as in muskie jerkbait fishing, twitching it in rhythmical sweeps of about ten inches. When you get good, you can make a Spook dance right over a bass's lair without moving toward the boat. Oh, bass *hate* that!

Floating minnow-type baits, like Lindy's Baitfish or Rapalas, can be worked as surface baits. These light baits will do a lot of kicking around without moving out of place, and that's often the best way to use them. They also dive when retrieved, and you sometimes pick up bass that way.

The Plummer Super Frog is the best surface bait for terrible, sloppy, junk-weed bays. With this frog, and with many other surface baits, you should set the hook only after the bass has taken the bait and turned sideways to run with it. Set too quickly, and you'll pull the frog right out of the bass's mouth. Bass often miss the frog on the first strike, so give them a second chance, with the frog again or (better) with a worm.

In general, the best "colors" for surface fishing are clear or light colors. At night, black is tops. In the daytime, don't give the fish too much to look at. A transparent Zara Spook, for example, presents a vague outline rather than a crude, definite shape. White, silver or white with glitter are about as good.

Big Baits

It seems strange to use huge baits for bass, but there's nothing strange about the results. Last fall, in northern Minnesota, using a giant musky-sized bucktail called a Buchertail, I took bass weighing 7 pounds, 2 ounces, and 8 pounds, 4 ounces. Up here, these aren't "big" fish—they're giants. These were strip pit fish. One came off the obviously best point in the pit. The other came off the best tree in the whole area.

Big baits, big fish. And fall is a key time to go for big bass. It's the time to throw nine-inch plastic worms, musky spinners, gigantic crankbaits or huge crankbaits of the type normally used for muskies or trophy northerns.

Live Bait

Partly because tournament rules ban live bait, many of today's anglers ignore live bait or hold it in contempt. Let's not argue about attitudes here, but I'd be letting you down if I didn't make it clear that *live bait can be extremely effective on bass*. At times, you either fish with live bait or you don't catch bass. Many guys who look down on live bait haven't tried it. When they do, they usually don't talk so scornfully about "minnow dunkers."

Like one time, not long ago, when I fished the James River near Richmond, in Virginia. My host had a pattern that worked early in the morning. Bass would come up on smooth sand/gravel points off islands. We would catch a few fish early, in the cool of the day, and then the bass would drop into deeper water along the river channel. Then my host tried to tempt them to take a plastic worm, but they were having none of it.

I suggested we try Lindy Rigs with minnows. "No way," said my host, "would I use live bait. If I can't catch 'em on artificials, I'd rather not catch 'em." I knew better than to argue, so I just quietly baited up with the standard slip sinker rig I've used to catch thousands of fish over the years.

My first bass didn't impress my host, though it was a real nice fish. He kept pretty cool when I caught the second one, too. But when I boated my third bass (these were fish from 5 to 6 pounds), he began to re-think his position on live bait. If any of his buddies had been in sight, he never would have lowered himself to use one of my Lindy Rigs. But they weren't, so he did.

It was quite a day. I can't begin to remember all the bass we caught. By moving around, I found several deeper holes, mostly inside turns along the river channel, where the bass were holding. They wouldn't look at a plastic worm, but they couldn't say no to live bait. Man, did we catch fish!

When we repeated this performance the next day, a live bait fisherman had been born. In fact, he talked some friends into trying it. Today there is a small, tight circle of enthusiastic Lindy riggers in the Charleston area.

Minnows are my favorite live bait for bass, and I usually fish them on a jig. In most environments, in fact, the jig-and-minnow is the *single deadliest bait you can use for all fish at all times of year under all kinds of conditions*. Other baits work well or even better at times, but there just isn't a more versatile or reliable bait than a jig sweetened with a minnow.

There are two major times I use the jig and minnow. One is after a bad cold front. The fish are deep in the cover. They're inactive. They won't strike anything unless it is small and smells good, and they'll not move more than an inch or three to pick up a bait. Tough conditions! Time to stick a spottail shiner on a Fuzz-E-Grub or some similar jig and start working carefully in the best weeds. The color of the jig head and body can be more important than you'd expect.

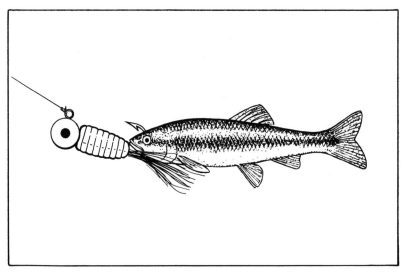

When bass are not active, especially after a front, you can hardly beat a jig-and-minnow.

You can't tease the fish into biting; they're going to take it or they're not. So keep moving. you're trying to show the minnow to enough fish, close enough, until you get it in front of one that is slightly more aggressive than the rest. This works best with a light jig (for a slow drop time) worked on a short rod with a light tip. The active fish will be scattered, so you have to roam about, straining the cover methodically.

I've also taken a whole lot of bass on jig-and-minnows, or minnows on live bait rigs, late in the year. With live bait rigs, you've got to have fairly open water to work with, or your rig will hang up. Sometimes a worm sinker (instead of the usual walking Lindy Rig sinker) snags up less. It sometimes helps, too, to switch to a weedless hook with a wire guard. In this fishing, you position the boat over the fish and slowly move it around, showing the bait to the fish.

Late fall fishing almost always centers on the steepest breaks in the lake. The nastier the weather, the deeper you'll fish, often on inside turns. If I had to fish an artificial, a jig-and-eel would be good, but I'd much rather use a jig-and-minnow.

A jig-and-crayfish can be deadly. Hook the crayfish through the tail. Move the boat slowly with an electric motor while you hop the crayfish along the bottom with pulses from your rod. The soft-shelled stage of crayfish is best, when available.

A large share of the biggest bass caught in the nation every year fall to huge golden shiners fished in a variety of ways. The best tackle and techniques depend somewhat on the size of shiner you get and some-what on the cover. Shiners as short as six inches can work, but the biggest fish are taken on shiners from 10 to 16 inches long (and these are hard to come by). Lines from 20- to 40- pound test are appropriate, with hooks from 2/0 to 8/0.

Shiners can be fished below a bobber. You want a lively shiner, so treat them carefully. A good, lively shiner will tell you when a big bass is around by its frantic motions. This rig has to be fished near the heaviest cover, and it requires very heavy tackle to pull a trophy bass away from that kind of stuff. You can anchor to fish a bobber rig or you can drift. Treble hooks are often used, sometimes with one hooked at the mouth and another (stinger) hooked lightly at the tail.

Often the best cover for big bass will be huge floating masses of hyacinths or hydrilla. You can't cast up under them, but you can sometimes tease a golden shiner into swimming up under these big masses. It is sometimes necessary to use a large single, weedless hook. Some shiners just refuse to swim under these masses, so you have to have a good supply of baits and switch until you get one that will.

One of the best ways to fish these shiners is on a free line (no bobber), with little or no weight. Hook a big shiner in the lips and toss it out softly, then move the boat with the troll motor to steer the shiner around promising cover. You cover more water doing this. When the shiner starts plunging around and running to the top, get ready! You've found bass. Then it often pays to anchor and fish the area more carefully, with golden shiners below bobbers. I recently used this technique to take a bunch of big bass from the lakes on the Disney World property near Orlando, Florida.

When fishing big shiners for bass, you have to set a hook as if you wanted to snap the bass' spine. You usually let the fish move with the bait on a slack line for a while. It is sometimes smart to maneuver the boat nearer the fish or away from obstructions before you close the reel, take in the slack and slam the hook home with a powerful set. Shiner fishing can be slow, but your next fish might be a 12-pounder. You don't want to lose that fish because you failed to set the hook.

Nightcrawlers are also very effective at times. An excellent presentation was worked out by my friend, Bill Binkelman, many years ago. Bill's "Nightcrawler Secrets" technique involves hooking a lively crawler through the nose with a sharp, light hook. Up the line a few inches, he clamps a split shot or two...just enough to make the worm castable and get it down. This clean, natural bait rig is then worked carefully along the bottom. You'll lose worms frequently no matter how softly you cast. It helps to "condition" your worms by putting them in a refrigerator in a container that alternates layers of damp newspaper with layers of crawlers. Chill them for a day or two before fishing. Keep the crawlers cool in your boat. Conditioned worms are firmer and fatter.

A modern adaptation of the Nightcrawler Secrets technique involves the same little mushroom jigheads mentioned earlier for plastic worm fishing. When fishing live worms, I *don't* bite the head of the worm off before hooking them. The barbs on the jighead keep the worm on pretty well, but you'll inevitably cast them off.

With either rig, fish the crawler slowly in areas that might hold bass. Because worms are fragile, these techniques are not appropriate in rougher cover.

There'd be no point bothering with live crawlers if a plastic worm worked as well. Sometimes they do, and then I'm happy to use them, but there are days when the results of fishing with real crawlers will make plastic worms look sick. I'm not too proud to switch then.

Leeches can also be excellent. Leeches are tough animals that stay on a hook better than any crawler, especially when you fish them in reeds or other raspy weeds. But leeches are small. The best leeches for bass are the very biggest ones. Keep them very chilly. Note: these are *bait leeches* that live on vegetative matter, *not* bloodsuckers! Don't be afraid of leeches. They're harmless to humans, but deadly on bass.

Several rigs work with leeches. Leeches can be fished under a bobber in very clear water where you need to keep your distance from the fish. A jumbo leech on a light, clean jighead is very effective. If you want to fish over the tops of weeds, a leech on a hook with a split shot up the line (a "light line" rig) often works well. When the weeds are heavier, use a hook with a wire weedguard.

Waterdogs (immature salamanders) have a special appeal to trophy bass. They are often used by guys who don't mind waiting hours between strikes because, when a strike comes, it will be a monster fish! Waterdogs can be fished on jigs, on weedless hooks or on plain hooks if you fish in open cover. To keep the waterdog on the hook, some fishermen put a plastic tab (cut from a coffee can lid) on the hook before and after the waterdog is hooked. The tabs keep the waterdog positioned right on the hook for hook for a good set.

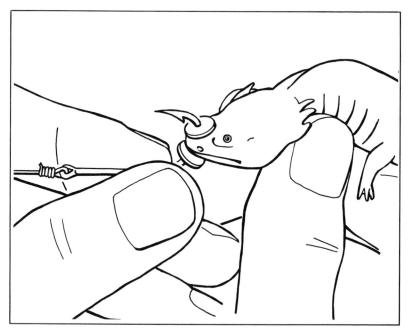

To hook a waterdog, insert plastic tabs above and below the waterdog to keep it in place on the hook.

Chapter 8
Understanding Pattern Fishing

Two boats are working the northeast arm of a reservoir. Eventually they end up side-by-side. The anglers in each boat can tell that the guys in the other boat know what they're doing. If these were inexperienced fishermen, they might look at each other and ask, "Doing any good?"

Instead, the operator of one of the boats pops open a frosty can of pop and asks, "What's the pattern today, boys?"

What's the pattern? That's the single most important fact every bass fisherman needs to determine when he hits the water. When you start fishing, you aren't looking for bass. You're looking for the pattern. A bass is just a bass. The right pattern is the key to happiness.

Until you know what pattern or patterns are best for the day, you're probably only going to pick up the occasional stray. When you've got the pattern, though, you can really have some fun.

As I said earlier, a pattern is a specific combination of *fish location* and *angler presentation* that will produce the best fishing possible at that time and place. At a given moment there's usually more than one good pattern, though some will be much better than others.

Pattern fishing is smart fishing. Smart fishing *is* pattern fishing. The more patterns you master, the better you will be at catching bass. When you really get good, you will discover new patterns of your own, finding bass where nobody thought there were any or catching them in ways nobody tried before.

I hope this book will teach you pattern fishing for bass, and it presents quite a number of specific patterns. But there's something bigger I want to pass along: an overall sense of what pattern fishing is. Get that, and you'll be able to move beyond this book. Here's an analogy. This book is like a cookbook, with lots of recipes. But being able to follow recipes is not the same thing, exactly, as being able to cook well. While it's nice to start with the recipes, you eventually want to go beyond them and do creative things.

Beginning fishermen have no concept of patterns. They see fishing as a confusing activity, with hours of "bad luck" occasionally interrupted by the happy accident of catching a fish. Ask a beginner where he caught that bass on his stringer, and he'll say, "In that big bay." And how did he catch it? "On a black jig." Well, that's as much of a pattern as he has: he knows a black jig will, once in a while, catch a bass in that bay.

Nice bass, but what did he tell you? If you listen well, bass will tell you where other bass can be caught.

Now let's ask the same question of someone who knows bass fishing. We'll have to be a little careful. If he's a good fisherman, he can tell fibs more convincingly than our beginner can tell the truth. Let's assume that our expert sincerely wants to help us. Perhaps I've run into my brother Dave on the water, and for once he isn't determined to jack me around.

He might say something like this: "Early on, we caught fish on topwater stuff fished shallow. But ever since the sun cleared the trees, the better fish have been coming on a 1/4-ounce single spin—green skirt, brass blade—worked slow over the cabbage beds in about seven feet of water near the dropoff. They're hitting pretty good, but mostly when we stop to let it drop into the pockets. Since I put on a three-inch white Ripple Rind, I've taken a few larger fish."

Hey, thanks Dave! *That's* a pattern. Unless I have a pattern that is working better I will follow my brother's tip and, almost surely, have a bending rod within minutes. On the other hand, I'll be sure to peek in his boat to check what he's actually fishing with. If everyone's rods are rigged with red worms on little jigheads, I'll know Dave's been jacking me around again and I'll owe him one back.

Understanding patterns is one key to catching good numbers of bass. The only thing *more* important is being able to put that concept into use. Here are key concepts of pattern fishing.

- *Bass are always where they are for good, specific reasons.*
- *When you find one bass in a certain kind of spot, doing a certain kind of thing, others are probably in similar situations elsewhere on the lake.*
- *The presentation that catches bass in one kind of location is likely to catch other bass in similar locations elsewhere in the lake.*

If you fish with no concept of pattern, every fish hooked will be a random event. When you understand patterns, each fish hooked will be telling you something. *In fact, he'll be telling you the most important thing you want to know: where and how you can catch your next bass!*

Of course, like fishermen, bass sometimes fib a little. Let's say you catch a bass on a buzz bait run quickly by the shady side of a boat dock in four feet of water. In a sense, that bass is telling you you can catch another fish by moving down the shore to the next similar dock and fishing it the same way. Maybe this bass is right. Maybe not.

Start by believing the bass you just caught. But if you fish eight similar docks without getting another strike, you might figure the first bass was a little flaky and you're still hunting for the pattern.

If you get a half-hearted slash from a small fish on the third dock you work, that fish is telling you something, too. He's saying, "We're here alright, but we're feeling kinda crummy and slow right now." According to this second bass, the docks are holding fish, but maybe you should switch to a lightly weighted Texas-rigged worm or a plastic salamander on a swimming jighead and work it very slowly.

Okay, believe him...for a while. One bass might lie. Two might lie. But if you keep asking the fish what the pattern is and paying close attention to what they say, you'll get it. By the time you've boated 12 or 14 bass on a particular pattern, you *know* they're not lying!

Scrounging Up Fish

Remember, when you first start fishing, finding *bass* is less important than finding *patterns*. Fortunately, you learn the pattern by hunting for fish. Where are the bass? How active are they? What's the best presentation for catching them?

You are a *hunter* of fish. The real catching part starts after you've found the pattern, not before.

You should be moving all the time, trying to find those fish, paying close attention to details. If you were hunting rabbits, you wouldn't spend half an afternoon bouncing up and down on the same brushpile ...but I've seen people fishing bass that way. Or if you hit six good brushpiles and didn't get any sign of a rabbit, you wouldn't go on hunting brushpiles all day, not if you know rabbit hunting. You'd check out the weeds near the corn, or maybe work some shelterbelts or creek beds. It just isn't smart to pound the same kind of spot all day when you're hunting...whether you're hunting rabbits or pheasants. Or *bass*.

And, like any good hunter, you'll concentrate on *edges*. An edge is formed whenever two types of habitat meet, and that's where bass tend to be. The front edge of a timber line. The back edge of the weeds. The places where thick clumps in a reed bank meet more open areas. The edges of docks, stumps, brush or timber. The edges of old creek beds. *Think edges whenever you are fishing.*

You are a hunter of fish, and your hunting should concentrate on edges.

You are looking for a *cover-structure combination*—that is, some major structural feature which has good cover on it that will serve as an ambush point for the bass.

Always start your hunt with the most likely spots, moving then to the next most likely spots. Time is precious, so work as efficiently as you can, fishing the places with the best chances of paying off. Sure, sometimes the bass are in oddball, unexpected spots, but avoid low-percentage cover until you've eliminated the most likely spots.

If you forget everything else in this book, remember this: *you are hunting fish, and the best place to hunt bass is along edges in their habitat where cover-structure combinations are best.*

The biggest problem facing any bass fisherman when he fires up his motor to start a day of fishing is *finding fish.* Where are the active bass? Begin with some educated guesses about where the bass will be. Consider the season, the type of lake (forage base, amount of cover, water clarity, etc.) and the recent weather.

Never forget the big picture. Combine what you know about *the nature of the fish,* the *possibilities offered by this particular environment,* the *influence of the season,* and *the impact of recent weather.* Those will point you toward the most likely patterns.

Don't get hung up on "rules" about expected location. Maybe you've read that early spring reservoir bass move up into the warmest coves. They often do, so check out the coves fairly well. But don't go on hammering coves for two hours without getting any encouragement from the bass. Maybe a cold front sent them scooting way back to the next big dropoff, half a mile from the ends of the coves. Remember, bass are *always* where they're supposed to be…fishermen often are not. Bass only seem to break rules because it is *our* rules, not *theirs,* that they break.

Keep moving quickly until you find the fish. Perhaps I suspect the bass are up in the reeds. Okay, I zoom in on a reed bed, drop the troll motor and start firing a spinnerbait into the reeds. I'll move the boat as fast as I can while giving the bait a chance to do its thing. I'll get casts in to the inside edge, outside edge and middle of the bed. I'll rush the bait through the dead water. In 15 minutes if I haven't seen a bass, *bye bye reed bed!*

Continuing the same example, if I really think the bass should be in reeds I might hit another reed bank next, probably one with some different characteristics. But if the first bunch of reeds I worked was a good one and I think I gave it a reasonable chance to produce, I'll move quickly to *another type* of spot—maybe some boat docks, maybe some timber, maybe a deep weedline. Wherever I go, I'll give that spot a quick check, looking for some reason to stick with it longer.

Now, in my initial searching if I find one negative little bass, I'll figure the hunt is still on. I'd rather not dink around all afternoon with bass that are small and off their feed, so I will keep hunting until I find an active school of good fish. Why settle for less?

Check out different types of cover. Don't spend the day fishing reeds unless you get some indication that's where the fish are.

I'm trying to scrounge up a fish or two to learn the location of the most active bass. I hate to fish slow when scrounging like this, so I'm going to use a lure that lets me work the water quickly—a spinnerbait, a crankbait, maybe a spoon or even a worm that I'll work as fast as possible. I'm *hunting* bass, and I'm not going to sit on one spot waiting until a bass comes by. No way!

One of Babe's Rules: *patience is rarely a virtue in fishing!* It pays to be patient when you *know* the fish are negative and you're going to be forced to work slowly and thoroughly for each one. But, that's rarely the case. Most of the time it pays to be impatient. Keep moving unless you're on fish. Bass fishing isn't supposed to be slow and dull. Don't accept slow, bad fishing unless you *know* that's the best you can do.

I don't have to catch bass to locate them. If a fish boils behind my spinnerbait, I've at least learned he was there. I'll have my eyes open, looking for bass that spook out of shallow cover or for signs of bass feeding. Maybe I'll see the wake of a fish just below the surface when I cast. Then it will be important to decide whether that fish was running away from something (a negative bass) or an aggressive bass that was chasing something. At certain times of the year, any bass in shallow water will be visible to an angler with good polarized glasses. So if I don't see the bass, I know they aren't there and I should keep on truckin' until I know I've found them.

One of Babe's Rules: it is possible to catch nothing by fishing where bass are, but you *never* catch bass by fishing where they aren't!

Look for details, the little things overlooked by most guys. The more you can figure out about *exactly* how the bass are using the cover, the more you'll enjoy your fishing. Attention to detail is a major difference between the pros and the weekend duffer.

Almost always, a locational pattern will be very precise. To nail it down, with each bass you catch you must ask some sharp questions. Why was the bass by a certain kind of stump? Which side? Was it the shady side? What was the bottom content there? What was the water color? Was there any wave action washing over that spot? How close to the stump was the bass? How close was the stump to deep water? Could there have been any current on the spot? Which way was the bass facing? How aggressively did he hit it? How deep was your lure? What food might have drawn the bass to that location? What other cover exists nearby and how likely is it that it was part of the pattern? Could this bit of cover hold more fish?

Get the picture? The more information you can accumulate, the more fun you'll have. Listen to the bass! Listen close!

Searching for the pattern is very much like putting the pieces of a puzzle together.

Hot, Cool and Cold Bass

Sharp readers will have already picked up on the fact that good bass fishermen pay a lot of attention to the *mood* of bass. And for good reasons:

- Bass are a very moody fish. All kinds of things (mostly weather) affect them.
- At any moment, bass are either hot, cold or more or less cool in their attitude toward feeding.
- Hot bass are fish that are actively feeding. They are extremely aggressive, "chasing" fish that leave cover to run down a lure.
- Cold bass are fish that are turned off, because of weather, because they just spawned, because they are cold and sluggish...or because of some other reason known only to bass. They shy away from lures and boats, stick extremely tight to cover and bite timidly.
- Cool bass are neutral, neutral-positive or neutral-negative. They are cautious but not paranoid. They may move a short distance for a lure, but you'll have better action if you don't require them to move far for it.

You must figure out the mood of bass each time you fish. Some anglers like to talk in terms of a "strike zone," an area that is mostly in front of bass which, if it is entered by an attractive lure, will draw a strike. Negative bass have tiny strike zones; hot fish have big strike zones; and most bass have medium-sized strike zone.

Think of this in terms of some weird sort of basketball game where, until you've taken a few shots, you don't know the size of the basket. When bass are aggressive, it is like you are shooting at a huge basket; even a sloppy shot goes in. When bass are negative, it would be like your shooting at a basket just barely bigger than the basketball; you have to be *right on* to get a bucket.

Mood also affects your choice of lure. Positive fish often respond viciously to flashy, loud presentations—a spinnerbait with a big willow leaf blade or a buzzer racing along just at the surface, for example. A negative fish might ignore everything but the slowest, quietest and most natural presentations—perhaps a jig with a pork eel worked super slow and deep in the timber, or a jig and minnow.

Mood dictates your retrieve speed. Hot fish try to kill anything moving in their area, but they are best caught on lures that move fast. Cold bass might respond best to a lure that moves super-slow or doesn't move at all.

One of Babe's Rules: we dream about finding hot bass, we dread finding that the bass are cold and we actually find, most of the time, bass that are more or less cool.

Another of Babe's Rules: no matter how lousy the fish feel, there will *always* be some catchable fish somewhere if you find the pattern!

And another: if you can't *entice them into biting*, try *forcing them into striking*. Oddly enough, negative fish can be triggered by a lure that explodes by them so fast they just forget themselves.

Nailing Down the Pattern

As soon as you see or contact some bass, you begin to learn how aggressive they are. Pay attention to the little things. Here are some clues to watch:

• If a fish spooks out of shallow water when it sees a lure sailing toward it, that's a bad sign. That bass, at least, is negative, and you want to keep moving to find some fish that aren't. Or try a different approach.

• Note exactly where you catch a bass. If you take a bass very tight to cover, you've got reason to think the fish are slow and you're going to be forced to fish right in contact with cover. If a bass dashes out five feet past a dock to nail your lure, the fish are probably in a chasing mood and you can really go to town with fast presentations.

• The *way* a bass strikes can clue you into how active they are. Active, aggressive bass bang a lure. You *feel* them hit it. Negative fish will strike short or diddle around with the tail of a worm. You'll catch negative fish sometimes by just feeling the action of your lure change or feeling something spongy or different at the end of the line. Every now and then you'll just surprise yourself by finding a bass is hooked up with you and you didn't feel anything, which is another indication that the bass are negative. Hey! You're not concentrating enough!

• When you catch a bass, note how deep it took your lure. It's a good sign if the fish really gulped that lure rather than just barely getting its mouth on it.

158

As soon as you begin homing in on the location and mood of the fish you can discover the best presentation. Here's where a good partner can be so valuable. You and your partner should never be fishing the same lure until you're sure you have the best presentation nailed down. Start with entirely different lures—you fish a worm, your partner a crankbait, etc.

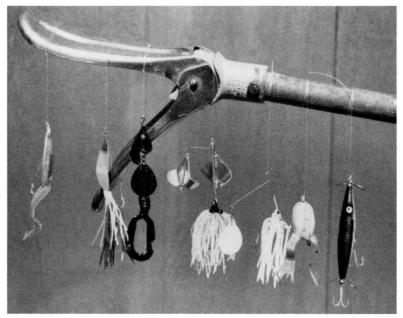

Which of these shallow water lures will be best? You can refine the pattern best if you check them out with the aid of a partner.

Fine Tuning

Okay, now you've found a school of bass. These guys are in a bunch of coontail in pretty deep water, and they're not terrifically active. Looks like it's time to peck away at the weeds with a worm on a little jighead, or maybe (if you keep getting snagged on the coontail) a Texas-rigged worm or a pork eel on a weighted weedless hook.

Keep experimenting to nail down the pattern. What worm? One of you can fish a straight grape worm while the other works a black firetail worm—something a bit different. All the while you keeping experimenting, maybe changing weights. One of you can try some scent attractant. One of you can swim the worm slowly while the other kicks his worm around to put action on it.

You and your partner are working together to ask the fish what they want. Eventually you'll get the presentation part of the pattern nailed down. It just gets more and more fun as you get a more precise fix on what is working best.

When that spot finally plays out, you've got a choice. If you've been getting fair numbers of good-sized fish, it's worth trying the same spot with a new presentation. Give 'em a different look. If you were catching fish on a red worm with a chartreuse firetail on it, put a jig 'n pig down there, or a little jig with a brown plastic grub on it. If the spot was only producing so-so fish and now it has gone dead, move on to the next spot you can find with the same basic depth and other characteristics.

Patterns and Patterns

We've presented the main concept of pattern fishing, namely that at any given time and place, there's a certain combination of location and presentation that will produce the best fishing. If you keep asking the fish where they are and what they want, constantly re-defining and refining the pattern, you're fishing smart. And, no matter what you hear, that's better than fishing lucky!

Now let's take that simple concept and make it a little more complicated.

Bass are individuals. Some of them are just naturally more aggressive than others. Some of them have a weakness for plastic worms, while others just can't turn down a spinnerbait. They have somewhat individual preferences in location. Some fish get in the habit of feeding at night, even though other bass nearby do not. When you catch a bass, it doesn't *automatically* follow that the lake has a thousand bass in the same kind of place waiting for the same presentation. Start by assuming that is true, but recognize that bass aren't mass produced to be identical.

So it's simplistic to think there is only *one* pattern working at a given time. There will usually be a good pattern or two for those slop bass, another good pattern or two for the deep guys and maybe another pair of deadly patterns for the gang of fish that never strays far from the huge weed flat on the north shore of the bay.

Sometimes you'll find that a hot pattern is only hot for bass of a certain size. Many tournaments have been won by guys who did nothing all day but pound the shallows with spinnerbaits. Doing this they rarely took big bass, but they kept racking up 12-inchers until

those inches added up to victory. Other patterns, often ones involving *big* baits fished in horribly thick cover, will produce only trophy fish.

It's rare to have *all* the bass doing the very same thing at the very same time. You can get that impression, but it's not often true. Bass don't even all spawn at the same time.

And don't expect the hot pattern to hold up all day long, much less for several days at a time.

It does happen, of course. Sometimes conditions remain stable long enough for a hot pattern to produce fast fishing for several days. Bass in deeper water are more likely to be receptive to the same presentation several days in a row than bass in shallow water.

Food chain reactions often cause bass to school up in tremendous numbers. For example, water temperatures in a certain weedbed might hit a certain special level, and suddenly tiny insects begin emerging from the silt. Minnows and sunfish are quick to sense this, and they converge to scarf up the bugs. Behind them come the bass. At this time, perhaps, these minnows and massed sunfish represent the best meal in town, so for five days the bass really grind on the small fish in this area.

If you were to come by with the right lure, you might be amazed at this tremendous school of active bass. Yet that school might not be there—or anywhere else—in a week. It arose in response to a food-chain reaction. The school disbanded when that reaction weakened.

Good bass fishermen anticipate that patterns will change and keep changing. Here are two examples.

Let's say it is fairly early in the year and you've got a reasonable number of bass in the shallows. At daybreak, your best pattern might be a surface bait twitched slowly on the surface in the shallow bays where the bass recently spawned. Then the sun begins to come up, and you might need to switch to crankbaits worked in medium-deep water. When the sun gets high, don't be surprised if the hot pattern is a jig-worm hopped just outside the weedline in deep water.

Another example. Let's say a cold front came through yesterday and, ever since, the bass have refused to open their mouths. You've scratched up about one nice fish an hour, though, by teasing a worm through the densest weeds, being very careful to fish as deep and slow as you can. Good. That's the pattern...for the moment. But every now and then you might want to slip up into the reeds in shallower water to see if there are any fish there feeling peppy enough to bust a spinnerbait.

Why? Fishing worms is generally a slow process. You do it when that's the best pattern going, and that's often. But sooner or later the fish are going to shake off that cold front and get more active, making a shallow spinnerbait pattern far faster and deadlier than the worm pattern that is working for you now. Since shallow fish are usually more active than deep fish, you always hope for—and check out—a good shallow pattern.

Patterns change. Sometimes a pattern will hold only as long as the wind is blowing. Some hot patterns go cold when the sun comes out, but return in full force when a cloud sails by and blots out the sun. Or something might happen with the forage base that you aren't aware of. Also, fishing pressure can change the location and feeding disposition of bass.

Sound confusing? It doesn't have to be. Don't take the attitude that all this change is bad. Heck, you could be fishing the wrong pattern and have things change so that what you're doing is right. If you understand a wide variety of patterns, you won't die when your favorite one fades. Be observant, keep moving and keep asking the fish what they want. You'll catch bass!

Chapter 9
Bass Patterns

Okay, let's go fishing!

By now, you should have a solid grasp of what pattern fishing is all about.

By now, you understand that your success will depend on your ability to find patterns that match up with what the bass are "up to" in a particular situation at a particular time.

By now you understand that, wherever they are found, largemouth bass have a basic nature that causes them to interact with their environment in certain kinds of ways (and not in others). Their annual cycle creates certain needs at certain times of the year. They'll be in the best combination of structure and cover their environment offers them.

And if you know bass, you can catch them.

A little story might make this more clear. A few years back, the first national B.A.S.S. tournament on *northern* waters was held in the Thousand Islands area of New York State. Southern anglers had been dominating the tournaments which had all been held on southern reservoirs. Everyone was saying, "Now the northern boys have a chance to teach these southern pro's a few lessons about Yankee bass!"

It didn't work out that way. It was the southern anglers who taught the lessons about catching Yankee bass. Why? A bass is a bass, after all, not a Yankee bass or a Dixie bass. The southern anglers had more basic bass sense. They came from an area where the largemouth bass was just about the *only* gamefish, and where bass could be fished every month of the year.

If you know bass, you know bass. If you can catch bass, you can catch them just about anywhere.

You want to know the most frustrating thing about travelling around the country giving seminars on fishing? It's all the guys who come up to me and say, "Well, your techniques probably work where you fish, but my waters have these special problems." Fellas, give me a break! Give yourself a break! Don't believe it. That kind of thinking is just an excuse for not applying yourself.

In the next pages I will give you a sampling of patterns that work well at different times and places. With a few appropriate adjustments, they'll work well just about *anywhere*. I have chosen a mix of patterns from spring, summer and fall. What counts is not so much the individual patterns as the way they can teach you to put together your own patterns.

164

Spring Patterns

Ice-out Bass, Natural Lakes

This will be your earliest fishing on natural lakes, coming maybe as quickly as a week after ice-out. The temperature on the main lake will be in the 40s—too cold for decent bass fishing—so you want to find those little bays that are the first to warm up. Because they warm quickly, they are the first place in the lake where insects become active. The bugs draw in minnows, and they draw in bass.

What kind of bays warm up quickly? They'll be shallow, with dark organic bottoms. They'll be sheltered, usually on the north, west or northwest shores of the lake because those bays get the effect of the spring sun earlier than bays elsewhere. Also, the cold winds come from the north and west, so those are the protected shores. These might be bays that fill up with lily pads and are too shallow and warm for bass the rest of the summer, but now they're prime. They'll be the same bays where you often find spring crappies.

Water temperature is the critical factor now. Unless you find water that's warmer than the main lake, you won't find active bass. A difference of even one degree can spell the difference between good and bad fishing! Check temperatures right next to shore, not way out in the middle of the bay. Usually, the best fishing will be in the afternoon after the sun has had a chance to warm the bays.

My water temperature gauge is now worth more to me than my sonar, plus I depend heavily on my troll motor. These are going to be shallow fish in clear water, so it's important to be able to sneak around silently. Good polarizing sunglasses are absolutely necessary. I'll not be looking for fish so much as spotting good places to drop a cast.

Your tackle should be fairly light, with the system based on whatever rod and reel you'd like to use to throw a spinnerbait of 1/8-or 1/4-ounce. I'd choose a light spinning outfit, maybe a rod about 5 1/2 feet long, and clear eight-pound Stren.

For a lure, my first choice would be a little single-spin spinnerbait, perhaps with a white skirt with a hammered silver blade (always a good choice in clear water). Little spinnerbaits with grub jig bodies under flexible arm spinners are good now, too. Or use those spinners with a little four-inch worm or curly-tail grub lure. Really, what you want is the sort of lure that later in the year would be good on big crappies. I've also done well with little floating minnow baits at this time of year, the smallest ones I can cast.

The actual fishing is pretty easy. The main thing is to find a good, warm bay and then do a decent job of casting to the banks. The bass are going to be tight—*real tight*—to the banks, almost with their backs out of the water. You've got a very short strike zone—just a foot or so, usually. The average angler comes in too noisily, fishes too quickly and drops his casts too far from shore. I'll often cast on land and then slide my lure into the water.

If I've been getting bass back in the bays and some cold, windy weather comes through, my bass will move back out to the first significant dropoff just outside the warm bays. Or sometimes I'll find bass staging along the dropoffs, waiting for the water to get warm enough to draw them in.

Compared to the bass up shallow in the little bays, these fish will be deeper, obviously, and negative. I'll go after them with similar tackle, maybe six-pound line, but a different bait. Now you can't beat a jig-and-minnow, the jig being a Fuzz-E-Grub (about 1/8-ounce) and the minnow being a shiner two-to three-inches long.

In this situation I'll probably backtroll, using the transom-mounted troll motor, fishing the jig-and-minnow carefully along the break. I will expect the bass to be tightly schooled. If the fish are shallow enough to be spooky, I'll throw a marker and then back off to cast to the spot. Sometimes casting is best; sometimes vertical jigging is best. This is a time when you want to use a good attractant scent.

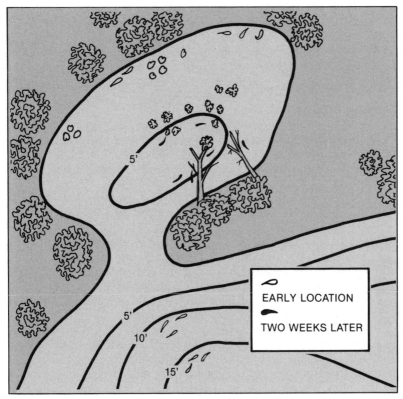

This diagram covers three conditions you might encounter when fishing ice-out bass. Water temperature is often the key factor.

If spring warming is progressing normally, the bass in the little "crappie bays" will begin to move in earlier and move around the bay more. You'll find them in there by mid-morning, for example. And instead of being tucked up with their tails on shore, they'll be in deeper water using any kind of cover that's around—brush, perhaps, or whatever's left of last year's weeds.

Now the little dark-bottomed bays on the *south* and *east* ends of the lake will be doing what the north and west side bays did two weeks earlier. These sometimes get overlooked by guys who aim their whole ice-out effort on the first bays to warm up, not realizing that the whole pattern will repeat itself on other bays a little later as more food chain reactions occur.

These fish will be more aggressive. You can use a bigger lure, maybe even a 3/8-ounce single-spin spinnerbait. Because these bays become more off-colored as the warmer temperatures produce more organic growth, I would use a more conspicuous color: like a chartreuse skirt below a hammered copper blade, or a yellow skirt under a nickle blade. My rod and line would be a little stouter.

Plastic worms will also start to work well. Use light (about 1/16-ounce or less) sinkers and throw the worm up shallow, *swimming* it back at mid-depths rather than hopping it on the bottom. Spinning tackle with six-or eight-pound line will cast these light lures better than baitcasting tackle.

Shoreline Walking

On many lakes, you can fish pre-spawn bass as well from shore as from a boat. Sometimes it helps to have hip boots or chest waders to let you get past high shoreline weeds, like cattails, to have open water to cast to.

You'll want to find the shallowest, darkest, warmest bays around. Then the challenge is usually to find a place you can cast from, and this is where hip boots can make the difference.

Many baits and different kinds of tackle work, but mostly this is light spinning rod stuff with little beetle spins, small weedless spoons with trailers or Texas-rigged worms, if you choose to throw artificials. You want lures that are small and active at slow speeds. Try casting to the center of the bays, but also try casts that parallel the shoreline because the fish might be in very shallow water.

But you'll probably catch more bass with live bait. On a weedless #2 or #3 hook, put a smallish minnow, say four-inches long. Just cast it out and let it sit on the bottom, twitching it from time to time. Keep the minnow free from any old dead weeds that might be around. You can let the minnow sit in place for a few minutes, but from time to time you'll want to slowly move it toward shore.

Keep alert. Bass will often grab the minnow and make a fast dash for deep water, and that's where you want to set the hook.

Pre-spawn bass can often be caught from shore. You'll have access to more fish, though, if you use waders.

John Powell, the well-known bass pro, once told me that, at this time of year, he'd fish a flooded cow track if he could get his bass boat back in it. The bass will go extremely shallow at times, so shallow you are actually better off walking than trying to work from a boat.

Pre-spawn Bass, Reservoirs

Reservoirs offer wonderful pre-spawn bass fishing too, and it is very similar to the fishing already described for natural lakes. Since many don't freeze up, we aren't really talking about "ice-out" any more. But bass in most southern reservoirs early in February or March are just like the ice-out April bass of northern lakes. They do the same things for the same reasons as their Yankee cousins.

Once again, water temperature will make or break your fishing. You're looking for the warmest temperatures you can find. The best pre-spawn bass fishing takes place in water that's anywhere from the mid-40's to the mid-50's. The bass will be sluggish because the water is cool, but that doesn't mean fishing can't be red hot. It can be!

Rather than little bays, you'll be fishing the far back ends of coves. The coves on the upper end of the reservoir will usually produce good fishing first. A cove receiving warm water from an incoming stream will warm earlier. A cove with a light, sandy bottom will maybe not warm up quite as quickly as a dark-bottomed cove. At the backs of

The key to finding pre-spawn bass in coves is determining how far back toward the end of the cove they are.

170

these coves you might find little lagoons and bays that behave exactly like the ones in natural lakes mentioned earlier. These little areas will sometimes draw active fish before the rest of the cove does.

Usually you'll be coming into these coves from the main lake, testing them to find out how far up the coves the bass will be. The most common mistake is not going back far enough. You might have to go way back in the shallow, brushy areas full of buttonbrush and all sorts of timber to find where the active bass are holding.

Several years ago on a promotional tour in Tennessee I failed to find bass in a little cove where I expected some action. Since the cove was getting really narrow and brushy, I beached my boat and walked the shore. I finally found my bass and had a heckuva afternoon with little minnow baits and spinnerbaits. The fish were jammed up at the extreme end of the cove where no boat could go. A little incoming creek formed a pool of water that was a bit warmer than the rest. The bass were so shallow I could only reach them on foot!

Same Situation, Bad Weather

When a cold front comes through, the active shallow water bass in these little coves often scuttle toward deep water. How far they go depends on how cold the water gets and how severe the cold front is.

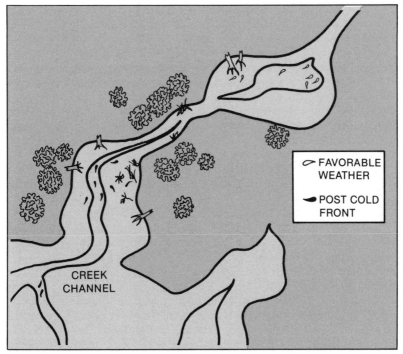

Two likely locations for pre-spawn bass in reservoir coves. If the weather has been favorable, they'll be way up in the coves. After a front, they drop to the deeper water of the channel.

If the front is minor, the bass might tuck down into the little creek channel in the cove, just trying to get a little deeper. They'll probably pull into cover tighter than they were. A jig-and-pig or similar snagless bait worked very carefully around the cover will score. Flipping often works well on these cover-hugging bass. Most of the time, though, I'll want to use conventional casting techniques to cover a lot of water and find the fish. Then I'll flip if the fish are so tight to cover they are hard to cast to.

A more severe front will send them out deeper to the main points on the creek channel. A worse front will drive them all the way back to the junction of that creek channel and the main reservoir.

Pre-spawn Channel and Canal Bass

On many lakes people have cut boat canals out of the banks, making what (to the bass) are simply small bays. Start checking these areas out about a week or so after the small marshy bays turn on.

Especially when they've been cut for larger condominium or housing developments, these boat canals can be quite large. For some reason, many people ignore these canals, maybe thinking the bass won't use them because they're artificial. Hummph! These are some of the best areas for pre-spawn bass, and the larger canals will go on holding fish for weeks after the spawn.

Slide into these canals with your trolling motor, approaching the fish as quietly as possible. Early in the spring, expect the bass to be right up along the banks. Sometimes the canal bottoms are cut with a natural slope, like a bay; if so, a spinnerbait might be best. Other canals have steeper banks, shored-up with rock or metal retainer walls, or possibly even undercut by wave action. In these canals your best presentation will be a very light worm rigged on a swimming jig head or hooked Texas-style and fished with little or no weight at all. Cast the worm right to the edge of the canal, sliding it into the water softly. As always, you'll want to look for little special spots that might serve as ambush points for bass.

The channels between major bays of a lake often turn on well before the lakes will in the spring. There will be current in these necked-down areas, mostly made up of the warmer surface water. The fishing usually gets good in the boat canals before it turns on the channels.

Some bass hang around in the larger boat canals and channels and will eventually spawn there. So they sometimes use these areas for extended periods of time. If so, the tactics that work at one time won't necessarily work later. Later into spring you will usually need to fish deeper water.

Tactics and tackle are much the same as I recommended for the marsh bays mentioned earlier. Little spinnerbaits are great. Other good lures for this situation: Lindy Legs jig in the 1/8-or 1/4-ounce size dressed with small pork spring lizards or pork frogs. You don't want a heavy jig here. A Silver Minnow spoon with a pork trailer can be great.

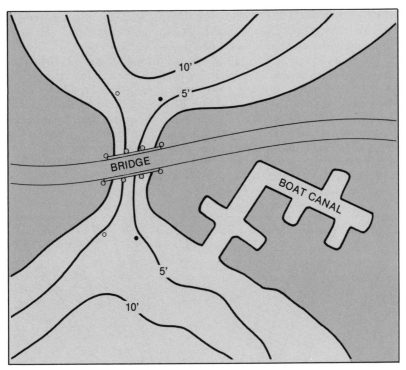

Boat canals and channels are among the earliest places to turn on in spring. They can be good later, too, if they don't get too warm.

Riprap Pre-spawn Bass, Reservoirs

This pattern has the potential to produce some very nice fish.

Many dams are constructed so the riprap face tapers more gently at the outside edges than at the middle. Very early in the year, those slowly tapered edges can attract bass. If there's a wind pounding in on the riprap, though, forget this pattern.

Bass move to the riprap edges for two reasons. These areas will be early to get insect and minnow activity. And when the water hits the mid-50s, crayfish often move up on the riprap to spawn.

The strength of this pattern depends a bit on how much riprap a reservoir has. In a muddy, shallow, small reservoir with some brushy cover near the only riprap in the lake, the riprap could be extremely important. On a big, multi-faceted reservoir with all kinds of structure-cover combinations, the riprap might not attract many bass.

Riprap will pull in small groups of roving bass. While nice schools sometimes come in to really work the riprap, they're the exception. More likely you'll find one here, two there, one over there, and so forth. So you want to move around with baits, like crankbaits, that cover a lot of water. Try to get your bait down, bumping bottom, but don't work it too fast. On calm, hot days, bass might go up extremely shallow near shore. Then spinnerbaits or a jig and pig might be best, but usually the crankbait excels on riprap.

I've enjoyed my best riprap fishing with small crankbaits fished on six-pound line, maybe eight-pound. Sneak in close to the riprap with your trolling motor and make very long casts parallel to shore. Keep the bait about two feet from shore. Riprap tends to be laid out uniformly. Do bass like uniformity in cover? Of course they don't, so be on the lookout for features that are just a bit different. Even small changes in shape and texture can be major draws for bass.

It's smart to visit riprap areas in fall when the water levels are low and photograph the dam area. You'll record those little features that can be so important to you in spring.

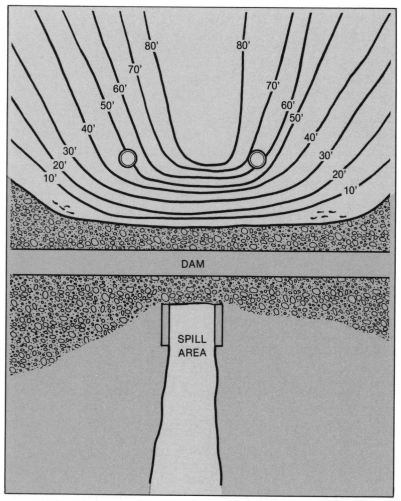

In reservoirs, I've had some great fishing along the tapering edges of riprap dams. How good the riprap is depends on what other cover the reservoir has.

Early in the year, but not extremely early, water levels will often rise in response to spring rains. This inundates new areas. In Santee Cooper Reservoir there's an area called "The Cow Pasture" which is just that most of the year, but which can be a hotspot for early spring bass when the water goes up. Other reservoirs, and even some natural lakes, have similar areas that get flooded when spring rains back up.

There are some special things to look for. In any cove, one side is usually steepish and one side will slope gradually. What you want is a cove where there is a gradual slope on the north side—the side most protected from wind and most exposed to sun. But that's not always the case; the bass will take what they can get.

Ideally, you are looking for areas with green grass and, especially, grass mixed with stumps, brush, logs or whatever. While grass will attract bass, the best situation results when brushy, timbered areas are flooded. But the flooded flats alone will attract fish, even without stumps or weeds. Typically good depths are one to three feet of water over the cover.

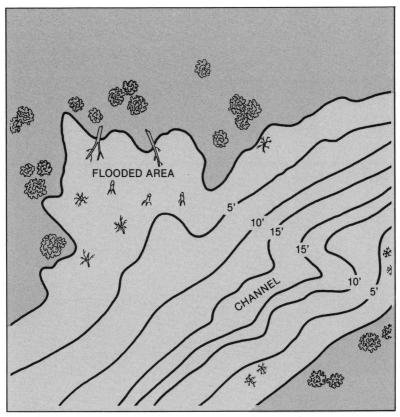

The best fishing in freshly-inundated fields will be around brush and timber, if they are present.

175

If you do find some cover on the flats, the bass will be holding right next to it. Cast parallel to these objects, using heavy baitcasting tackle and a single spin spinnerbait with a huge (#7) Colorado or willow leaf blade. Because the water will be colored, 12-pound line won't be too thick.

Work the spinnerbait very slowly past the cover. If you are casting to logs or stumps, cast past the object and bring the bait slowly to it. Let the spinnerbait drop for a few inches right by the object before moving it again. I've turned up some monstrous bass this way.

In areas of recently flooded grass, use light spinning tackle. I like a short rod with a medium heavy butt and a medium light tip. Use a floating minnow bait but retrieve it with an erratic, snapping action. Barely turn the reel handle while snapping the rod tip to put as much action on the bait as possible without bringing it back toward you (although you'll have to retrieve some to keep tension).

Another good bait for flooded grass is a good-sized spinnerbait with a big blade to put out a big thump at slow speeds. Bring it back with a pumping retrieve.

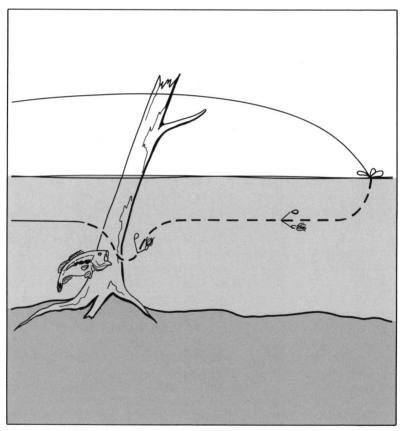

In this situation, the best retrieve is to put the spinnerbait past the cover, retrieve and then let the bait drop briefly right where the bass should be.

Dragonfly Nymph Migrations

Early in the year, when water temperatures are in the low 60s, on many lakes the dragonfly larvae become active. They migrate to the shallows, attach themselves to solid objects such as reeds or timber, and crawl up near the surface. They soon hatch out as adult dragonflies. Rock-piles near reed banks are particularly likely places for these migrations.

You know this migration is "on" when you see many dragonfly nymph husks on rocks, reeds or timber right about at the waterline. These are easy to spot and identify.

As you'd expect, this migration draws the attention of the bass. This is an example of an unusually specific and narrow predator-prey relationship. Bass go crazy when these big, plump nymphs are available.

I first caught on to this pattern on big Lake of the Woods, on the Minnesota/Ontario border. I'd noticed lots of dragonfly activity in a marshy, necked-down area between major sections of the lake. I figured that there couldn't be *that much* insect activity without the bass being interested, too. They were. I used ultralight tackle and a leech hooked on a #10 weedless hook and split shot clamped to the line. In a single afternoon I caught 76 bass, up to 5 pounds.

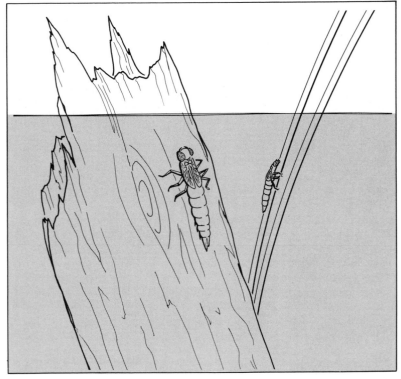

Dragonfly nymphs crawl to the surface to shuck their husks. When you see this, fish with live bait or a grub jig.

Since then I have found the same thing happening in lakes all around the country. You need that low 60s water temperature to bring this off.

I think the light, simple leech rig mentioned above is probably the best for this pattern, but it is the kind of pattern that is flexible. You can do well with a dark grub jig or small curly-tail body on a weedless hook. This is one of the few patterns that gives a fly fisherman a good crack at nice-sized bass, and lots of them.

You'll often find a lot of floating debris around at dragonfly nymph time. If there is, the bass will be under it. With good sunglasses you can spot the fish.

Lily Pad Bass

When I started bass fishing everyone said lily pads were *the* place to catch bass. Years of fishing have taught me pads can be good...or a big waste of time. You have to know when and where to fish lily pads.

Late in the pre-spawn time, pad bays can provide great fishing. Bass come into pad bays for pre-spawn feeding. They might stay to spawn down in the root masses of the pads. The key: you need to find bays with the *white-flowered* pads, not the *yellow-flowered* ones. What's the difference? The root systems of the white-flowered pads are much more attractive to the fish. Bass often make their nests quite often in these tangled root systems. The white-flowered pads have root systems with all sorts of wild, twisty roots that make places for a bass to get down into. These root systems look like a big pineapple with lots of twisty growths, all covered with hairlike roots.

Lily pads offer great fishing at times early in the year, but you have to know your pads. Look for white-flowered pads.

I use different baits in pads, depending on the mood of the bass. A Texas-rigged plastic worm is often tops. I like a worm that has built-in swimming action, rather than a straight body, with a 1/16-or 1/8-ounce sinker. A spinnerbait often works well. You also can have loads of fun fishing a topwater bait in pads, something like a Zara Spook (for extremely aggressive fish) or a Tiny Torpedo (for neutral bass). And minnow baits are good at times.

The first time I ever fished Florida, almost 20 years ago, the best pattern I found was this very lily pad pattern that I had fished for years on lakes near my home. I'd been expecting some difficulty adjusting to a whole new region. I caught a bunch of nice fish in those pads, and let me tell you, I felt right at home!

A variety of baits will work in pads.

Newly-Forming Reed Beds

As you know by now, bass like to spawn over solid bottom areas. Since reed beds grow out of hard-bottomed areas and provide cover, they are often "key" spawning areas for bass. When water temperatures reach the high 50s or low 60s, bass move into reeds in anticipation of the spawn.

Spawning bass always situate themselves near an object if they can. Larger objects offer protection against egg-stealers, but bass even hold beside something like a stick three inches in diameter, *if* that is the most substantial thing they can find. Logs, deadheads or big boulders attract spawning bass. With good glasses, you'll be able to spot clumps of thick growth and various objects in the reeds. Look for anything that gives an edge effect in the general context of the reed bed cover.

Babe demonstrates this pattern for his "Good Fishing" television audience.

Three baits are best. First would be a spinnerbait, 1/4-or 3/8-ounce, perhaps with a white blade and white skirt, on an outfit with 10-pound mono line. Second, try a floating minnow bait that has a nice wobbling action and doesn't dive more than about three feet. You will be working it slowly, just fast enough to bring out the wobble.

Or use a six-inch worm with a 1/16-ounce sinker pegged in place with a toothpick (to minimize tangles). Use such a light weight that the worm just flutters on down; it won't catch much if it drops quickly in that shallow water. For the worm rig, six-pound line is best (last year's reeds will have been cut off by ice or lying down).

I won a tournament years ago in this kind of cover. I caught 52 "weigh" bass by using a 1/32-ounce weight on a six-inch worm while my partner caught a single fish on an identical worm. He used a 1/8-ounce weight because it was "too much hassle" to cast the light rigs in the wind. My almost weightless worm fluttered down slowly instead of plunging down like his.

Sometimes when you move through the reed bank you'll spook bass out as you go. That's okay. Remember exactly where the bass spooked from—a certain clump of reeds, a spot with a dark rock, or whatever. Come back in an hour or so, fishing those spots very carefully and quietly with long casts.

Be cautious. The water will usually be clear and the cover is often not well developed, so bass will be super spooky.

Pegging a worm weight in place with a toothpick. This will reduce hang-ups.

Post-spawn Flats

This is a major pattern, though not one that produces that many lunkers. The biggest fish are usually semi-dormant or feeding at night when this pattern gets hot.

After recovering from the spawn, bass of both sexes often scatter across the flats in water from 4 to 12 feet deep. Fresh green weed growth, especially cabbage and coontail, on the flats provides some cover. Bass are in transition from being focussed on the shallows to being more concentrated in the depths, along the weedlines.

Logically enough, often the best flats will be those near good spawning locations. Much of the spawning by species bass like to eat will take place near the same areas where the bass had spawned earlier. The flats nearest those bays will concentrate the adult baitfish that have just spawned. For example, a flat in front of a a marshy bay, in a lake with good perch numbers, will attract perch that have just spawned. Flats in front of reed banks, another good baitfish spawning location, attract post-spawn bass. Incoming creeks also attract spawning fish, so good flats in front of them are also good. In addition to the baitfish, the main thing concentrating bass on the flats is the succession of insect hatches that take place there.

181

On these flats, look for *the best new weedy cover around.* These thicker, weedy areas put out the most oxygen, and that—plus the cover itself—is very attractive to bass *and* forage fish. And crustaceans. Crayfish eat vegetation, and when the flats are newly developing the crayfish find much there to attract them. Bass are always on the lookout for crayfish, so they aren't far behind.

Many bass use these mid-depth flats. They may concentrate on the deeper water edges during "off" periods, then move right up on the flats when actually feeding.

I fish these flats with small shallow-running crankbaits and light tackle. I like medium-light baitcasting equipment with eight-pound line, light to make long casts possible. Several baits will work, but I'd start with Lindy's Snipes, Bagley's Killer Bs or the small Bomber Model A lures. I'll make a point of experimenting with different retrieves. Since the water will still be chilly, slower speeds might be called for. Yet on another day, or a different time in the same day, medium or fast retrieves could be better.

This is a dynamic situation, with fish that are often migrating back and forth. On the flats— as in other open water, chasing situations— the fish won't be sitting in one spot, but moving around. Many baits will take them, but none are as versatile or fast-working as crankbaits.

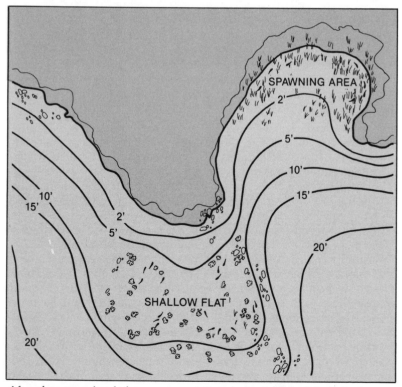

After the spawn but before summer patterns get established, look for bass on shallow shoreline flats, as shown here.

For a period after the spawn, the bass are scattered and difficult to locate. This is one of those major transition moments. Fishing is tough in transitions, because even when you find fish, you will rarely get a good concentration of them.

But one of the likeliest places, in those waters where this weed occurs, is in patches of wild celery, called *Vallisneria americana* by biologists. It is better known to hunters than fishermen because wild celery is a favorite food of waterfowl.

Wild celery is a long, thin, flat grass-like weed. It grows in relatively shallow shoreline areas, and in a short amount of time grows so long it droops over and lies along the water in long strings that point the way the wind is blowing. It is a terrible weed to fish in, because it is so thick and rubbery. You'll get tangled, no matter what you do!

Wild celery is tough to fish in, but it holds bass after the spawn. It lies flat along the top of the water in long, stringy ribbons.

But if that's where the bass are, that's where I'll fish. The fish are drawn there in many cases by the good cover and by the presence of spawning sunfish and bluegills. Look for edges where the celery comes together with bulrushes, fallen logs or lily pads. As thick as celery is, there will be pockets and alleys in it where you can work a lure. You drag the lure over the thicker patches, letting it drop into any kind of opening.

183

Bass in wild celery will sometimes be out roaming the beds, but you should look for them first near cover or in clumps of thicker weeds.

Yet celery is such good cover overall that, unlike some weed types, you can just pitch lures at the main body of grass. The whole celery bed has potential for holding fish. The bass can be scattered all over, and they'll often find a way of shooting through the weeds to engulf the lure.

The only lures to use here are those that are most snag-free. Even a spinnerbait will get tied up in weeds. A better choice for a searching lure is a weedless spoon, like the Johnson Silver Minnow fitted with either a spring lizard pork rind or a rubber skirt. In color, a silver spoon with a black rind on it is good. On other days a gold or black spoon (still with a black rind) might be better. Experiment.

Tie your line directly to the spoon, using no snaps, to minimize tangles. The Silver Minnow has enough weight to work down through the weeds and draw strikes from the bass. Sometimes you want to throw the spoon right over the very thickest patches, maybe where the celery is lying over, and haul it back, making a big wake on the surface. Bass will sometimes blast right through the celery to kill that spoon.

My favorite tackle for the spoons would be 12-pound line with medium-heavy baitcasting tackle. The tackle has to be heavy enough to horse the fish in through the grass.

When the fish are aggressive, the spoon will score. When they aren't you'll need a worm. Rig up a second outfit with a weightless plastic worm, just a six-inch or seven-inch worm with a hook buried in the worm Texas-rig style. My favorites are black, black-grape or dark purple. To throw such a light worm you'll need to work with spinning tackle. The rod will need to have enough authority to wrestle a bass out of the celery, even though you'll want a line only about eight pounds in test. Sometimes, bass just dive into the celery so fast you can't do anything about it, and then you need to go in with the boat and try to free the fish by hand. Push poles, the kind duck hunters use in heavy marshes, help you maneuver in this stuff.

If you get a clear indication the fish are aggressive, the spoon will take the most fish because it covers more water in the same amount of time. But you'll get a lot of missed strikes with the spoon, especially if the fish aren't aggressive. The worm will get the negative bass. Often the best technique is to fish the spoon until you get a slash from a fish...then drop that outfit and bang that worm in there as quickly as possible but *right in the rings left by the striking bass*.

In this cover, when you hook a bass your problems are just beginning! You've got to do two things as quickly as possible—get the fish's head *up* instantly, and then get that fish moving your way.

Summer Patterns

Early Summer, Inside Turns

The fish have come off their post-spawn behavior. The lake is setting up in a summer pattern, which means that the new year's vegetation is getting established and the water is becoming organized into warm, cool and cold layers.

To a very great extent, the active schools of bass will congregate on the inside turns in weeds on breaks near the shore. These inside turns can be small, but not necessarily; in fact, some are quite sizable. *Inside turns are the key to your early summer bass fishing.*

The inside turns that hold the most and biggest bass are those with the *thickest new weeds and the fastest drops into deeper water*. Basically you'll be fishing 6 to 12 feet of water, but check down as far as 20. Bass often concentrate right in the center of the inside turn.

The weedy structure with the inside turns in it can occur in the middle of the lake or close to shore. Of the two possibilities, structure connected to shore (like a big point with one or more inside turn on it) is better than a weedy reef.

Use a four- to six-inch curly-tailed worm on a light line (six- to eight-pound test) with 1/8- to 3/32-ounce mushroom jigheads. Choose the stiffest rod that will be able to cast the light worms, generally a short graphite rod with a fast tip.

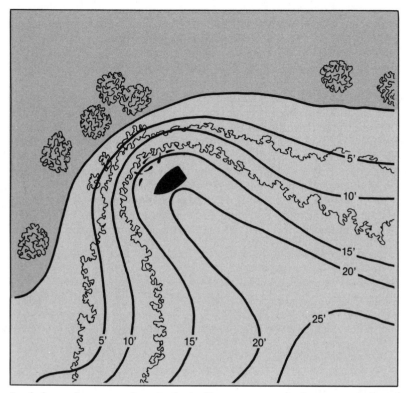

Look for early summer bass in the inside turns, near the best new weeds and closest to the deeper dropoffs.

Position your boat a short distance off the weeds, in deeper water, right off the inside turn. Tease the worm through the tops of the weeds with a swimming motion. Let the swimming worm parallel the contour of the tops of the weeds. Where the weeds drop steeply, stop retrieving long enough to let that worm drop. A sharp snap of the rod tip will usually free you when you snag up.

The fish can be spooky. An overcast sky is better than a bright one. A wind that puts a moderate chop on the water definitely helps. If the wind gets too brisk, you won't be able to feel the difference between weeds and fish, so you should switch to a small crankbait. At this time, bass are most aggressive when rough or overcast conditions cut down on light penetration.

Usually you will cast *in* toward the weeds. But when the fish are tightly grouped at the base of the weedline, put the boat on the weedline and cast parallel to the weeds.

At this time of year, the active bass will be tightly grouped, and *they'll almost always be on an inside turns!* Inside turns might be physically small, but they're huge in terms of importance. Since bass roam around from spot to spot, check out all parts of the inside turns carefully, from one end to the other.

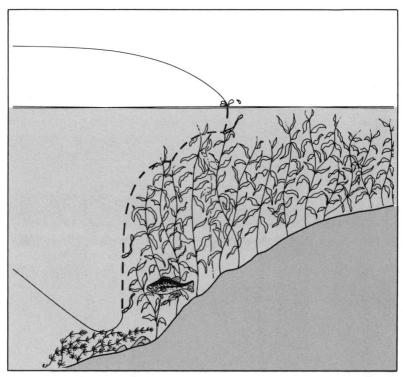

Work your worm along the top of the weedbed, then bring it down the front face.

Creek Channel Bass

As spring turns to summer in reservoirs and flowages, bass that spawned way back in the coves begin to follow the creek channel out toward deeper water. The later it gets, the more they locate toward the main body of the reservoir instead of the shallow cove ends. Since some coves are many miles long, the bass won't leave them quickly, but they make a fairly steady migration away from the cove ends toward the lake center.

The creek channel guides their migration like a highway. And certain key spots along the channel will stop or hold them. Here are two examples:

Where the channel swings in close to a stand of timber you have, in effect, an inside turn next to a flat. If the flat has good cover on it, it would be very attractive to migrating bass.

Or, as the bass move along one creek channel, they might encounter a junction with a second channel. If water depths at the spot range from six to 20 feet, bass will hold there.

Once you locate a school holding in an area, you can have good fishing for several days. Bass will hold in fairly deep water near the channel, making frequent movements shallow to feed. Sometimes they

One of the best areas for fishing creek channel bass is on a flat adjacent to the creek bed, especially if the flat has timber.

go some distance up a connecting creek to forage before dropping back to the safety of the creek channel. You can catch them deep or up shallow, and you'll have to check out both areas.

One of my favorite baits for this situation is a jig with an exposed hook and a grub body, like the two- to three-inch long Mann's Sting Ray grub. I'll work the grub on eight-pound line with a graphite spinning rod between five and six feet. My second choice would be a pork frog on a snagless jighead. Finally, I'll use a Texas-rigged plastic lizard (or "salamander" or "water dog") or perhaps a plastic lizard on a jig with an exposed hook.

Choose your bait according to the heaviness of the cover. If the creek junction is full of brush, a bait with a protected hook is best. If you spot the bass on your graph lying at the edge of cover in deeper water, use the pork frog or plastic bait with the exposed hook rigs.

No matter where you fish—a strip pit, a big lake, a stock tank or a reservoir—underwater points are terribly important in summer. The points we can see with our eyes are often good too, mainly because they continue into the water as underwater points. It is the *underwater points* which we can see with sonar that we're talking about now.

Points offer bass several environmental conditions in a small space. In one general area they have access to shallow and deep water, for example. Winds from several different directions will stir up baitfish action on points, too. In early to midsummer, points concentrate bass.

Points can form in reservoirs in several ways. Often, points are created by the meeting of the main river channel and a cove mouth. As the river channel comes near a bank it will form a fairly steep drop. Then, if the mouth of a cove intersects such a drop, you have an underwater point. Such a point will be near the river channel, near the cove mouth and connected to the shore. Obviously, it has a lot going for it. And if it has some stumps up on top, as so many points do, so much the better!

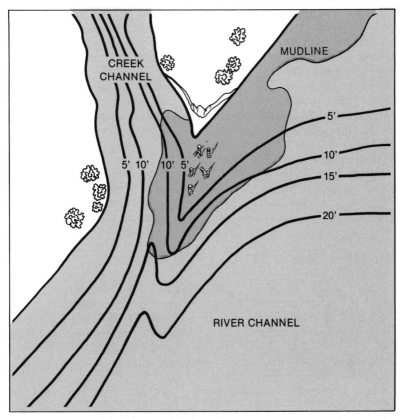

This illustration shows a mudline on a reservoir point. The two places to expect bass are shallow, up on the point, or along the edge of the mudline.

When winds cause waves to roll over such a point, they create a mudline and a current line as the water moves around the tip of the point and heads into the cove mouth. The mudline and current draw bass out of deep water, concentrating them on the point.

Boat control will not be easy. Most bass boats have motors so big they can't be used except for running from spot to spot. In that case, you better have a powerful troll motor and lots of poop in your battery. If I'm fishing out of my Ranger 1600 V-II, I can hover off these windy points by keeping my Mariner Fifty running slowly in reverse.

Bass will come extremely shallow on a muddy point. On most points, winds from the south (and southeast and southwest) are better than winds from the north. If the wind has been working on the point for most of the day, the best fishing tends to be in the afternoon because by then the water has been stirred up sufficiently to draw large numbers of forage fish in there.

Incidentally, this pattern is so strong it can even hold up during those brutal post-frontal conditions (usually caused by a wind from the North). After a front has come through, though, you will have to work your bait more cautiously. After a front, I'd swim a jig-and-pig or a jig with a plastic lizard slowly across the point.

Usually you need to check out two areas thoroughly. Work the *top of the point*, checking various depths, but primarily the water from a foot to about four feet deep. Secondarily, look for bass *along the current line* formed by the wind going past the point. The mud and current line creates an edge effect.

To fish this situation, I start by throwing vibrating crankbaits, like the Cotton Cordell Spot or Lewis's Rat-L-Trap, on ten-pound line. These are fast, shallow-running lures that really grab aggressive fish. I'd use medium baitcasting tackle with a reel with a fast retrieve ratio. Whenever possible, I'll bang my crankbaits on the sides of the stumps on the retrieve.

After checking the shallows, I'll go back with a deeper-running crankbait. Good ones include Lindy's Snipe or Bomber's Deep Runner Model A. Look for bass in the same places (on top of the point and along the current/mud line), but go a little deeper.

Buzzing Early Morning Bass

This is a particularly fun pattern, one that might work over a long period of the summer, and one that can produce huge bass.

Early in the morning, from fairly early summer all the way through late summer, bass will slide up out of deep water on shallow flats where they scatter to feed. They'll frequently make their move before the earliest hint of dawn comes, so you can actually start fishing this pattern as a form of night fishing.

Many fishermen think that warm water drives the bass into the depths. While there's some truth in that, it is misleading. Bass will come up into very warm water to feed in summer, which is one reason this pattern works so well. In fact, buzzbaits will tear up the bass (and

Use a vibrating crankbait to fish these muddy areas. Bang it into existing cover to attract bass.

northerns, if they're around) in the summer shallows where temperatures exceed 80 degrees. This pattern doesn't get going until water temperatures are 65 degrees and gets better when the water is warmer and the bass are more inclined to nail a fast-moving bait.

Early morning is a calm time of day, which is a good thing because this pattern depends on a smooth lake surface. Forget it if the wind is putting a big chop on the water; bass can't pick up a surface bait well enough then to hit it. The best mornings are muggy and still, the kind of morning when water beads up on your boat and you know you'll need the air conditioner running in the car on the way home.

191

A flat is a broad, table-like area of uniform water depth. In natural lakes, good flats will often be covered with coontail, cabomba or cabbage weed. But reservoirs have flats too, and a shallow flat covered with timber or brush will draw bass in early in the day just as a shallow weed flat does. Many reservoirs, for that matter, have extensive weedy flats whose coontail, milfoil or shore weeds attract bass. Flats don't have to be absolutely flat on top. A very broad weedy area in front of a reed bank that slowly tapers off into the depths is, in fact, a flat...and a very good one.

Would you like to catch a trophy bass? Start here. The biggest flats with the best cover will attract the greatest numbers of bass. The very thickest cover on the biggest flats will often hold the biggest fish in the lake. If you find a particularly thick clump of weeds or a particularly attractive stump that is close to deep water on one of these big flats, you're in lunker country! For this reason, I like to approach flats from the deep water side, being careful to work the most promising spots first as I come in.

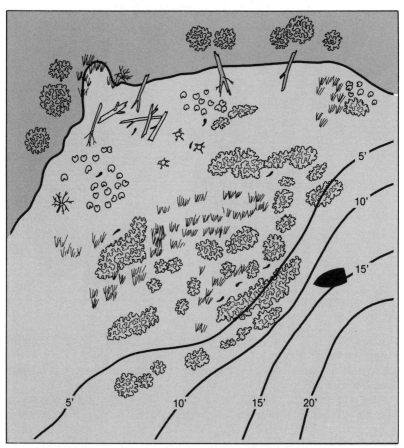

The best places to use a buzzbait for bass are large shallow flats with plenty of cover leading in to shore. Approach from the deep water side.

Bass up on shallow flats can be spooky, so go easy. Make as little noise as possible, though you want to cover a lot of water. Keep a low profile. Make long casts. You want the bass to be aware of your buzzbait but not you or your boat. Medium strength baitcasting tackle is fine for this pattern. I like a slightly light line for longer casts—about ten-pound test. I'd prefer Prime for this situation because long casts complicate hooksetting.

You should have two types of buzzbaits. The original buzzbait was the Harkins Lunker Lure, and it's still a good one. I also like Lindy's Clacker. The Clacker and the Lunker Lure are both all-metal and both have a large delta blade (with two wings). They are best for fast, noisy retrieves, especially if your blades strike the bait's body on the retrieve.

But at times you'll need a slower, quieter retrieve. Then choose one of the lighter buzzers with more lift. A buzzer with paired blades will stay up well, or one with a three-bladed spinner (such as Bill Norman's Triple Buzz). These triple- bladed spinners stay up at the surface when you are only crawling the buzzer along.

Speed, you've probably already guessed, is one key variable in this pattern. Erratic retrieves are not appropriate, as bass need a certain consistency of speed to nail a moving target. Some days they'll want the buzzer barely moving and other days they'll want it flying as fast as you can move it.

Buzzbaits are best in fairly shallow water, but they can pull bass up out of water 12 to 16 feet, too.

Color is the other critical variable. If you start fishing when it is dark, use a black or purple buzzer. Later, in dim light, I like a yellow or chartreuse buzzer. Still later, when the sun is up, white is a good color, especially in clear water. Under a bright mid-day sun, I've also done very well with sky blue buzzers.

Keep checking color preference, as this changes from moment to moment. And keep experimenting with speed until you've got a tight fix on what the bass want.

You will *always* want a trailer hook on your buzzer. And *sharpen* it!!!!

Flipping Heavy Cover

This is a great way to catch fish in cold water, even after a cold front. In fact, one of the best examples of how this technique worked is also probably the most famous flipping story. In the mid-70s, a Californian named Dee Thomas won a B.A.S.S. tournament on Bull Shoals with a new technique, called flipping.

People might not have paid so much notice if conditions had been normal or even poor, but they were much worse than poor. Bull Shoals had just been hit by one of the worst cold fronts I've ever seen. Winds of about 35 miles an hour were just part of the problem, and many boats swamped. A few days before the tournament we had six inches of snow. How bad was it? Well, with 180 of the nation's best anglers fishing there, each day about 150 came in *skunked!*

So when Dee Thomas weighed in with over 36 pounds of bass, *people noticed.* And flipping was on its way to becoming a national craze.

How'd he do it? Thomas knew that there are always some bass fairly shallow, and he knew that cold fronts send bass crawling into the the thickest, tightest cover they can find. In a way, that was to his advantage, since he was prepared to fish with a meticulous, tight-to-cover technique that would not be possible with conventional gear.

Thomas motored back to the far ends of coves, looking for the most impossibly thick cover he could find. He finally found some tangles of logs and sawdust left over from logging. Using his special flipping tackle, he'd drop a jig into the very middle of the worst cover. Thomas used a fairly heavy jig to penetrate the surface crud and sink on down to where the bass were hugging stumps below. Then he would dance and tease that jig in place, never moving it far because he knew the bass weren't going to be anywhere but right in contact with the timber. When his jig got feeling slightly funny, he'd rare back and horse the fish out of the timber jungles.

The technique still works. If anything, it works better now than it used to since bass fishermen have discovered scent and rediscovered pork rind. As good as Thomas' technique was, it might have been better if he had put pork on his jig and smeared some scent on it.

In this pattern, you need enough weight on the jig to get down through the cover to the bass. Snagfree, rubber-legged jigs of 3/8- or 1/2-ounce are usually best. Put an Uncle Josh Flipping Frog or Flipping Crayfish on the jig and add scent to it. Dark colors are best most of the time. My favorite colors, for both the pork and the jig, are black, brown or purple. It's smart to give the bass a little choice, so I might go with a black jig and a brown frog or some other mix of dark colors. When the water is very clear and the skies are bright, I've had some luck with lighter colors, like yellow, so it pays to experiment. Because you'll be rubbing the line against timber and because you want a slow drop, use an abrasion- resistant mono in 17 to 25 pound test, maybe a little heavier.

Flipping is particularly effective when bass are tightest to cover. So flipping shines after a cold front has made other techniques relatively worthless. Exactly *where* you find the bass will depend, of course, on what general areas of the reservoir the bass are using. If they have pulled back from the back ends of coves, look for bushes and timber along the sides of the main channel. This is a game of inches. You've got to fish *in the cover*, not just near it.

Flipping shallow cover. After a front, bass will be right up against or under the cover and will not chase. Work a jig-and-pig slowly, dropping it to the base of the cover.

A very similar pattern occurs on natural lakes. After a cold front, bass often tuck up in the dense, floating masses of cattails or cane. You want to find floating bogs of cattails or cane with two to four feet of water in front. This stuff is not as thin and open as reeds or rice, and you just can't cast right into the middle of the heavy cover. If you do, you'll be fishing up in the air several feet off the water, which is farther than a post-frontal bass will move for a bait!

Occasionally, in lakes with clear water, you can get these post-frontal bass off the deep edges of floating vegetation using conventional tackle, casting in to the front edge of the cover. That may be your only option, since bringing a boat into flipping casting range would spook the fish.

Flipping after a front to the pockets in a cane weedbed. Pockets like the one right under my left hand are the targets to hit.

But if there is any color to the water, flipping is superior because no other technique allows so many casts to be made per minute and no other technique allows casts to be placed so precisely. That's what it takes.

There are two differences in tackle if you are flipping cane masses in natural lakes. First, since you aren't penetrating cover with your jig, it should be lighter. A jig of 1/8-ounce is about right. And your line can be lighter since you aren't horsing fish out of woody cover.

Move your boat along the front edge of the cane, flipping repeatedly to the little pockets in the cover. The front face of the weeds may look like a solid, smooth wall, but it isn't. Look hard enough, and you'll find little cracks and crevices where your jig-and-pig can drop slightly deeper into the cover.

You won't find fish schooling at times like this, so you're always on the hunt. Some areas will be better than others, so occasionally you'll pop two or three fish in a general area. If so, be sure to come back in an hour or two to see if more bass have moved in.

Another good example of cover where flipping is more efficient than other techniques. The bass will be within inches of the cattails and rushes.

Docks can be dynamite for those who have mastered the challenges of fishing them. While there aren't a lot of reliable "rules" about dock fishing, three basic principles will lead you to the best fishing. First, *docks are best in midsummer,* not in spring or fall. Second, *docks are far better on lakes that have submerged weeds but no timber or emergent weeds.* Third, *not all docks are equally productive,* because not all docks offer the same number of ambush points.

Let's say that in a different way. Bass like to move in and out of docks. They do this in summer, mostly on lakes where there are submerged weeds in front of the docks but no bays with emergent weeds. And bass use certain docks more than others.

What docks are best? For every rule there is an exception, but here goes. Straight, simple docks aren't as good as more complicated shapes—the L or T shapes, for example. Docks that sit high off the water aren't as good as lower docks. Docks with metal posts aren't as good as docks with heavy wood posts. Docks with big canopies with pontoon boats moored to them are better than docks without those shade-throwing elements. Docks that end in or near deep water are better than docks that end in shallow water. Docks with a lot of human traffic (they've got beach toys, fishing rods, towels, etc., on them) are not as good as docks that rarely get used. Finally, a dock in a stretch of shoreline with several good docks grouped together will be better than if it sat off by itself.

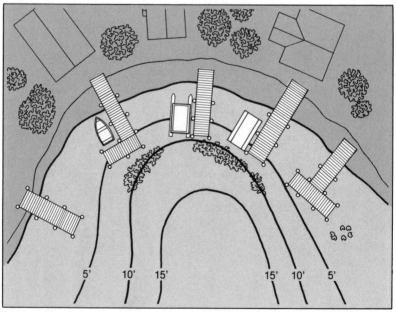

The dock at left would probably not hold bass, whereas the others are good. But when several good docks exist together like this, each becomes better than if it were alone.

Docks can give you all-day fishing. Since some patterns only work well early or late in the day, it's smart to work docks hard in the bright sunlight hours. If anything, a bright sun will help you by concentrating bass under the docks.

Bass use docks for two reasons: shade and food. All docks throw some shade, and remember that the shade is usually not directly under the dock but off to one side or the other. Remember, too, a boat moored at a dock is just another part of the dock to the fish. Pontoon boats are especially good.

Dock bass are often *feeding* bass. If they'd wanted to rest in security, they could do that in the deeper weeds. Instead they came shallow to ambush the minnows and small panfish attracted to the shade and cover of the dock.

To fish docks, I want no less than two rods rigged up, maybe three or four. Every rod has to be fairly stiff because I'll have to muscle the fish away from those posts, yet I need a flexible tip to give me the necessary casting accuracy. I often cast under and around docks from a position right in front of the dock and close. I like a snapping, underhanded cast that fires the bait way back under the dock.

If I've got two outfits, they will be a spinnerbait baitcasting outfit and a spinning outfit with an unweighted Texas-rigged worm. The spinnerbait gets the active, aggressive fish, while the worm danced slowly around the dock posts gets the others. I might have another rod rigged with a Johnson Silver Minnow with some dressing on the tail.

An excellent way to fish docks is with a flipping rod and jig-and-pig. Flipping forces you to fish methodically, which fits dock fishing perfectly. A good flipper can work down a line of docks, fishing behind two or three other boats, and he'll catch some nice bass because he'll be hitting the little corners more accurately and doing a better job of letting the lure drop along the dock posts.

Work a dock systematically. Since the most aggressive fish will often be along the front face of the dock, your first cast should sweep past that face, *as close to the dock as possible*. Work the shady water carefully. When the fish are hitting well, I'll get a lot of bass with quick moving spinnerbaits fished near the surface. But if they're more neutral, I'll need to work the spinnerbait slow and low. Or maybe the worm will have to swim right by the fish's lair to draw a strike. After checking out the front face of the dock, cover the lanes along the sides of the dock.

Dock fishing is a game of inches and seconds. You simply *must* cast accurately to hit the right spots and keep from wasting all your time with casts that wrap around canopies. If you happen to drop a cast on the dock, just slide it into the water and go on fishing. After making a cast, you can use your troll motor and rod tip to steer the bait right through the best cover.

The clarity of the water determines how close you can work to the dock. In dirty water, you can run a boat right up to the dock. If the water is clear, you may have to hang back a bit and make longer casts.

Don't quit fishing a dock when you take a single bass. If you get one, in fact, there's all the more reason to think she had some company under there.

Dock fishing is a game of inches and seconds. Fish as close as possible and work systematically to get the most casts per pass of the boat.

Slop Pockets, Eutrophic Lakes

One summer, several years ago I was invited to Fargo, North Dakota to help the state make a film about their fishing. My partner was a good angler, Dave Jensen, of Bismark. We'd be fishing a eutrophic reservoir called Sweetbriar. Local anglers told us we'd have fishing for a few moments at daybreak, then the day would be over because the bass all ran up under Sweetbriar's floating mass of algae.

We started at eight in the morning. While the other guys were launching boats, I stood on the dock and threw a buzzbait out to the back edge of an open pocket in the mung. I turned the reel handle about three times and—*whoom!*—a 4-pound bass was all over it. I caught three bass standing on that dock while the guys were getting the boats in!

In Sweetbriar, as in many lakes and reservoirs, summer fishing is plagued by sloppy, mungy masses of growth—I wouldn't want to call it "weed" growth because it's not that respectable. Eutrophic lakes have more nutrients than is good for them, and as a result in summer you see these vast, mossy algae blooms. In Sweetbriar these form canopies of floating glop that extend a hundred yards from shore. If your lure touches this stuff it is instantly enmeshed in this stringy, yucky mass. Like the character in "Ghostbusters," you've been *slimed!* So the local anglers stayed away from it.

We didn't. Dave and I mostly ran the boat along the front edge of the slime, casting in to the pockets we could reach. If we'd had to, we could have rammed the boat in with push poles and reached more spots inside. Our targets were open pockets that ranged from a few inches to as much as four feet across. We used heavy baitcasting tackle because we needed power to make casts long enough to hit the pockets.

We started fishing with Lindy's Clackers, fairly heavy buzzbaits. They took the more aggressive fish, which was most fish that day. When action slowed down, Dave and I switched to black Silver Minnows with pork rind trailers. The spoons let us fish just a bit slower, and that was good for a few more fish.

And what a mess of fish we got into! The biggest we landed was over 6 pounds. Dave lost one we thought was 8 pounds. We landed a bunch of 5s, and nobody kept track of the 4s. In all, we took 78 bass. At the end of a perfect day of filming, the cameraman dropped the camera in the lake and we never got an inch of film. But we'd proved a point about fishing eutrophic slop.

Most of what you need to know is in that anecdote. Aggressive fish hit buzzers, and less aggressive fish go for slightly slower baits like spoons or a Texas-rigged worm. After a front, use a floating bait like a Super Frog which you can let sit in place, twitching it until a fish bashes it.

There are two points to keep in mind. First, *you must cast accurately*. Your casts not only have to hit the open pockets but have to hit the *back edge* of the openings. Otherwise you don't get any kind of travel time for your lure, and the bass don't get to hit it even though they want to.

Second, expect to get slimed. That's part of the experience. After your lure has travelled the few inches or feet of open water it will inevitably get munged up, so you have to strip the stuff off. Big deal! For 78 bass, I'll put up with being slimed. In bass fishing, you have to fish where the fish are, and in eutrophic lakes under a bright sun they're going to be up under the slop.

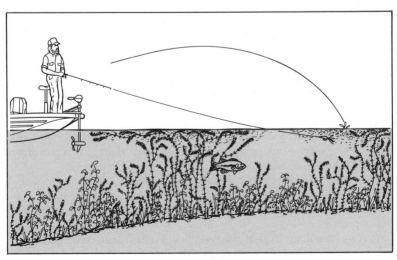

Actually, the pockets in mungy cover aren't often this big, but this illustration shows the concept of fishing in slimy eutrophic cover.

This is one of the most fun and consistently effective patterns in bass fishing. Throughout the summer on lakes with weedlines, this will tend to be the prime pattern. One of the bonuses is that this pattern allows you to catch big bass on light tackle.

Most natural lakes develop weedlines. We already know that a weedline has a front, back and top surface. Where the weeds stop on the front, deep, edge is the *deep weedline*. It's the key spot for much summer fishing, for bass and other species. The deep weedline is shallow in lakes with dark water and deep in clear lakes.

Deep weedlines naturally attract bass, as they are the most important *edge* in a summer bass's world, the spot where the security of deep water meets the cover and food of the weeds. These deep weed edges are not uniform. The weedline will have lots of projections (fingers) and indentations (inside turns). At the base of the taller weeds you usually have scraggly weeds or grass.

Your weedline fishing should be keyed to any *irregularity* in this weedline. Coontail may give way to cabbage weeds. Maybe there is a pocket in the weedline. Maybe there is a change in the bottom, or possibly a clump of rock rubble comes near the weedline. Again, you are looking for any little difference in the weedline.

One lure works so well that I'll not mention alternatives. I like to use a light jighead (1/8-, 3/16- or 1/4-ounce) with a short plastic worm, no more than six inches. The mushroom jighead, such as those made by Gopher Tackle, are tops for coming through the weeds without fouling.

Worms with straight or action tails are fine, and I've also used the four-inch Mr. Twister Sinsation with its pair of curly tails. Sometimes straight colors are best and sometimes a firetail is hotter. Experiment. In clear water, I'll start with light purple, ice blue or strawberry red. In dark water I'll try brown, black or a very dark purple. With the mushroom jig I usually bite the nose off my worm for a snugger, snagfree fit. In this slow style of fishing, an attractant scent often helps. Some days, in fact, the bass seem fussy about which flavor of scent you use.

To throw such a light worm you need medium spinning tackle with a rod from five to six feet long. Use a good graphite rod with a sensitive tip and lots of feel. Spool up with six- or eight- pound monofilament in a highly visible color.

The two critical factors in your presentation will be worm color and jig size. You want your jig weight to be exactly right, not 1/16 of an ounce too heavy or too light.

Boat control is important. If the weeds stop at, say, 15 feet, you'll want to hold in about 18 or 20 feet of water, using a front troll motor to move along the weedline, using a bow-mounted sonar unit to keep at that depth.

Your casts will go in past the weedline itself. If the weeds stop at 15 feet, for example your worm might hit at the ten-foot level. Ease the worm through the weeds. Let it drop, pick it up, let it drop...until it

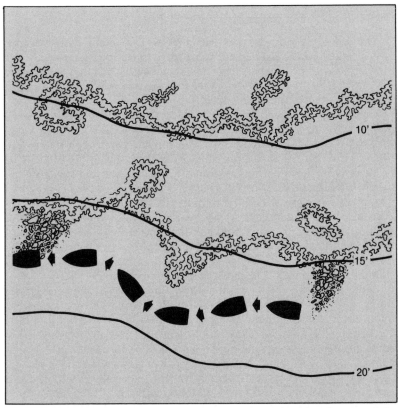

Holding the boat a few feet away from the weeds, you should probe around the little pockets and points or other irregularities in the weedline.

falls to the very deep front edge of the weeds. To fish a deep weedline efficiently, you want your worm to spend as much time as possible swimming and slowly dropping in those weeds just behind and along the deep weedline.

How deep into the cover you fish depends on the type and density of the weeds and the weight of your jig. When fish are negative and deeper, sometimes you'll need a heavier weight to get the worm *into* the weeds more, and you need more weight if gusty winds are interfering with boat control. Otherwise, go as light as you can.

Most strikes come on the drop, including the drop on the initial cast. Watch your line! Most takes make the line twitch. When that happens, set the hook immediately and get the bass moving away from the weeds. This is a style of fishing that lets you enjoy the full fight of a six pounder on six pound test.

Reed Bank Bassin'

Bass don't *live* in reeds, they *eat* in reeds. If a lake has good deeper weeds, that's where bass spend most their time. In lakes not so well blessed, bass spend much of their time on dropoffs. But they go to reeds for one reason: to feed. When you find bass in reeds, you've found some active, very catchable bass.

One thing about reed beds: bass are in them or they aren't. There's no point fishing reeds if all the bass are off in deep water. As mentioned earlier, you rarely find bass in shallow reeds when high waves are pounding in there. You often need to check reeds several times a day to be there when a school has migrated in. Because of the shade of the weeds, sunlight is not a problem in reed fishing. Hot reed fishing can take place any time of day, even under a bluebird sky.

Time of day does affect how you work a bank. If you hit a reed bank early in the morning, you'll find fish roaming around. Then a spinnerbait run through the open areas and even the water just outside the reeds will produce well. When the sun is high, you'll need to concentrate much more on the specific clumps of cover in the reeds.

Some banks are better than others. Sparse, open reed banks are rarely as good as ones with thicker growth. Reeds with weeds growing under them are not as good as reeds on a clean, hard bottom. But bass can't choose the lake they're born into, and on some lakes these weedier reeds are the only reeds the bass have available to them.

Four baits work best. A Texas-rigged worm is very good. Spinnerbaits are super for the more aggressive fish, especially if you've got a good number of open pockets or alleys to run them. The Silver Minnow with a pork trailer is another great reed bait. Finally, the jig-and-pig has become one of my favorites.

The rest of the equipment is standard. Since you'll have to muscle fish out of strong reeds, abrasion-resistant lines of at least 12 pounds are needed, with fairly strong baitcasting tackle to do the muscling. A strong bow mount troll motor with a weedless prop will get you most places, but serious reed fishermen also carry push poles.

The true art of reed fishing consists of spotting the little areas that will hold bass and then hitting them perfectly with the first cast. Accurate casting counts for a great deal. Long casts don't pay off. You just end up getting fouled up, and even if you hook a bass on a long line you can't control him.

Though a reed bank may look uniformly good to you, it isn't. Within the bank will be clumps of thicker cover, and they are often key spots. When bass are holding tight in these clumps I like to dump a jig-and-pig in there and just shake it around without pulling it out. Sometimes you'll do better running a spinnerbait through the open alleys and pockets. Don't fish randomly, just covering water. The fish are concentrated in special spots. You should always key your effort on those spots.

When reeds are this thick, fish elsewhere in low light hours and then hit the heavy cover when it's bright. Bass will hit all day long in cover this thick.

Too many reed fishermen confine their attention to the front edge of the bank. That's often the worst spot. Get *in* the reeds and work the places that are a little different. Don't be afraid of running all the way up to the far back (shallow) edge of the reeds. That edge often has the thickest, best reeds, and you'll sometimes find logs and other cover lying around back there. When a good school hits the reeds, some fish will move all the way to the edge nearest shore. I've caught big bass in shallow reeds, almost on shore.

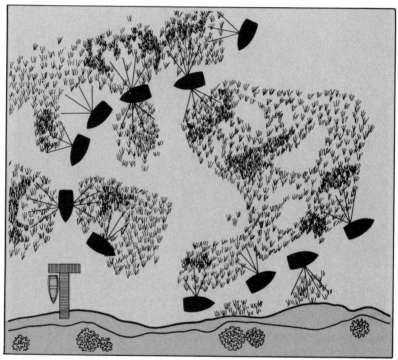

Look for key spots in a reed bank such as clumps, pockets, and alleys, and then make short accurate casts. Don't be afraid to work the inside edge.

Topwater Baits at Night

This pattern can be a problem solver for tough lakes and difficult conditions. It can also produce *huge* bass. But they aren't going to jump in the boat! You'll have to fish smart and hard.

Two conditions make night fishing good in summer, whether you're working reservoirs, farm ponds, strip pits or natural lakes. Warm water is one such condition. When water temperatures get around 80 degrees, bass often revert to night feeding part or even all of the time. This, of course, happens more often on southern waters.

Extremely clear water also makes night fishing good. In this case, the bright sun will deter bass from being active in the middle of the day, so they make up for that lost time with nocturnal feeding.

Many summertime lakes and reservoirs come alive when the sun leaves the water.

Obviously, a reservoir with warm *and* clear water is sure to come alive at night. Some "play lakes" that get terrific waterskiing and pleasure boating pressure during the day will turn on at night. So, night fishing can solve some tough problems.

Night fishing also offers the potential for catching trophy bass. Lots of lakes have big old females that hole up in secure cover during the day and just don't make the kinds of mistakes that little fish make. But they lose caution at night, cruising the shallows away from cover.

Dark, dark nights are best. I love night fishing on hot, calm, muggy nights when there is no light at all coming from the moon.

Running around in the dark can be dangerous. Fish a lake at night only after you've learned it in the day, and even then it might take a trip or two to learn to navigate by shoreline silhouettes.

The best areas will be *moderately deep to shallow* and *free of cover but near it.* In other words, a shallow tapering flat or point that gradually drops off to deep water will be good. In reservoirs, try points with brushy, deep water close by. In reservoirs if the water is really warm you won't do well unless there is cooler, deep water nearby where the bass can hole up during the day.

Stay away from cover. At night, big bass do a lot of moving through relatively open water. They won't be hiding in the shade of stumps and they won't be buried in the weeds. You'd have a tough time catching them there, even if that's the kind of cover they used at night, but it isn't.

Night bass are notorious for coming very shallow, yet you can't forget the moderately deep water. I've pulled bass up out of 15 feet of water at night. The whole zone from two to about 15 feet can be productive.

Of course, your tackle can and should be fairly heavy. You're looking for trophy fish and you're going to be fighting them without seeing them. Lines of 14-pound test are not too heavy. I prefer fairly heavy baitcasting tackle.

For fun and to keep out of snags, you should fish surface baits. A good night bait has to have several qualities. It should be *big*. I usually use musky baits, such as the Musky Jitterbug. It should be *noisy* so the bass can locate it. Big buzzbaits are effective, as are huge chuggers or Zara Spooks. A night bait should be *noisy even at slow speeds* because the bass will miss the bait if it races along too quickly. In buzzers, for example, use only the lighter models with triple blades. Your bait should have a *consistent action*, not an erratic one. Bass will hit a musky jerkbait at night, for example, but many of them are too irregular in behavior for a night-feeding bass to nail. Finally, your bait should be black. Carry dark purple or dark blue if you want, but black is *it*.

I like to fish with a partner at night. It's nice to have company if something goes wrong. It's nicer to have company if something goes right...for netting fish at night can be tricky. I've got lights on my boat to help land fish. With experience, night fishermen learn to avoid the use of lights as much as possible except maybe for netting fish.

Worming the Crappie Holes

This pattern is useful all summer on reservoirs with little cover. These days, that's a lot of reservoirs, as many are so old the original timber has rotted and been brought down by wave action.

On cover-poor reservoirs, many lake owners stake down brushpiles in front of their docks so they can catch crappies at night. As you'd guess, bass use these brushpiles during the day. The worse the cover is in a reservoir, the more likely you are to find crappie brushpiles in front of the docks...and the more important to bass they will be.

You can spot the docks that are likely to have the brushpiles. If there are bait cans, poles or especially pole holders on the dock, check for a brushpile. Look, also, for docks that have bench seats on them.

The brushpiles will be within comfortable casting distance of the dock, usually right in front. You'll need to look around the area out to about 20 feet from the dock. I usually "look" for brushpiles with a lure like a jig-and-pig, casting until I feel them.

Don't bother trying to fish the piles seriously when you first locate them. You first need to locate a series of brushpiles in a cove. Later, you can come back and fish down the line, running a "milk route" of maybe 25 brushpiles in a day.

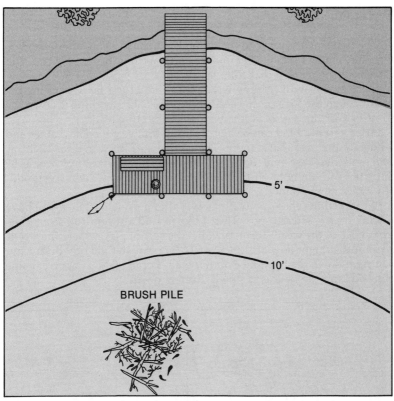

BRUSH PILE

On cover-poor reservoirs, brushpiles put down for crappies will offer some of the best bass fishing.

It's critical to get a good fix on the brushpile before you come back to fish it. Once you locate it, take sightlines until you're sure you can come back and locate and make accurate, effective casts. Bass spook out of brushpiles easily. You want to be able to slip up to the brush quietly and place your first few casts just where they ought to be.

Expect the bass to be tight to the cover in reservoirs with clear water. They might be sitting right *in* the brush. If the water is murky, you will pick up bass around the edges of the brushpiles.

Two lures are best. The Texas-rigged worm is the classic choice. If you peg your sinker in place with a toothpick you'll hang up less. My other favorite is a jig-and-pig.

The weight of your jig or sinker should be matched to conditions. If you are finding thick, strong brushpiles and the bass are right down in them, you'll need heavy tackle. That is, your bait will have to be heavy enough to force its way into the brush. And you'd need correspondingly heavy tackle—a line of about 17-pound test and a stiff baitcasting outfit. If the bass aren't right in the brush or if the brush is lighter, lighter outfits will be better.

No need to drop an anchor and sit on one brushpile. Just slip in quietly, make a few well-placed casts, and zip on down to the next pile.

The best single answer to the difficulty of bass fishing after a front is live bait. I often fish a jig and minnow after a front, but for *big* bass you can't beat the pattern that follows.

Once again, we'll fish the weedlines of a natural lake, working the bait through the tops of the weeds but, especially, working it down the front face of the weeds all the way to the bottom.

After a front, wind can be a problem. If you've got cool weather and moderate breezes, that's good. The ruffled surface won't pass light as well and the bass will be more aggressive. Boat control won't be difficult. You can hold off the weedline in deeper water and fish gradually tapering weedlines.

Yet sometimes the wind really howls after a front, and then you have to look for a sheltered spot. Then I like to find a sheer drop so that the front edge of the weeds forms a wall—the sort of place where the weeds go almost straight down to 10, 12 or 14 feet of water. I'll be working my bait right down the front face of that wall, hoping that a bass will come out and grab the bait as it slowly flutters down.

After a front you can catch bass on a jig and live bait by fishing along the tops of the weeds and down the front. In a bad wind, look for a steep drop.

For big bass, you can't beat waterdogs as bait. The best size for this fishing is four to six inches. Bass hit waterdogs as if they hated them, and maybe they do. With waterdogs you'll get amazingly vicious strikes from big bass, even after a front!

I fish the waterdogs on a light jig, about 1/8 ounce. Hook the waterdog up through the lips. Sometimes you have to use a weedless jig, usually not. With the light jighead and light tackle, like eight-pound line on a spinning rod, you can get a slow drop and your waterdog will swim around a bit as it goes down.

Fish close to the weeds. Bass aren't going to move far for a bait, even a waterdog, after a front.

Fall Patterns

Turnover Bass

This pattern is a problem solver. It doesn't last a long time, but is interesting because it shows us how bass respond to a tough situation. It is also a classic example of how *you* can respond to a tough bass fishing situation. This is a pattern for those terrible days during and right after the fall turnover.

Cool fall weather, especially cool nights, will lower the temperature of the surface water and cause it to sink. Ultimately this mixing process goes all the way, exchanging top and bottom water. This special moment is called the turnover. You can recognize it by the rotting vegetation in the water, by the sudden drop in water clarity and by the foul smell that accompanies the turnover. It is notorious as a time when bass cannot be caught.

The turnover causes cool bottom water to come to the surface, and that in turn causes a dieoff in the submerged vegetation that has been home to the bass throughout the summer. The dying of the weeds forces the bass away. Where do they go?

They go down. From wherever they were, the bass move deeper, abandoning the security of weeds in favor of the security of deeper water.

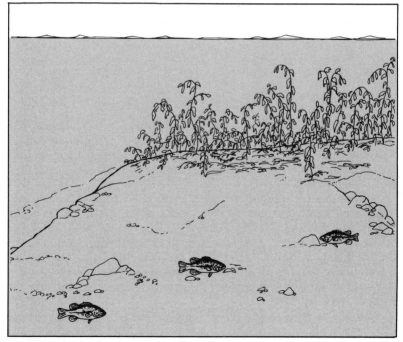

During turnover, bass move out of the dying weeds and take up residence in deeper water.

Let's take an example. Say you had a nice point with cabbage or coontail weeds on it. The weeds stopped at 14 feet, and that was your key spot for catching bass all summer. Right after the turnover, those bass will drift down to the 20, 25 or 30 foot level on that same point. I've caught them as deep as 40 feet at this time.

These are *not* tightly schooled or aggressive fish. They'll school up a little later. These turnover bass are fish that have just been forced into cooler water and away from their favorite haunts. They'll be negative to neutral about feeding, and they'll be somewhat scattered right after the turnover.

You should be able to guess part of the answer to catching these fish. Whenever bass are in an "off" mood, live bait will outfish artificials. In this case, the best baits are probably huge leeches — the very biggest you can find—or big, healthy nightcrawlers. Since we want to move around (to cover more water) slowly (because the fish will not be aggressive), the best way to present this live bait is a regular Lindy rig. This is just like fishing for negative walleyes. The rest of the tackle is identical to walleye tackle. You want a sensitive little graphite spinning rod and line of six-or eight-pound test.

Boat control is important. The best way to move around on the structure is by backtrolling, using a transom-mounted electric motor. You can do it with a bow-mounted motor, too.

This pattern only holds up for about a week. Yet that can be an important week for you. If you snoop around the structure down deeper from the bass's summer haunts, you can have excellent fishing.

Big Baits, Big Bass

About a week after the turnover, you might nail a trophy if you fish with a huge bait. Perhaps you're thinking you would probably do as well with smaller baits. So did my friend, Paul Vinton. Paul's a good bass fisherman. But when he heard me talking about musky-sized baits, he shook his head.

So we ran a friendly little contest. Paul fished a 3/8-ounce spinnerbait on conventional bass tackle. I grabbed an outfit I'd set up in August for muskies. It was a stiff "pool cue" rod, with 46 pound dacron, a wire leader...a musky outfit, all the way! For a lure, I chose a Bucher Buzzer, a musky buzzer made by Wisconsin guide, Joe Bucher. It was a huge thing, with an orange blade over a black body. We went to a strip pit for our little contest. I was so confident I let Paul take the front of the boat.

Well, it was no contest after all. Paul caught 14 bass. I caught two. Paul's biggest bass was two and a half pounds. My first bass went just over eight; the second went almost seven and a half! Paul agreed that he'd be willing to settle for only two fish if they were two fish like that.

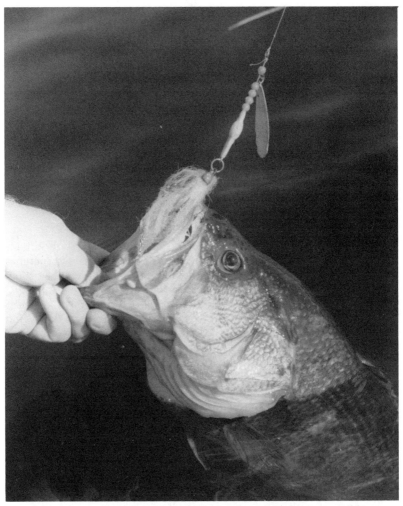

A huge muskie spinner took this large fall bass. Your bait can hardly be too big.

Here's my point: both those fish had turned down Paul's spinnerbait. He was fishing very carefully ahead of me, and the first fish came from an area he'd combed through. The second fish came off a stump that had given Paul a little bass. After catching that one, he made five more casts to the stump. Sure there was nothing else there, he moved on and gave me a shot at the stump. Boom! I took the other trophy. *In fall your bait can hardly be too big* for a big bass.

You have to have decent conditions. Once the bass have been sent deep by cold weather, they rarely come shallow again unless it has been warm for a day or two. When you get those nice "Indian Summer" days, calm and warm, that's the time to crack out the big baits and go lunker hunting. Afternoons are better than the low light hours, just as it was in spring.

Big bass want big baits in fall. But they aren't moving as quickly as in summer, so you want to keep your retrieves slow. My Bucher buzzer was running about six inches below the water, making a big fuss while going slow. I have seen fall bass snatch red-winged blackbirds in reeds, so I've always liked a black and orange lure. For whatever reason, that combo has been good to me in fall.

Cold Water Cranking

Here's another super fall pattern. In this one, you'll go after the bass with crankbaits in the last green weeds of the year.

You should be looking for big flats with good weed cover. Throughout the summer, cabbage is often the most attractive weed. But cabbage dies off faster than coontail. So in fall, it is the coontail flats, sometimes with some cabbage mixed in, that you want to find. You will be fishing flats in water only two, four or five feet deep on the warmer fall days.

Because the water is cold, the afternoons of bright days are best. Don't worry about sun penetration. You want a calm, warm day. Wind will knock the bass right out of these shallow areas.

Medium-light spinning tackle is best. Above all, you want sensitivity. Choose one of the best modern one-piece graphite rods with a soft enough tip so you can feel every throb of the crankbait. A line of eight- or ten-pound test is ideal. Long casts are often best in this clear water. If your line is too thick you lose important casting distance.

For this pattern, you want a crankbait. Not just any crankbait, but one with a fat body and a fat but short lip. The idea is to use a bait that wiggles a lot but doesn't dive much on a slow retrieve. I like the Lindy Shadling for this, and there are several other crankbaits that do the job, including some of the balsa-bodied fat crankbaits. Another good one is Bill Norman's Big N.

Experiment with color. I've done well with chartreuse, chartreuse/ brown and brown/orange finishes. Minnow patterns can be good, like white with a black back or white with a blue back. Sharpen your hooks until you can't tie a knot to the bait without getting hooked.

The bass that drift up out of the weeds to check out your crankbait will be cold and sluggish. To trigger a strike from these fish it is very helpful to have some kind of scent on the bait.

There are two keys to this pattern. The first is a s-l-o-w retrieve that just brings the crankbait back across the top of the weeds. Again, these are cold, sluggish fish.

The second key is intense concentration on the feel of the bait as it works. The strikes will be soft and the bass will usually be swimming toward you as they gently mouth your bait. You won't feel a savage slash. What you will feel is usually a soggy, "odd" sensation. Your line might go slightly limp or you might just sense that the bait isn't throbbing like it was. Hey, that's a strike! Set the hook!

214

A good fall pattern involves working crankbaits slowly with light tackle. After-noons are best.

River Channel Bluff Points

This pattern can be fun. Hit it right, and you can catch a tremendous number of bass. Bass seek out areas in fall where, while staying on one structure and not moving much, they can rise up shallow or go very deep. This pattern takes advantage of that.

On reservoirs, where the creek channel sweeps in close to shore, it forms a point with a leading and a trailing edge. But what you need for this pattern is a particular kind of point, a *bluff point* with an extremely steep dropoff to deep water. The point should drop down sharply in a stairstep fashion, almost straight up and down. If you're lucky, the bass might be only 30 or 40 feet down. But in spots like this, I've taken bass as deep as 60 and 70 feet!

To feel a bass at that depth, you will need light, sensitive tackle. Use a highly visible four-pound mono on a one-piece ultralight graphite spinning rod. Some ultralights are wimpy, and that's hardly what you need. The rod has to have some spine.

The best bait is a grub jig, something like the Sting Ray. Add scent to the bait. Put that grub on a jighead of 1/8-or 3/32-ounce, and take an extra moment to stroke the hook point until it is as sharp as you can make it. Hook the grub jig so that the flat side of the tail will slow down the drop of the jig. You want a slow, lazy drop.

There are two parts to this pattern. You start by moving slowly around with your troll motor, trying to find a school of fish. With the boat in deep water, cast up to a shallower part of the bank. Strip line off your reel so the line does not interfere with the free fall of the jig. When it hits a stairstep and stops falling, gently pull it toward deep water to set it dropping again. You just let it drop, drop, drop, stripping out line, until the jig gets all the way down below the boat. Or until you see the line twitch to signal a take.

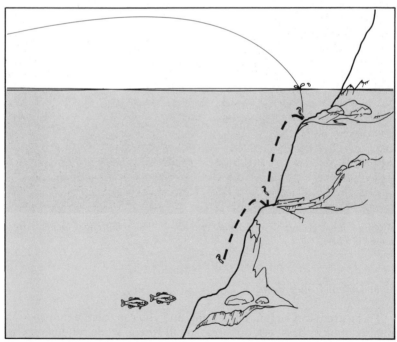

Dropping a grub jig down a stair-step bluff point. This is very much like live bait fishing.

You are fishing that little jig as if it were live bait. You're not adding action at all, just letting it fall freely. Obviously, you have to watch the line like a hawk.

It takes a heckuva good set to put a hook in a bass when you've got that much mono out. Mono stretches a lot, especially light mono. For a good set on a long line it isn't important to set quick or hard so much as to take up the slack and sweep the rod a long distance to get past the stretch.

Once you've found the bass and have a fix on their depth, put the boat directly over them and hold it in place with the troll motor. Now, instead of casting, you can jig vertically below the boat. This is usually when you can put a lot of bass in the boat.

Because of the finesse required to see a pickup at these depths, this pattern is strictly a calm weather affair. Wind will wipe you out.

Spinnerbaiting the Fall Marshes

On all types of lakes and reservoirs, the amphibians (frogs and salamanders) make a fall migration to the marshy bays to burrow into the muck and hide from winter. This is known in some areas as "the frog run," and it sure draws in the big bass.

I have to think of one October day on a central Minnesota lake when I ran into this situation. I'd found one bass at 30 feet and another in shallow weeds, so I kept moving around looking for a *concentration* of bass. When I got to the back of a reed bed at the mouth of a marsh, I noticed a boil on the surface.

I threw a big spinnerbait at it and saw what every bass fisherman loves to see—a big wake running right *at* my bait! That bass went almost 6 pounds, an exceptionally big fish in Minnesota. But the next bass was the same size. I got really excited. Who wouldn't? On some casts, I'd have three or four wakes zooming in on the spinnerbait as the bass competed for it!

In one hour I caught *42 bass over 3 pounds!* One was close to 7. Four were over 6. In that hour I caught a dozen over 5 pounds, which is more than most anglers take in a lifetime of fishing northern lakes.

Yet I keep remembering the one that got away. In the heat of the action, I neglected one of my firm rules by failing to check my line. After catching so many big fish I should have broken off the last few feet and retied. Should have. I didn't. The fish that broke me off was the biggest northern bass I've ever had on...probably a 9-pounder, and she was an easy 8. But she popped the line at a point about fifteen feet from the bait. Since my line was a bright fluorescent mono, I could see it trailing around in the shallows behind her. I chased her with my troll motor. Three times she came up and tossed that huge head, trying to throw the bait. I was just a rod length from the line when she jumped the fourth time and shook the bait free.

Frog run fishing in fall marshes can be dynamite! Don't forget to check out the shallowest water, almost on shore.

This is another pattern that depends on warm weather. An Indian Summer day in October is ideal. You will be looking for a shallow, marshy bay with a soft bottom, and you'll be fishing in water from four inches to just over a foot. For this fishing, as in so much bass fishing, good polarizing sunglasses are worth their weight in gold.

You'll want fairly heavy baitcasting tackle with line testing 12-to 14-pounds. Heavy line helps keep your bait from dropping, and that's a plus since the key to this pattern is moving the bait as slowly as possible. The bait is special. Use a spinnerbait, from 3/8-to 1/2-ounce, with a #7 or #8 Colorado blade. Not many spinnerbaits are sold that way, so you'll need to switch blades. The bait will roll if you retrieve it too fast, but you don't want to do that anyway. You should retrieve it slowly enough you can just about see each revolution of the blade.

Bright, sunny days are good, not bad. Bass will not hold tight to cover but will be out roaming around, so you should make long casts and try to cover a lot of water. Often you'll spot boils or wakes that will tip you off to the locations of big fish.

When cold weather comes, bass using shallower parts of a reservoir make a major migration along creek channels toward the depths of the main reservoir. They'll move along the channels until they hit the junction of the creek channels with the main river channel. That junction is often where they stay, if water depths are right. Or, if the creek channels wind around in deep enough water, the bass might hole up next to the steep drops of the inside turns.

Whether the fish are in the inside turns of the channels or at the junction of the channels, you're looking for much the same thing. Winter bass holes will be *deep* spots, from 20 to 50 feet deep, *next to steep structure*. Sometimes a winter bass hole will have timber or other cover, but not always. The hole alone is enough to attract and hold the fish. Bass and shad both spend the majority of winter in these holes.

One of the best things about this pattern is that you can really clean house when you get the location worked out. That is, when you find bass holding in one kind of winter hole, you can go looking for other similar holes and find bass in exactly the same kind of spots.

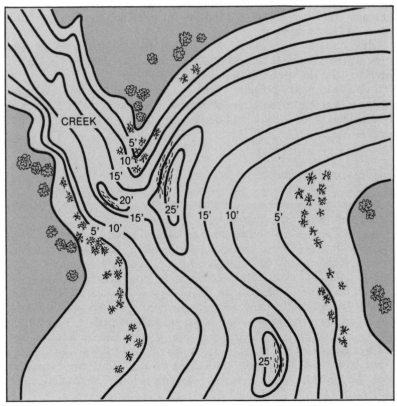

Late fall or winter reservoir bass will sit in deep holes along the river channels. Tailspin lures or jigging spoons are best.

This is classic structure fishing, for which you need a troll motor and some kind of fishing sonar. Use the troll motor to hold your position or to move around slowly while you look for fish. Wind is not as troublesome for this pattern as for other fall patterns we've covered.

My favorite lure is a jigging spoon, like the Hopkins Spoon. I like to put a split ring or light wire snap on the head of the spoon to let the spoon tumble freely on the fall. If you're fishing around timber, as you often will be, use a fairly light wire hook so you can pull the lure free when it snags up. As with other cold water patterns, scent will help you.

You want a fairly stiff graphite rod with lots of sensitivity. In timber, I'd use 14-or 17-pound test. In more open areas, 12-pound line might be better.

To jig your spoon, lower it all the way to the bottom, take up a foot of line and then snap the jig up about three feet. Give it a good, sharp crack. Then you *almost* let it fall free. Don't lose contact with the falling spoon entirely, but don't apply enough rod tip pressure to kill its action.

Bass will not hang on to a metal spoon long, so you have to be lightning fast on the set. Sometimes you'll feel the take, which almost always comes on the drop. Sometimes you'll see the line twitch. You have to *concentrate* to feel the soft takes. It takes experience to sense the take and suddenly reverse the motion on your rod to slam the hook home. Set fast and hard.

Often enough, a jig-and-minnow will outfish the jigging spoon, and some fishermen like a tailspin lure, like the Little George. If I don't catch bass on the spoon I'll try the jig-and-minnow.

If you've located a promising hole and you don't turn any bass there, move up into shallower water right above the hole, working the lips of the channels. Then, if you still don't have the fish pinpointed, go find another hole.

Bull Frogs and Big Bass

This simple pattern can produce some awfully large bass in fall. Once again, it involves live bait.

Essentially, you are looking for the places where a steep drop to deep water meets a good reed bank. As we've noted, fall bass like steeply tapering structure and deeper water. And, again as we've noted before, they'll come shallow in good weather to fatten up for winter.

Look for the reed banks with the deepest water nearby. Then look for spots where that deep water comes nearest the reeds. Usually there will be an open flat in between. Now, to make it perfect, find a little pocket or shelf on that flat. Anchor your boat in deeper water within casting distance of the reeds, in front of such a pocket or shelf.

For bait, use a large frog, the largest you can find, on a weedless hook. Your tackle should be heavy—a medium heavy baitcasting outfit with 12-to 14-pound test line.

You will be casting right to the edge of the dying reeds, then dragging the frog through the open area toward the dropoff to deep water. The

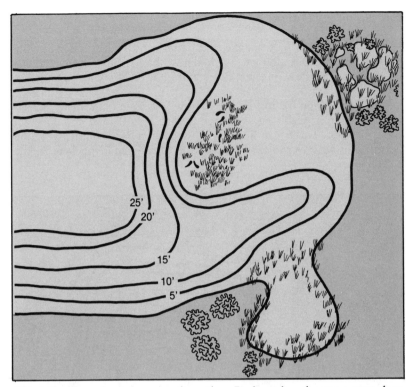

This fall pattern depends on good weather. Find good reeds near a steep drop and work the edge and in front of the weeds with a frog on a jig.

bass will come from the reeds and usually grab the frog in the open water between the reeds and the depths.

The one complexity to this simple pattern is that you must handle the hookset with care. Since the frog will be huge, you can't count on the bass getting the whole thing in his mouth at first. Let him grab it, turn and start heading back toward the reeds. Most people set too soon. I let the bass run two to six feet before closing the reel and getting set. Then you whip the rod up to set the hook. *Cross his eyes!* You have to explode the hook through the frog and into tough bass mouth tissue.

When you hit the fish it will be heading into the tough reeds, so you have to get it coming your way. Just as soon as you set the hook you need to put on the power to get the bass moving to you. If you are late or wimpy with this move, the game is lost. The bass will wrap you up in the reeds so fast you can't believe it. Your only chance lies in getting the fish coming at the boat before it knows it is in a fight. You can let the bass run, jump and fight as much as you want, *after* you've gotten it away from the reeds.

Like many fall and spring patterns, this one is best in the middle of the afternoon or later, when the water has warmed enough in the shallows to pull the bass up. Calm weather is better than high winds, but a little ruffle on the water is more good than bad.

This is a late fall pattern, the best pattern for the last fishing of the year on natural lakes. In fact, I've had great bass fishing on this pattern when there was snow on the ground and I had to break ice to launch a boat!

You'll be fishing the inside turns of the last remaining weeds, which will be coontail. Cabbage is always first to die off, and coontail will always be last. This is just like any other pattern based on the weedline only now you have to find *inside turns*, those small pockets in the weedline.

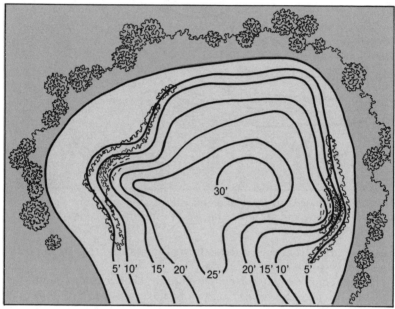

For the diehards, this is a great late fall pattern. Look for inside turns in coontail weeds.

As you'd expect, the best bait now is live bait worked slowly. I like a 1/4- or even 1/8-ounce jig with a minnow. A fathead or shiner minnow, about four or five inches long, is ideal. My favorite jig is Lindy's Fuzz-E-Grub in brown/orange, purple or (in clear water) white. Sharpen the hook.

Your equipment has to be light and sensitive. A short, one-piece graphite rod is best, with six-or eight-pound mono. You don't dare use a metal leader, as that will put the bass off, but you will get a number of bite-offs from northerns.

Using the troll motor, hold the boat off the weeds and toss the jig-and-minnow up past the weedline. Work the bait back, swimming it slowly over the tops of the weeds, then let it drop into the pockets on the outside edges of the weeds.

Usually at this time of year you don't get to pick your weather. You just take what comes. But an ideal situation is a light wind coming at the weedline, something to reduce light penetration and stir up the fish a bit. A really heavy wind will make fishing just about impossible and a totally calm, bright day will send the bass deeper on the break.

One nice thing about this pattern is that you don't have to lose any sleep to work it. This is a "banker's hours" situation, with the best hours being from mid-morning to mid-afternoon.

The real challenge is feeling the takes. These sluggish bass will drift up out of the weeds and gently mouth your jig, swimming along with it. You'll just about never feel that definite "ka-chunk" of a real strike. What you feel, instead, is a soggy, slightly heavy feeling. Snap your wrists sharply to set the hook!

Chapter 10
Improving Your Skills

The sport of bass fishing involves both your head and your body. When you're still trying to learn the sport, your head doesn't know what to tell the body to try to do. When it does, the body gets it wrong. In bass fishing as in tennis, getting on top of the game depends on perfecting a number of specific skills.

Reading Your Sonar

It takes experience to understand what your sonar is telling you. With the best unit in the world, you still won't know much more than how deep the water is until experience has shown you what those other signals mean.

Of course, you have to first learn how to install the unit and adjust the various settings. Beginners almost always run the power (sometimes called "gain") too low on their units. These and other topics are covered in depth in my *Comprehensive Guide to Fish Locators*. I'd urge anybody who owns a fishing sonar unit to look at this course. There's nothing else like it on the market.

The course also helps you interpret the signals, but you also need a lot of time on the water to learn that. Reading sonar is like playing the violin—no matter how much experience you get, it always seems there are more potentials and new frontiers if you put in more time and thought with the instrument. I doubt that one angler in a thousand understands *everthing* his sonar is trying to tell him.

Visualizing Structure

The underwater world comes in a huge variety of shapes—bluffs, slow dropoffs, humps, islands with projecting fingers, holes, saddles, points that run straight and points that take bends, flats and so forth. Translating your sonar's signals into accurate and detailed pictures of the underwater world takes time and experience.

It takes practice to interpret the signals coming from your fishing sonar. But, heck, that's fun...not work!

In the early days of structure fishing, people used to patiently map out the shape of a piece of structure by dropping six, eight or more marker buoys along it. That gets tedious, though it is certainly an educational experience.

Few people want to fish that way anymore, but the average guy could still do much better by carrying a few marker buoys. When you hit a fish while working a point or some other underwater structure, throw out a single marker buoy to serve as a reference point. It's usually best to throw the marker in shallower water than where you caught the fish. You aren't trying to mark the very spot the fish came from, but rather to make it possible to snoop around the area to check out the shape of the structure and the position of the school on it.

No matter how carefully you watch your sonar or the shore, you'll not be able to work the area methodically and intelligently without that reference point. If few other boats are around, it sometimes pays to leave that single marker out on a spot where you took a few fish. If you come back a few hours later, you might find active bass on the spot again.

Bass fishermen often get to fish in places where they can use their eyes to find spots that might hold bass. We can *see* timber and bulrushes, and their shapes often tells something about the shape of the bottom. With good polarized glasses, we can often see underwater vegetation or even the bass themselves.

Which is all fine. There *are* a few lakes where you can afford to fish visible structure all the time and ignore what's happening deeper. But *darn* few. Sooner or later, if you mean to develop your skills, you're going to have to take your fishing deeper than your eyes can see—much deeper. You're going to have to learn to visualize the shape of what's below you...first the big and obvious features, then the all-important little things that are so often the things that attract bass. The sooner you learn, the better.

Casting

I've tried to indicate how important accurate casting can be. A story might make the point. In a tournament several years ago, I found bass way back in a marshy bay. The fish were tucked up in tiny openings in the wall of cattails growing there. These pockets were from six inches to a foot wide. Since there was milfoil growing in front of the cane, I often was casting to openings the size of a football. A regular overhand cast splashed down too hard and spooked the bass. Instead, I made underhand casts with a black Silver Minnow spoon. The trick was to skip the spoon back into those pockets, getting back as far into the cattails as possible. I only had an effective retrieve length of about a foot. That was literally a situation that was "a game of inches," and anyone whose casting accuracy was only fair was just not going to catch a bass.

There is no substitute for experience for teaching casting. None of us fishes as often as we'd like to, but you can get experience by casting on your lawn. Most people to make practice casting too easy. That makes the practice fun and it's probably good for building confidence, but ultimately it doesn't teach us much. When I was learning the underhanded cast, I used to set nine ice cream pails around my yard. I'd stand on the front steps and fire casts at those buckets— thousands and thousands of casts—until I could finally drop the plug in all nine buckets within 60 seconds.

Practice should be realistic. You should *always* have a specific target. Otherwise it is too easy to think you're doing well when you really aren't. Switch around so you aren't always casting the same practice lure. If you've got a crankbait that refuses to run true—and who doesn't?—take the hooks off it and use it to practice with. You'll learn more than if you work with a heavy practice plug that has no wind resistance.

No single casting style is going to do it for you in all situations. The most popular cast is probably a high-arching cast which lands softly. It has its place. But so does a low, hard-driving cast that can fire a weedless spoon through a reed bank and not leave a lot of line up top to get tangled in reeds when you retrieve. When you fish in a wind around

Accurate casting has to be second nature, especially when working in the shallows, casting to visible cover.

227

timber, reeds or other high cover, you quickly learn that high casts are disastrous because the wind will foul your line no matter how accurately you place your lures. Around docks I depend heavily on an underhanded snap cast that skips a bait up under a dock. I execute this cast "upside down" with my rod tip just barely off the surface of the water. This cast starts low, stays low and is very quick.

Sidearm casts are also important at times. They're nothing all that special, except sometimes you have to be able to bring a cast in from the far left or far right side of your body when you are working around obstacles such as timber or docks.

Flipping is a style of casting unlike any other. Few people have trouble learning it, though the special flipping reels work differently and take some practice to master. You can flip with conventional spinning or baitcasting tackle, but for extended flipping, nothing beats the specialized tackle. Flipping allows outstanding accuracy; it takes no great amount of skill to drop a jig in a coffee cup at normal casting ranges if you flip.

Flipping has certain advantages over other casting techniques. It lets you make more casts per minute than any other style of fishing. Your casts will be more accurate and they'll land softer. Because you have so little line going out on each cast, it doesn't take long to make the retrieve. That cuts down on the amount of "dead water" retrieving you are doing, and it makes you concentrate on where you place your casts.

The main reason flipping is so popular, in my opinion, is that it forces people to fish certain kinds of cover the way they should. Perhaps you can tell, though, that I don't see flipping as the answer to all problems. To flip, you have to work very close to your fish, and often the water is so clear the fish won't let you get that close. Flipping is absolutely the best way to fish certain kinds of bass cover. At the same time, you can catch a lot of fish with conventional gear if you make many short, accurate casts.

In many forms of bass fishing, accurate casting is critical to good fishing. Imagine your boat is moving past some rice, the troll motor humming, and suddenly you see a tiny pocket in a rice bed. You've got about one or two seconds to get the cast off, and it has to be *dead solid perfect* or you'll get wrapped up in the rice. Let's also image that there's a six pound bass in that pocket. Can you make the cast? How often? Remember, it's usually the first cast into an area that does the trick...or spooks the fish. You want to be good enough so your first cast almost always goes where it should.

Ultimately you want to become so comfortable with your casting that it becomes automatic. You should be able to drop your baitcasting outfit and instantly make a perfect cast with a light worm on a spinning outfit—*without thinking about it*. If you're mind is dealing with the mechanics of casting, it can't be concentrating on cast placement as much as it ought to be. Bass fishing then becomes something like trying to scratch your head and rub your tummy at the same time. Casting should be as second-nature and unconscious as sneezing.

The same goes for boat control. It has to be right, and it has to be second nature. You can't afford to *think* about moving the boat because you're going to need 100 percent of your mind thinking about bass fishing.

In bass fishing, boat control is mostly done with the troll motor. I don't want to argue remote foot control versus the simpler manual models here. Both have good and bad points. I use the manual. With either type, you probably want to get a stand-up "bike" seat for the bow. These seats are safer and more comfortable than simply standing up there in the bow. Have you ever been running a troll motor fast, standing without a seat, when you hit an unseen deadhead or something else below the surface? And did you do a neat dive over the bow right into the water? Me too! That's one reason I sit on a bike seat whenever I can.

One of Babe's Rules: *the average bass fisherman runs his boat too slow and his lures too fast.* When you're just starting, you can't force yourself to move the boat quickly because your skills just aren't at that level yet. But that's something to work for. Your aim is to be as efficient as possible, getting your lure in front of as many active bass as you can.

In most cases, bass fishing is best done with a trolling motor. Resting on a bike seat is safer and more comfortable than standing.

The two biggest problems facing you as you maneuver your boat are *wind* and *obstacles* (including obstacles like stringy weeds that clog up your troll motor). The best bass boats for maneuvering are light, short, narrow and low (so they have a small "sail" area). For handling wind or clinging weeds, it is always smart to have more power in your troll motor than you think you'll need.

Wind, that old bugaboo, can be used to your advantage at times. In some situations where bass are holding in clear, shallow water, they can be hard to approach even with an electric motor. I'll sometimes let the wind blow my boat silently toward them.

Just as with casting, you should become so skilled that you can fish a whole day and not give the use of the troll motor a single conscious thought. You haven't mastered boat control until you do it almost perfectly without thinking about it.

Sensing Takes

Don't count on equipment to sense light takes for you. Today's rods and lines are far better at giving us a sense of feel than older tackle, but knowing when a bass has touched the lure starts with concentration and experience. A beginner with the best boron rod in the world won't feel takes as well as a bass pro with sloppy, 1950s equipment.

Don't get me wrong. Equipment helps, and I work with the best I can get. But you can't *buy* a sense of feel. You have to earn it.

When I fish with a beginner I'll be aware of more of his takes than he will...and I don't have his rod in my hands. That gets frustrating! At times I want to dive across the boat, grab the rod and set the hook for him. The bass is saying "I'm here! I'm here!" while the beginner is telling me stories about some magic crankbait he's read about!

Watch a heron fishing sometime. He is severely limited in fishing technique. A heron will go hungry unless a fish swims right under his beak, and then his strike has to be swift and accurate the first time. As a fisherman, that heron's got almost nothing going for him except concentration. *But he has that!* When he's fishing, his mind isn't on his girlfriend or a ballgame. When the moment comes, he's always ready.

It takes concentration to sense takes. To fish a worm or a jig well, you have to work some mind games that most people don't understand. Forget your body, the boat, the scenery...all of it! Is there a mosquito on your left ear? Forget it! You've got to enter the world of your bait, and actually see things the way your bait is. Pretend you see the weeds, the bottom, the brush. Are there any bass nearby?

Sometimes I actually think my mind has the power to make a bass appear and strike. If I'm really concentrating, I can almost say *"Now!* and make it happen. There's probably another explanation for that, but all I know is how it feels. It seems to me that I can enter that world and actually relate to the bass.

Beginners have many, many takes that they never feel. Good equipment helps sense takes, but concentration is still important.

Sensing takes requires experience. Since bass fishing is almost always done in some sort of cover, our lures are always bumping against stuff— weeds, rocks, timber, etc. A small portion of what our lures touch will be bass. Sometimes a bass takes a lure with a really distinctive feel and you get that *ka-chunck* of a definite take; but often there is just the tiniest difference between the feel of a bass pickup and the feel of jig scraping a stump or a wispy weed.

The best experience is lots and lots of bass fishing with these baits. We're not all lucky enough to have that opportunity, but other fish will serve the same purpose. Feeling light takes is like learning to ride a bicycle; once you learn, no matter what fish you learn with, the knowledge never really goes away. Try tossing light jigs for crappies or even flyfishing for bluegills. You'll be a better *bass* fisherman for it. One of Babe's rules: practice doesn't make perfect, but *perfect practice* does. Concentrate, even in your practice.

Fortunately, these things are fun to learn! You just have to apply yourself. People often ask me how to learn to use a worm, where both sensing takes and setting hooks requires skill. I usually tell people to go fishing for a day or two with nothing but a handful of worms, weights and hooks. Bear down on the skills needed to use worms without giving yourself the easy way out of switching off to whatever bait you already feel confident with.

Hooksetting

Beginners typically do better with fast presentations than slow ones because on fast presentations the bass often do us the kindness of hooking themselves. It still takes skill to feel a hit on a spinnerbait or crankbait and set the hook with consistency, but worms and jigs require that much more skill. Yet these are skills that pay off *big* when you get them!

We used to think we had to let a bass run with a plastic worm to get it all in his mouth, before setting the hook. Now we know better. Scuba observers long ago learned that bass come up behind a worm and suck it in, *all* of it, with an inhalation—sort of a large-mouthed vacuum cleaner. So there's no reason to wait before setting the hook , though it pays to pause for a second to gather yourself for a solid set. The bass will hang onto the worm long enough to let you do that if you don't just yank reflexively and weakly when the line jumps.

The best hookset technique with jump baits is to lower your rod tip to the water, reel up most of the slack and then set with a snap of the rod. This generally takes one to four seconds. If your rod tip can whip up through air for a few inches before the line comes tight, you get a "running start" that helps explode the hook through the worm (or whatever) and into the fish.

How hard should you set? Well, I've seen people set foolishly hard, but for every guy I've seen doing that I've seen 99 guys use a wimpy set. If you want to practice this, use four-pound mono and try to *bust the line with every set*. Really. Tests of the best tournament fishermen have shown that they consistently slam the hook home with eight pounds of pressure. I've checked, and that's what I hit, too.

You need all that power. Fishing scientist Paul Johnson has studied this topic. While there are places in a bass's mouth where a set of only two or three pounds of pressure might sink a hook home, the tough tissue on the very top and bottom of the mouth is another story. It takes eight pounds of force to get a hook into that bony material. With line stretch and a hook that isn't razor sharp, even the hardest set won't always do the job. Remember: it's darned difficult to set too hard, but easy to set too soft.

It is easier for right-handed anglers to set a hook powerfully with spinning gear because their stronger arm is doing the hitting. Setting powerfully with baitcasting gear takes more experience and technique. Most good anglers use pretty much the same technique, but it's one I haven't seen written up anywhere else. Watch a good angler on television setting a hook with baitcasting tackle. Very likely, he will slam the butt of the rod against his chest, arch his body backward, and lever the rod away from the fish, using the strength of both arms and his back to do it.

I set a hook by planting the rod butt against my chest and arching back. It is possible to set too hard, but almost nobody does that.

The force needed to seat a hook is related to what kind of tissue the hook point hits, and that's related to the sharpness of the hook. Since you can't guarantee the hook will contact softer tissue, you should sharpen your hooks to let them do their job with less force. *Always!*

The best tool for this is a fine metal file. Fortunately, someone is selling a great little file for fisherman. Luhr Jensen markets this file in two sizes. It really removes unwanted metal quickly. If you've only tried slow, clumsy stones for sharpening hooks before, forget that experience! Just try the files, and see the difference.

Always stroke toward the point. Take metal off one side of the hook, then the other. Then you might stroke the outer surface of the hook point too, creating a roughly triangular point. It is too tricky to try to sharpen the curved inner surface of the hook point, so ignore that area. If you get the other three surfaces, particularly the two sides, you've made the hook a lot more effective.

Test for sharpness by sliding a hook along your thumbnail. If it catches, the hook is sharp. In general, if you can tie knots to your lures without getting slightly hooked from time to time, your hooks are dull.

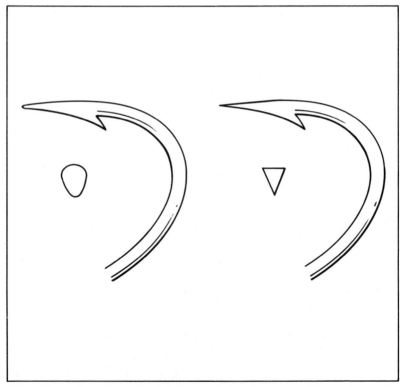

These illustrations show a hook before and after sharpening. Sharpening hooks is the easiest way to improve your fishing.

It isn't important to know 14 knots. It is important to know three or four good ones and be able to tie them properly, quickly and reliably. The average angler knows only one knot, the Improved Clinch, and it really isn't very good (as tied by most guys). Actually, an experienced man can get good performance from the Improved Clinch, but few of us are that skillful. So other knots are better.

Certain baits, especially crankbaits, work better when tied with a loop knot of some sort. Two of the best are the King Sling and the Duncan Loop.

Most of the time you'll be tying directly to a hook or split ring. Some of the best knots are the Palomar and the Doubled Improved Clinch.

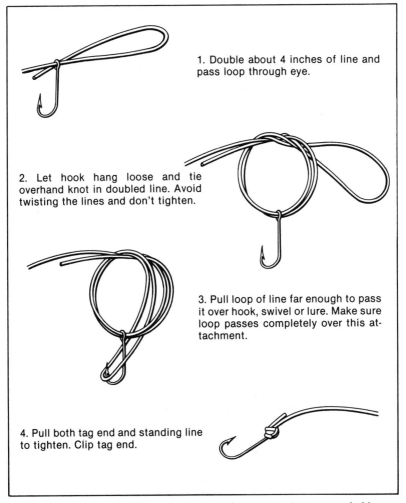

1. Double about 4 inches of line and pass loop through eye.

2. Let hook hang loose and tie overhand knot in doubled line. Avoid twisting the lines and don't tighten.

3. Pull loop of line far enough to pass it over hook, swivel or lure. Make sure loop passes completely over this attachment.

4. Pull both tag end and standing line to tighten. Clip tag end.

The Palomar knot is the simplest strong knot to tie. It is very reliable.

1. Pass the line through the eye of hook or lure twice.

2. Wrap the tag end around the standing line 5 or 6 turns.

3. Pass the tag end through the loop just above the hook.

4. Hold the tag end while pulling the knot tight against the eye. Clip the tag end.

An outstanding knot is the Doubled Improved Clinch. It is far stronger than the standard Improved Clinch.

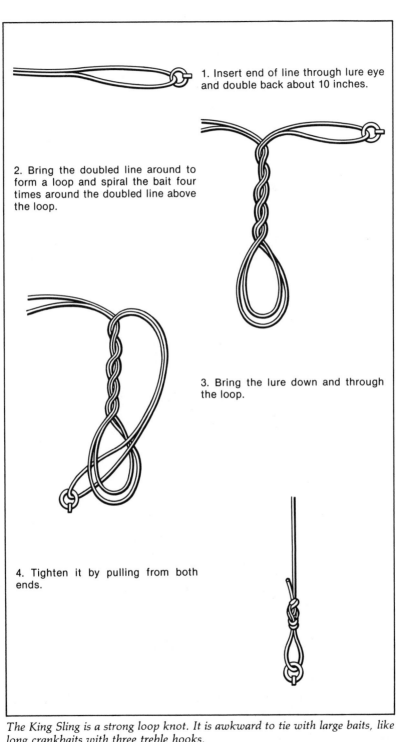

1. Insert end of line through lure eye and double back about 10 inches.

2. Bring the doubled line around to form a loop and spiral the bait four times around the doubled line above the loop.

3. Bring the lure down and through the loop.

4. Tighten it by pulling from both ends.

The King Sling is a strong loop knot. It is awkward to tie with large baits, like long crankbaits with three treble hooks.

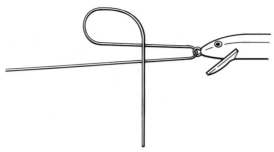

1. Pass the line through the eye of the lure, then bend it back toward the eye to form a closed loop.

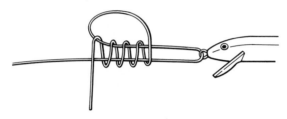

2. Holding the loop and standing line between your thumb and forefinger, wrap the end of the line around the standing line and through the loop four or five times.

3. Start to tighten the knot by holding the lure while pulling alternatively on the standing line and tag end.

4. Slide the knot to the desired position by pulling on the standing line.

5. Cinch the knot in place by pulling hard on the tag end with pliers; trim.

The Duncan Loop is another good loop knot that allows you to change the size of the loop. Loop knots are preferred for crankbaits.

Fish Fighting

This skill is the most fun of all to practice. Fighting bass is not especially tricky, with the exception of a couple of points. Tournament fishermen can actually horse an 8-pounder into the boat in seconds. Of course, they use heavy tackle and are not fishing for fun in the usual way.

A lot of bass are lost on jumps. Especially if a bass has a heavy lure to shake—something like a big crankbait or surface lure—they can get that lure flying so many different directions that it pops free.

Tournament anglers, who might lose a small fortune on one thrown lure, have learned to minimize losses on jumps. Usually you can anticipate the jump. Unless the fish is already in very shallow water, you'll see your line slicing toward the surface. But *before* the fish gets out of the water, reach forward with your rod tip, tighten the line and sweep the rod sideways with force to turn the fish's head. Your best chance to turn that fish is just before it breaks free of the water.

If the fish gets up on you, though, it's too late to try to stop him. Let it happen. If you yank the line hard now you might help the bass jerk the hook out, for the head of a bass thrashing in air moves faster and with more force than when it is thrashing in water.

The biggest problem, though, is losing bass to cover. The worst situation of all is when you've made a long cast way up into some heavy cover. When a bass hits, if you don't do the right thing and do it *now*, you'll be fighting the cover instead of the fish.

Many bass get away by wrapping the line around some obstacle, such as a troll motor or cover. Here I'm trying to keep a good fish from the motor prop.

In heavy cover, there's just no choice: you've got to horse the fish to you. Specifically, you've got to get the fish's head out of the water and keep the fish coming at you so quickly that the bass has no chance to turn back into the water and go for cover. One of Babe's Rules: a bass can't go anywhere its head doesn't go first! Control the head, and you've got control over the bass. In heavy cover, then, you get that fish's head up on top and *without pausing* you skid the fish right toward you.

It's just instinct for bass to dive into cover when threatened. One reason they turn get tangled so often is that they naturally turn sideways to get more body surface area to pull with. However and whyever they do it, they do it *fast!* You sometimes find yourself firmly hooked to a stump or some weeds almost the very instant you know you've had a strike. Man, they can be quick!

When fishing in cane, reeds, pads, timber and similar cover, use enough tackle to handle the fish. Lines of 12 to 20 pounds are needed, matched with strong rods and reels with drags screwed down tight.

More and more, I find I'm passing by that kind of tackle, though I used it a lot when doing more tournament fishing. These days I try to use tackle that will bring a fish out, but no heavier. When fishing for fun, I'd rather avoid situations where I have to horse my fish. But sometimes the bass give you no choice.

In heavy cover like reeds, get the bass' head up and then keep it moving toward you. You can skid a big fish this way.

There is a final trick for getting bass out of impossible situations even if the fish gets wrapped up in heavy cover. It doesn't always work, but few tricks *always* work. Once a bass has driven into cover and gotten rid of the pull of your line, it gradually relaxes and will sooner or later seek to swim free. The fish doesn't want to stay there forever with its nose in the slop. So you just let your line go slack. Every now and then, test the line cautiously to see if the bass is still tied to cover. If he is, go slack again. If you can feel the fish's head moving, fool him with a smooth but forceful pull to get his head coming your way again.

Learning the Game

There are lots of ways of learning bass fishing, and I guess each one has its place. One of the less effective ways is reading magazine articles, yet I've learned a *lot* doing that over the years and I'll go on reading the more promising ones.

The instructional video cassettes have many advantages over the written word. Mainly, you *see* what is being taught. If someone is telling you to fish in a certain kind of weed, you see what it looks like. It doesn't take a lot of imagination for you to realize you've been passing by weeds like that all your life, either thinking there were no bass in them or being afraid you couldn't fish effectively there. I sell video cassettes on bass, as well as for other species (for ordering details, see the back of this book). There are some other good ones on the market, too.

I also sell a line of audio tapes on fishing, including bass fishing. You'll find information on ordering them in the back of this book. They are handy to pop in your car tape deck and just listen to several times. Stuff you miss the first time through will suddenly pop out at you.

The best fishing books are better than magazine articles because they put things in perspective. Articles often make it seem like the particular pattern being talked about is the hottest thing going. Often it's a minor tactic that struck some editor as being new. But I'm not saying you should ignore articles. They're especially good for teaching you the newest developments, if you just keep a sense of perspective.

Seminars are fun, partly because they're usually held in the off-season when there's no bass fishing to do. You'll get the most out of seminars if you take a tape recorder along and *ask questions* about stuff you aren't sure about.

Fishing with good bass fishermen can be a tremendously educational experience. You'll be fishing your own kind of water, and almost surely you'll learn new techniques or new wrinkles on old techniques. Do this whenever you can.

But there's a hazard with this approach. Someone else is running the boat. Someone else is watching the sonar and deciding where the fish are likely to be. Someone else is making the key decisions about where and how you will fish. You'll likely catch a bunch of bass and gain in both knowledge and confidence. Yet there is a very real limit to how much you can learn if you let someone else do the hard stuff. Fish with experts whenever you can, then go out and practice the same techniques in *your* boat, making *your* own decisions.

No matter how you try to learn, don't expect it to come to much unless you go fishing. Every source of knowledge is worthwhile—audio tapes, video tapes, books, articles, seminars...all of it. But nothing counts without BIB (Butt In the Boat) experience!

There comes a point in the development of most anglers when they begin to stagnate, when they get stuck at one plateau of skill. Nothing will kick you out of a rut like that as well as competitive fishing. In every part of the country where there are bass, there are bass clubs. Almost surely, there's a club near you where the fishing competition is friendly and fun.

And educational. You never learn so much as when fishing competitively. First of all, you'll reach down and find new levels of concentration and inventiveness you didn't think you had in you. And, more often than not, you'll come in behind some other fishermen who worked out a problem that defeated you. That's okay. That's how we all learn. In club fishing, the learning takes place at a terrific rate.

Fishing with other good bass fishermen in a club can be an educational experience, and give you a taste of competitive fishing at a low cost.

Chapter 11
Pass It On

As a bass angler, you hold two heritages in your hands. One is physical, and the other is not. Both are precious and in some trouble.

Bass For Tomorrow

When I was getting serious about bass fishing, the message coming out from fisheries managers was that "you can't hurt a lake with a hook and line" and that "most fish grow up and die without having seen a fishhook."

To those of us who were really fishing hard, that was welcome news. We were all eagerly trying for stringers of big fish. We killed those fish, of course, and we ate them. We were proud of what we'd accomplished. After all, biologists told us these were fish that would have died of old age if we hadn't caught them.

And then some of us began to have our doubts.

We'd notice that those lakes we'd been hitting the hardest were just not putting out fish the way they used to. Were the fish getting smarter? Had they move to new spots in the lake? That's what we wanted to believe. Yet more and more, we began to suspect that smart fishing pressure could definitely hurt a lake.

I think the better anglers caught on to what was happening before the fisheries managers did. After the most skilled and dedicated anglers were starting to change their habits, the managers were still emphasizing the fact that fish are a renewable resource and that angling pressure was not excessive.

Part of the problem was the mentality of the managers. Many of them were—heck, still *are!*— locked into the idea that bass were being "wasted" if they weren't being consumed. Others kept pointing to data that showed people were still catching plenty of fish, ignoring the fact that the size of those fish was going down drastically as angling pressure removed the larger bass that make the sport so interesting. Apparently the colleges and universities that teach our fisheries managers their profession don't have much to say about *quality* angling.

Finally there came some changes in the scientific community, too. Some population studies were published that confirmed our fears about the vulnerability of fish to modern fishing pressure.

It takes patience and forethought to teach kids to fish, but I can't think of anything more important for us to do well.

Years ago it was believed that fishing pressure couldn't hurt a lake and good anglers eagerly put that theory to a test. I have to admit that now I'm ashamed of pictures like this one.

Fishing pressure definitely has an impact on fish populations. Believe it. In fact, in many lakes it is the main determining factor in how strong bass populations are.

Any lake can support only so many fish. In a given body of water, there might be about 15 or 20 pounds of bass per acre. Most of that poundage would be made up of a bunch of little bass, fish less than a foot long. A few will weigh 2 pounds. Fewer still will weigh 3 pounds. A very small percentage will weigh 4, 5 or 6 pounds.

Fishermen have funny ideas about bass size. I don't care where you go in this country, and I've fished around a lot, it isn't easy *anywhere* to catch a lot of bass over 4 pounds. Bass occasionally get huge in Florida and other southern states plus some areas in California, but nowhere in this country will you find easy fishing for bass 4 pounds and up. A bass that big has survived long odds.

Anglers also have funny ideas about how many fish they are "supposed to" be able to catch in a day. They see magazine articles with stringer photos—articles that often depict those rare moments of peak conditions—and then the average fisherman goes out thinking he's a failure unless he catches a limit of fish like that.

It just doesn't work that way. Consider the statistics of B.A.S.S., kept over a number of years, that show us *the best bass anglers in the nation catch three-tenths of a pound of bass per hour* in competition! Admittedly, they're working under unusual conditions of extreme competition, but those guys are *good* fishermen. When you go fishing, don't expect the moon!

More to the point, don't be unhappy if you're not filling the boat with big bass. I hope people understand that my fishing show, like all the others, is edited. Yes, we do actually catch those fish, but before we release the shows to be broadcasted we edit out many minutes of fishless footage. I worry sometimes that we give the impression fishing is easier than it actually is.

The best effect of tournament fishing has been the way it has encouraged bass anglers— particularly the best ones—to release bass. The really good anglers are no longer killing whole stringers of bass like they used to. They'd be ashamed of themselves if they did. Today, the damage is being done by casual anglers or the guys who are just getting it together and who want to show other people they can catch fish.

Catch-and-release fishing is a very new idea. It started with trout fishermen in the 1940s but didn't have any impact on people who fished for bass until the 1960s. Even then I can remember lots of people who thought it was stupid and funny to go to all the trouble of catching a fish if you just meant to throw it away. Even ten or fifteen years ago, some people actually got upset when I released fish.

Of course, there's nothing crazy about working hard to catch fish and then releasing them. Golfers enjoy golfing without eating golf balls. Skiers enjoy skiing without eating snow. The fact that fish taste good doesn't alter the fact that fishing is a *sport* in its own right. If a fishing trip ends with fillets in the skillet, that's an attractive bonus, but it doesn't *have* to be the reason we fish. And I'd rather eat panfish than bass, any day.

Many people understand that now. I'm amazed at how popular catch and release fishing is becoming. On a big lake near my home, people are even starting to release big *walleyes*. The trend will surely continue, and it has to continue. We've got to see fishing as a recreation and fish as a precious resource.

I'm surprised that some people don't seem to understand that catch and release has to be a year-round practice. You say that, unlike some people you know, you don't kill big bass on the spawning beds? Good! But if you keep a nine-pounder taken in early October, you've done just as much damage. I'm primarily concerned about the big bass, those really special fish that make bass fishing so exciting. Heck, they don't taste that good anyway!

There's no reason to get all preachy about this. Ultimately, it's just a common sense thing. In most lakes, there's nothing wrong about taking an occasional bass to eat. Bass are a renewable resource that, whether you kill them or not, will not live forever. I occasionally eat bass and don't feel ashamed about sharing some of the bass I catch with my

When you catch a trophy bass like this, the future of the sport is quite literally in your hands.

family. I keep some fish long enough for pictures at the end of the trip, for that's all part of my business.

But I watch it. I almost never keep a bass unless it would die anyway because of being badly hooked. Every now and then—well, three fish so far—I keep one for mounting. I feel it's okay to eat a few bass from time to time, but eat the ones under 3 pounds and release larger fish. Obviously, some lakes have better populations than others, but *no* lake can take much continuous catch-and-kill fishing. We've proven that, all too well.

If fishermen wait for managers to come up with regulations that truly protect bass, we probably won't like those regulations when they come because they will probably be very restrictive. The smart thing to do is regulate ourselves now by limiting our own kill of bass. The more proficient the average and better-than-average anglers become, the more important it is for all of them to exercise sportsmanship. It just makes sense!

Pass It On

Good bass fishermen these days understand that, with no bass, there will be no bass fishing. Fewer fishermen have given any thought to the fact that the future of the sport depends on new fishermen entering it. Yet it is a fact.

If the sport of bass fishing is to endure, we need young anglers in the sport.

249

As a nation, we are getting increasingly urban. More and more kids are growing up in a world dominated by television, rock music and video arcades; fewer kids these days have ever experienced the fun of dinking around on a swim dock with a pole, a bobber and a bunch of sunfish.

When today's kids get into the school system, they are recruited into various team and individual sports—football, soccer, tennis and so forth. That's mostly a good thing, except many sports have a high potential for injuries, including injuries that last a lifetime, and many of those sports cannot be practiced when our kids have left school.

You may think there are too many anglers now, but statistics show something interesting. Interesting and alarming. Every year, the average age of the angler gets about a year higher. Which means that there are few young people entering the sport.

The long-range implications are troublesome. What if there are not many anglers in the future to speak against development schemes that would destroy lakeshore? If anglers become a tiny minority, who will consider the needs of fishermen when setting water-use zoning regulations? Who will pay for expensive fisheries management when there aren't enough license-buying anglers to do it? Some day "animal rights" extremists might lobby for anti-fishing laws on the grounds fishing is "cruel." Will there be enough anglers to successfully defend the sport then?

If that is one reason for teaching kids to fish, it's just one among many. And there are many others that are probably even more important.

Fishing is a lifelong sport. It can be enjoyed individually or with friends. It is a form of recreation that brings together family members of different ages in a wholesome, shared good time. It teaches kids to understand and care about the workings of nature.

This is a sport too worthwhile and positive to be allowed to fade away!

You are the carrier of one of the world's oldest and richest traditions, the tradition of sport fishing. Pass it on.

The best way to do this is with your personal involvement, but it isn't the only way. Not far from my home there is a camp where kids are taught to fish. "Camp Fish," in Walker, Minnesota, allows kids of all ages to share in the pleasures of angling. It is a safe, well-run operation that is working for the future of angling while it teaches the campers the skills and attitudes that will allow them to enjoy fishing the rest of their lives.

We all should share our sport with our kids. When you do, forget about your own fishing and make sure the kids have fun. Keep the trips very short and sweet until you hear complaints from the kids that they'd like to stay out longer.

The choice of whether or not my girls care to fish will be theirs, but I'm taking them out for short trips to make it possible for them to learn to love fishing. And to tell the truth, I get as big a kick out of seeing my youngest daughter catch a sunfish as I do out of catching a big fish myself.

Pass it on!

I don't claim to be able to predict the future. It's enough of a challenge to decide how deep the bass will be tomorrow. But if I know anything, it is that the world will be a lot healthier if the future has lots of bass swimming in healthy lakes and lots of folks who enjoy fishing for them.

You and I have been blessed with a special resource and sporting tradition. Pass them along.

The "Facts of Fishing" Video Library

The **Facts of Fishing Video Library** is the only video tape series that teaches a *complete system* for catching fish. Each fantastic tape outlines a specific area of fishing and features a complete understanding of the methods and techniques for successful angling. 18 Unique and exciting titles to choose from. $39.95 each

VT01—**Walleye I**—Waging War on Weed Walleyes, Suspended Walleye of Lake Erie, Beaver House Walleye, Deadliest Method for Trophy Walleye, Minnow Madness for Walleye, Trophy Walleye of Lake Sakakawea

VT02—**Largemouth Bass I**—Cattail Bass, Bullrush Bassin' Tactics, Coping with Cold Fronts, The Fall Bonanza, Lily Pad Bucketmouths, Understanding Weedline Bass

VT03—**Great Lakes Salmon and Trout**—Kings of the Great Lakes, Chinook Stocking Builds Fishery, Early Season Lake Trout Secrets, Ski for Steelhead and Lake Trout, Fall Run Pink Salmon

VT04—**Smallmouth Bass I**—Early Season Tactics, Cranking Summer Smallies, Fall Run River Smallmouth, Autumn's Bronze Bombshells, Smallmouth Bassin—Great Lakes Style

VT05—**Walleye II**—Bill Binkelman—A Fishing Legend, The Great Lakes Walleye Breakthrough, Creating a Walleye Bonanza, Dr. Loren Hill—pH & the Walleye, A Unique Pattern for Big "Weed Walleyes," Porkin' Out Walleyes—A Totally New System, Walleye Secrets from Around the World

VT06—**Largemouth Bass II**—Bass & Rice—A Unique Combination, Dr. Loren Hill On pH & Bass Fishing, Bustin' Bass Off the "Flats," Flippin for Timber Bass, Boat Dock Bassin', Frog Run Bassin', Jig & Pig Bassin'

VT07—**Panfish I**—White Bass—The Silver Scrapper, EZ Summer Crappies, Whitefish...Panfish of the North, Small Pond Panfish, Deep Water Slab Crappies, ABCs of Ice Fishing

VT08—**Northern Pike I**—Fight'n Pike of Manitoba, Trophy Pike Tackle, Monster Northerns of Recluse Lake, Reindeer Lake—BIG Water, BIG Pike

VT19—**Jig Fishing**—Jigs—The All-Around Lure, Jigs & Walleyes...a Natural, Jiggin' Leeches, Jigs...Crappie Magic, Quiver Jigs & Smallmouth Bass, Jigs & Crawlers for Walleyes

VT20—**Northern Pike II**—Bucktail Spinnerbait Secrets, Jerkbait Pike Trolling Tactics, Trophy Lake—Trophy Pike

VT21—**Smallmouth Bass II**—Jig & Leech Smallies, Smallmouth Gold, Minnowbait Tactics, St. Clair Smallmouth, Spinnerbait Smallmouth

VT22—**Live Bait Rigging**—Back to Bobbers, Floater Rigs, One Deadly System, The Crawler "Hauler"?, Time Tested—The Lindy Rig

VT23—**The Basics of Fishing**—A Beginners Guide To..., How to Get Started, Basic Tackle, Basic Skills, Fish and Their World, Babe's Pattern Fishing Principles

VT24—**Fishing—The Electronic Age**—In the Beginning, Sonar...Which One For You, Big Water Electronics, Battery Maintenance, Electronic Accessories, Future Electronics

VT25—**Atlantic Salmon: A New Brunswick Angling Tradition**—In the Canadian province of New Brunswick, there is an angling tradition so important it borders on religious. Fly-fishing for the acrobatic, immense atlantic salmon is a sport handed down to today's anglers by the fanatic, gentlemen casters of the past.

VT26—**Canoe Country Fishing: Angling in the Quetico-Boundary Waters**—Come fish a place where there are no motors, no sounds except those made by animals and the wind. The experience of wilderness is the same as it was when this expansive natural garden served as the water highways of the rugged voyagers.

Babe Winkelman gives you everything you need to know to make such a trip yourself. Through leading authorities, you learn: how to plan; why it is best (and less expensive) to work through an outfitter; how to paddle and portage a canoe; how to select a camp site; and, of course, Babe himself teaches you how to fish the scrappy smallmouth bass and abundant walleye.

VT27—**Fishing Ontario: It's Incredible!**—Ontario! The name alone conjures up images. Lakes, crystal clear and rimmed with rock and pine. Fish as long as your arm. The lonely cry of the loon. Join Babe Winkelman as he catches fish from one of his favorite places on earth. He feels the pulse of this world, capable of giving up numbers of huge fish. It is a fragile yet bountiful environment and this is a tape you will love. Species featured are walleye, lake trout, northern pike, and brook trout.

VT28—**Understanding Walleye**—The name is simple, but the subject a constant source of fascination and frustration for anglers throughout North America. Learn the complete story of this fish from the man who built an international reputation for catching them! Babe Winkelman lays a foundation of knowledge that is a basis for future walleye videos to come. This is the angler's encyclopedia of walleye information from seasonal movements and the basic biology of the species to, most of all, tips and secrets for catching them under all conditions. If you only have one walleye video, this is the one to have!

Babe Winkelman's "Fishing Secrets"

Babe introduces a sizzling new video series titled, *Fishing Secrets*. Each action-packed video is crammed with facts, tips and fishing's best-kept secrets. *Fishing Secrets*, at a very affordable price, contains the type of "inside" information anglers are looking for from a man they know they can trust...except with their secrets! Approx. 50 min. each. $19.95

VT100—**Land of the Midnight Sun: Saskatchewan Fly-In Fishing**—The rugged beauty of a wilderness land untamed by man comes to life as Babe Winkelman offers a special journey into the heart of fishing's dream land. Explosive and awe-inspiring segments on northern pike, arctic grayling, and lake trout.

VT101—**Water Wolves of the North: A Northern Pike Spectacular**—Babe Winkelman entertains and teaches viewers everywhere to catch savage northern pike. Contains thrilling non-stop action footage of some of the largest pike ever captured on video.

VT102—**Wilderness Walleyes: The Lure of Ontario**—In a home video destined to be a scenic and educational classic, Babe Winkelman teaches four separate modern approaches to finding and catching the fish he built his reputation on: the walleye. Spectacular underwater footage.

VT103—**''Summer Heat'' Bass: No Sweat!**—Most fishermen have trouble catching bass in midsummer. Babe Winkelman teaches his time-tested methods for catching big bass, in a variety of locations, during the scorching days of summer.

VT104—**The Great Lake Erie: A Fishing Success Story**—Babe Winkelman shows you more than one way to catch walleye and smallmouth bass from Lake Erie and tells the amazing story of the lake's comeback from environmental disaster.

VT105—**Trophy Time: Fall Fishing Bonanza**—The crisp weather of fall stirs the biggest lunkers into action and Babe Winkelman shows how to be in the right place at the right time. Take this personally guided hunt for those rod-busting brutes of autumn! Features walleye, bass, and crappie.

VT106—**Land of 100,000 Lakes: Manitoba Magic**—Come fish the land where legends are born, with legendary fisherman Babe Winkelman. Yes, Manitoba is a huge land of huge fish. If you love fishing, or ever plan to visit the *Land of 100,000 Lakes,* let Babe show you what the legends are all about.

VT107—**Cold Water — Hot Action: Ice Fishing Fever**—Ice fishing has undergone a recent revolution in techniques and knowledge unlike anything in the history of the sport. Today's winter fisherman is more mobile and scientific in his approach. Get the inside scoop on today's tactics for catching fish through the ice from Babe Winkelman, a true northern son.

VT108—**Fishing the Canadian Shield: The Ultimate Experience**—Babe Winkelman has long been considered *the* expert on fishing the bountiful yet fragile lakes of the Canadian Shield. Join Babe as he experiences a fishing smorgasbord in the rugged, pristine waters of Ontario. Catch smallmouth bass and stop for shore lunch, and then watch as one of Babe's fishing partners hooks a big surprise he didn't quite bargain for!

VT109—**Bronzebacks of the North: Smallmouth Spectacular**—Built like a bullet and muscled like a prize fighter, the smallmouth bass is everything you are looking for in a gamefish. Join Babe Winkelman on a tour of the scenic, unspoiled waters "smallies" inhabit. He will share a complete system for catching these bronzed acrobats.

VT110—**Spring Fishing: The Cure For Cabin Fever**—After a winter of dreaming, the first day spent fishing on open water is a time to savor. Join Babe Winkelman in a celebration of spring in the north country. Unleash a winter of pent-up energy with this entertaining and fact-filled video guaranteed to cure your cabin fever at any time of the year!

VT111—**Big Water Bounty: Great Lakes Fishing Made Easy**—The huge, sprawling Great Lakes are home to a breed of fish that is used to its freedom. These fish wage a battle they don't intend to lose, in some of the most spectacular fight scenes ever! Babe Winkelman, the man everyone seeks for angling advice, shows you there is fantastic Big Water fishing within easy reach of the average angler.

VT112—**Family Fishing Fun: Sharing the Good Times**—This tape will help the entire family learn about fishing together. Babe Winkelman, despite his busy schedule as a professional fishing educator, knows the value of quality time with his wife and four daughters. Join the Winkelman family on a houseboat trip where they find a renewed appreciation for the traditional values that make fishing the most universal and endearing lifetime sport of all.

VT113—**Fishing the Flow: Wonders of the River**—The flowing peacefulness of a river draws the heart and soul of a fisherman deeply into its grasp. Babe Winkelman is at home in the ever-changing world of river fishing. In the style that has drawn him an enormous following, Babe shares his secrets for catching fish from the river's currents.

VT114—**Great Plains Reservoirs: Fishing Midwestern Impoundments**—Some of the most fabled names in fishing history belong to a group of relative newcomers: the flood-control reservoirs. Let Babe Winkelman unravel the secrets to catching walleye and bass in a world where river fish have become lake fish. Or have they?

THE LIBRARY OF FISHING KNOWLEDGE
COMPREHENSIVE GUIDE SERIES

Babe Winkelman, America's most renown fishing educator, brings you the highly acclaimed **Comprehensive Guide Series**. These are without question the most authoritative books on freshwater fishing ever produced.

Each book contains concise, detailed information put together into a total system for understanding, finding, and catching more and bigger fish...a system that's guaranteed to improve anyone's fishing results! $11.95 each.

Jig and Live Bait Fishing Secrets—The basic fundamentals of jig fishing and live bait rigging are covered in Babe's easy-to-understand style. But this book goes well beyond, into the tips and secrets that can help you become a master fisherman. 288 pages.   BK06

Fish Locators—A complete A to Z course on the use of sonar (graphs, flashers, and LCDs). Babe explains everything from installation to the finest points of interpretation. Learn how to get the most out of your electronic investment. 216 pages.   BK07

The Strictly Fish Cookbook—Not just another cookbook—this book includes illustrated "how-to's" on cleaning, filleting, and preparing. Includes smoking, pickling, canning, grilling, and other unconventional cooking methods. 256 pages.   BK05

Walleye Patterns—This finicky, highly prized critter is Babe's specialty. His unusual methods and patterns are explained in detail. Includes valuable material never before in print. 304 pages of solid walleye knowledge.   BK02

Fishing Canada—The angler's roadmap that unlocks the mysteries of the vast Canadian wilderness. Babe shares his secrets and information on all major species. This book is a MUST if you're planning to fish "God's Country." 230 pages.   BK01

COMPREHENSIVE GUIDE SERIES GIFT PACK

A new six-volume set of the entire **Comprehensive Guide Series**. $71.70 retail. Sixpk

"Good Fishing" Audio Cassette Series—Four 1-hour tapes feature Babe answering some tough questions about catching panfish, bass, walleye, northerns and muskies. Babe explains how his "pattern method" works throughout the seasons. This one-of-a-kind item is the perfect companion at home, in the car, or even on the water. $24.95. CT01

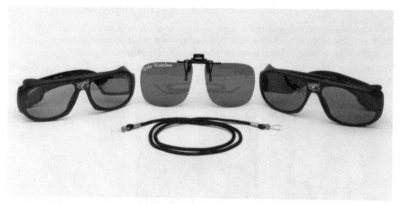

BABE WINKELMAN'S "FISHERMAN'S FAVORITE" POLARIZED SUNGLASSES

See what you've been missing with Babe's **"Fisherman's Favorite"** polarized sunglasses, now in two sizes: large (regular) and new medium size for ladies or smaller men. Both styles feature high quality *glass* lenses in two colors, gray and amber. Floatable case included. $19.95.

SG01-A: regular size, amber   SG03-A: medium size, amber
SG01-G: regular size, gray   SG03-G: medium size, gray

Eyeglass wearers! At last you can enjoy the benefits of polarized glasses with Babe's Clip-on Sunglasses. These high-quality scratch resistant plastic lenses are fitted to a sturdy flip-up style frame. Includes a floating padded case. $14.95.

SG02-A: Clip-on, amber   SG02-G: Clip-on, gray

Keep sunglasses handy and secure with Babe's new **Sunglass Lanyard,** worn comfortably around the neck. Nylon 24" cord with plastic retainers slide directly on bow of glasses and cinch down tight. $1.49 retail.   SG05